The Politics
of Public Policy

RICHARD P. **BARBERIO**

Associate Professor of Political Science, SUNY College at Oneonta

PEARSON

Boston   Columbus   Indianapolis   New York   San Francisco   Upper Saddle River
Amsterdam   Cape Town   Dubai   London   Madrid   Milan   Munich   Paris   Montréal   Toronto
Delhi   Mexico City   São Paulo   Sydney   Hong Kong   Seoul   Singapore   Taipei   Tokyo

Editor-in-Chief: Ashley Dodge
Senior Acquisitions Editor: Melissa Mashburn
Editorial Assistant: Courtney Turcotte
Director of Marketing: Brandy Dawson
Executive Marketing Manager: Kelly May
Marketing Coordinator: Theresa Rotondo
Managing Editor: Denise Forlow
Program Manager: Maggie Brobeck
Senior Operations Supervisor: Mary Fischer
Operations Specialist: Mary Ann Gloriande
Manager, Central Design: Jayne Conte

Cover Designer: Karen Salzbach
Cover Art: Wim Wiskerke/Alamy
Director of Digital Media: Brian Hyland
Digital Media Project Manager: Tina
  Gagliostro
Full-Service Project Management and
  Composition Service: Abinaya Rajendran/
  Integra Software Services Pvt. Ltd.
Printer/Binder: Courier
Cover Printer: Courier
Text Font: 10/12, Sabon LT Std Roman

Credits and acknowledgments borrowed from other sources and reproduced, with permission, in this textbook appear on the appropriate page within text.

Many of the designations by manufacturers and sellers to distinguish their products are claimed as trademarks. Where those designations appear in this book, and the publisher was aware of a trademark claim, the designations have been printed in initial caps or all caps.

Library of Congress Cataloging-in-Publication Data

Barberio, Richard P.
  The politics of public policy/Richard P. Barberio, associate professor of political science, SUNY College at Oneonta.
    pages cm
  ISBN-13: 978-0-13-615775-5 (alk. paper)
  ISBN-10: 0-13-615775-0 (alk. paper)
  1. United States—Politics and government. 2. Policy sciences. 3. Political planning.
I. Title.
  JK421.B27 2014
  320.6—dc23

                                                                              2013016968

10 9 8 7 6 5 4 3 2 1

ISBN 10: 0-13-615775-0
ISBN 13: 978-0-13-615775-5

BRIEF CONTENTS

CHAPTER 1   Introduction to the Text   1

CHAPTER 2   Politics and Policy   13

CHAPTER 3   Approaches to the Study of Public Policy   39

CHAPTER 4   The Policy Environment   67

CHAPTER 5   Agenda Setting and Massing of Interests—Actors Outside Government   95

CHAPTER 6   Policy Formulation and Execution: The Inside Players   131

CHAPTER 7   Policy Evaluation   165

CHAPTER 8   The Future of the Politics of Public Policy   193

CONTENTS

Preface   ix

CHAPTER 1
Introduction to the Text   1

Defining Public Policy   7

Politics, Again   9

Plan for the Text   10

Summary   12

Discussion Questions   12

Notes   12

CHAPTER 2
Politics and Policy   13

Politics and Policy: What Is the Difference?   15

A More Politicized Policy-Making Process   17

The Transition from Programs to Policies   18

The Government as a Policy Maker   20
The Size of Government   21
Who Works for an Expanding Government? The Rise of the Contract Workforce   24
Policy Promotion and the Permanent Campaign   25

Human Values, Ideology, and Policy Making as Politics   29
Freedom   32
Equality   33
Political Ideology   34

Conclusion   35

Summary   36

Discussion Questions   37

Notes   37

CHAPTER 3
Approaches to the Study of Public Policy   39

Power   40
Formal and Informal Versions of Power   40
The Degree of Concentration of Power   42

The Degree of Change   44
   Non-Incremental Change   45
   Incrementalism   48

Public Policy Typologies Based on Outputs   53

Public Policy as the Result of a Process   55
   System Analysis   55
   The "Textbook" Approach: The Stages or Phases Model   56

Other Views of Public Policy Making   57
   Garbage Cans and Policy Streams   58
   Rational Choice Theory   59
   Punctuated-Equilibrium   61
   Advocacy Coalition Framework (ACF)   61

Conclusion   63

Summary   64

Discussion Questions   65

Notes   65

CHAPTER 4
The Policy Environment   67

The Structure of US Policy Making   68
   Federalism   69
   Separation of Powers   72
   Political Culture   74
   Demographic Changes   80
   Communications   81
   The Economy   85
   ***BOX**   The Recent Financial Crisis   87*

Conclusion   90

Summary   91

Discussion Questions   92

Notes   92

CHAPTER 5
Agenda Setting and Massing of Interests—Actors Outside Government   95

Problem Identification   97
   ***BOX**   What Is the Problem? Oil Scarcity, Pollution,
   and the Promise of Hybrid Cars   99*

Setting an Agenda   101

Agenda Setting: The Importance of Outside Players   105
> *Corporations   106*
> *The Media   109*
> *Interest Groups   112*
> *Social Movements   114*
> *Citizens   116*
> *Other Actors   118*

Cycles of Power   119

Conclusion   124

Summary   125

Discussion Questions   126

Notes   127

CHAPTER 6
Policy Formulation and Execution: The Inside Players   131

Policy Formulation   133
> **BOX**   *The Regulation of Wall Street and the Politics of Formulation   135*
> *The Need for Legitimacy   138*
> *Formulation: The Degree of Change Sought   138*

Implementation   139
> **BOX**   *The Politics of Policy Implementation   143*

Patterns of Power: Executive Policy Formulation and Implementation   145
> *The Rise of the Executive: State Governors   146*
> *The Rise of the Executive: The Presidency   148*
> *The Contraction of Power: The Policy-Making Role of Legislatures in an Era of Executive Ascendancy   155*

Conclusion   159

Summary   160

Discussion Questions   161

Notes   162

CHAPTER 7
Policy Evaluation   165

Policy Evaluation or Analysis?   166

Policy Outputs and Outcomes   166
> *Evaluation from the Outside and the Inside   167*

Winning and Losing: A Valid Framework?   171
> *World War II and the Cold War   172*
> *The Auto Bailout I and II   174*

Losing but Winning? Reforming Social Security   *179*
Success and Failure — Moving the Goalposts   *180*
BOX   Shifting Goals of US Policy in Iraq   *183*
Success or Failure — Pulling the Goalposts Out of the Ground   *185*

Conclusion: The Politics of Outcomes   186

Summary   190

Discussion Questions   191

Notes   191

CHAPTER 8
The Future of the Politics of Public Policy   193

The Degree of Change and the Policy-Making Environment   194

The Appropriateness of Policy Solutions   197

A Less Political Policy World?   203

Conclusion: Wither Politics?   206

Summary   206

Discussion Questions   207

Notes   207

Index   209

PREFACE

Jumping into the complexity of the academic study of public policy with its attendant theories and schools of thought can and does frustrate students. A way to draw students into the study of public policy is to make use of their sincere, if inchoate, fascination with politics. "Wow, that last presidential election was exciting!" "The reaction to the health care reform package sure got a lot of people riled up!" "The wrangling over the budget sequester really got ugly." These musing are highly commonplace and also highly political in and of themselves. They reflect an interest in power, competition, fairness, and personalities—the things that make the political world interesting for most of us. These statements also have numerous connections to the policy process and to policies themselves. It is a basic tenet of this text's approach that most of us come to study public policy not because we want to know more about public policy as an academic subject, but because we are intrigued by politics and we infer that there is a link between the two. While this is true, it is sometimes obscured in the way public policy is written about in textbooks and taught in the classroom. The "policy as politics" approach offered here works along these lines: First off, as political science students, policy scholars, and related seekers of knowledge, we all share in a basic pursuit to better understand the nature of our political system and our democracy. Second, the only way to really understand either of these is to see them in political terms. This does not mean partisan or ideological terms. Politics is about power, who has it, who doesn't, how it is used, etc., and this does not always translate into who is right or wrong and what party affiliation they hold. Third, studying public policy in a framework of political phenomena and concepts gets us closer to an important related objective—getting a better understanding of the American political system and American democracy.

The thematic approach taken by this text is reflected in its structure, and the result is something different than what is available in many contemporary texts. Most policy textbooks contain a set of conceptual chapters followed by a selection of issue areas that are designed to act as illustrations of the concepts found in part one. I've used this approach many times in the past but became frustrated with it. Too often I would find it necessary to return to basic concepts from the early points in the semester in order to get my students to see that what we were reading about in one of these issue-area chapters was an excellent illustration of a nondecision in the agenda-setting phase of the policy process or some other conceptual nugget. It was as though the course was really two courses: the first part immersed in the abstraction of the parts of the policy process and largely divorced from the real bare knuckles world of policy making, especially its political aspects, and the second part, a mix of real-world examples dealing with health care, immigration, the environment, education, and so on. I would even jokingly tell my students that we needed to get through the "boot camp" of theories and models to appreciate the richness of the real-world examples we would soon encounter.

Over time my approach changed. Why not infuse each section of the course concerning the conceptual aspects of the policy process with a sustained set of real-world examples? I did this in my teaching all the time, often literally tearing an ongoing episode in the policy process from the day's newspaper. I felt that my students needed the reinforcement of a text for the theoretical framework of the course—all those new terms, ideas, and theories are daunting and not always easily assimilated—but I was frustrated that the set of chapters at the end of the text often went underutilized or unread altogether because I was doing more to illustrate the phases of the process with other material as we went along. The issue chapters often assumed too much prior knowledge about the policy process for them to work well as illustrations of specific aspects of the process, or the chapters covered the process from beginning to end, making them unsuitable as examples of one part of the process. I began to seek out books that just gave my students the nuts and bolts of the policy process with no issue-area chapters. I then used articles and even short books on a particular policy area broken into useful blocks as the illustrations of the concepts. I kept looking for a text that would provide the conceptual framework and the examples together in balance. I did not find one that provided the integration of the two in a way that met my needs. This text is my attempt to create a text that provides that mix.

A blended approach helps engage students in an ongoing way. Concepts are not abstractions that need memorization for their own sake; instead, they are part of a set of real-world events and actors that are far more likely to be retained and work as the basis for expanding the student's analytical skills along with an extended knowledge of the intricacies of our political system.

It matters little if an instructor uses this text in the traditional pattern with concepts up front followed by longer illustrative readings in the later part of a semester, or if he or she uses it in the way I do, by elongating the discussion of the process of policy making over the course of the semester and injecting supplementary material as one progresses. In either case, a blended text improves the students' ability to access the more challenging abstractions of the policy process and to build upon that knowledge. This, coupled with the policy-as-politics approach to the treatment of the material, provides a highly accessible text for undergraduates and maximum flexibility for instructors in terms of topic focus and emphasis, while still providing a rigorous treatment of the breadth of theory and practice of the study of the policy process.

ACKNOWLEDGMENTS

This text has been years in the making and involved a lot people, probably more than I know. Lists are tricky because they imply completeness and ordering that seldom reflects the complexity of something as multifaceted as writing and publishing a text. Given these limitations and with a great sense of who I will doubtlessly leave out, here are a few of the people to whom I owe a debt of gratitude for their efforts, ideas, and patience. I would not have gotten my start at writing this or even thought that I was suited to writing a text without Dan Shea's encouragement and introduction to Dickson Musslewhite, the editor who first signed me to write the text after seeing something in the public policy chapter I wrote for Dan's American government text. My succeeding editors all added positive contributions to this work and Eric Stano is notable for his ability to make me rethink what the text could be. Many other people had a hand in the refinement and completion of the text and were incredibly helpful and supportive, including Amada Zagnoli, Stephanie Chaisson, and Toni Magyar.

I would also like to thank the reviewers of this text for their helpful feedback and criticisms: Mary Lou Adams, University of Texas at Austin; Joseph Appiahene-Gyamfi, The University of Texas – Pan American; Eric Austin, Montana State University; K. Lee Derr, Pennsylvania State University – Harrisburg; Euel Elliott, University of Texas at Dallas; Jodi Empol, Montgomery County Community College; John Grummel, University of South Carolina Upstate; Marilyn Klotz, SUNY Geneseo; Martha Kropf, University of North Carolina at Charlotte; Glen Krutz, University of Oklahoma; Marilyn Lashley, Howard University; Bruce Rocheleau, Northern Illinois University; and Bruce Stout, The College of New Jersey.

Most of all I must thank my family. My mother and father, Millie and Nick Barberio, were both educators and instilled a love of learning in me that forms the bones of my teaching, research, and this text. Eva, my daughter, was a constant inspiration for going forward and persevering in the completion of this work. Most of all I owe my wife, Christine, all the thanks in the world for her help and patience in the writing of this text. She read many drafts of what you see here and her keen editorial eye and knowledge of politics immensely improved the final product.

This text is available in a variety of formats—digital and print. To learn more about our programs, pricing options, and customization, visit www.pearsonhighered.com.

Introduction to the Text

S V Luma/Shutterstock

CHAPTER OBJECTIVES

When you finish reading Chapter 1, you should be able to do the following:

- Define what is meant by politics
- Distinguish between public and private policies
- Illustrate how a nondecision is still an exercise of power in policy making
- Summarize the ways in which the process of policy making helps to clarify the workings of our democracy

"The first rule of Fight Club is you don't talk about Fight
Club. The second rule of Fight Club is that you don't talk about
Fight Club."

In the iconic movie *Fight Club*, the characters create a world that they feel is more real
than the one they turn their backs on when they enter into the realm of bare-knuckle
brawling as a release from the oppression of a mundane, workaday life. Devotees of the
movie instantly recognize the often repeated line about keeping the underground club a
secret. It neatly sums up two of the main ideas that draw the characters to the club in the
first place: Do not talk about the subject with anyone outside the sphere of participants,
because doing so will spoil the secret. (Secrets are mysterious and rather exciting things,
especially if you are in on one.) And, if you do not know the secret, then you do not matter
all that much in the first place. (Secrets create exclusivity, a very sought-after item in
many circles.) Many students look at public policy making as a sort of secret, one that
they know exists, but one that they have not been let in on yet. Those who are adept in the
language and concepts of public policy making and the stuff of policies themselves sometimes seem to be communicating in a foreign language. This text is going to let you in on
the "secret" of public policy making.

You may be reading this text for any number of reasons, but it is probably
safe to assume that at some level you think that politics is important or at least
is something worth knowing about. Many times we—even academics who
study, write, and teach about public policy and how it is made—tend to com-
partmentalize politics and policy so that the connections between the two are
obscured. The dominant way that public policy making is taught to students
is to place the process within the framework of a set of steps. That works well
as a heuristic or type of "shorthand" way of thinking about the complexities
of the process. However, using this model to understand the policy-making
process sometimes gets many of us—both students and instructors—caught
up in the abstraction of the model rather than the reality that the process of
public policy making is, first and foremost, a political process. Public policy
making is really the intersection of what are traditionally thought of as the
"political" players and forces in the United States, such as the power of the
presidency, Congress, and the courts; the influence of interest groups and lobbyists; and the impact of elections. Other players and forces are less conventionally thought of as "political" in nature but are still key parts of the making
of public policy. Examples range from the transformative effects of the new
communications environment of the Internet and social networking to the fundamental shifts in demographics now taking place. Public policy making is *the*
process that features the interplay of these and many other actors and forces.

Simply put, if you want to get a deeper understanding of politics and government in this nation, you need to study public policy making. Three main
points support this claim: First, as political science students, policy scholars,

and related seekers of knowledge, we all share in a basic pursuit to better understand the nature of our democracy. Second, the only way to really understand our democracy is to see it in political terms. This does not mean partisan or ideological terms. Politics is about power—who has it, who does not, how it is used, etc.—and this does not always translate into who is right or wrong and what party affiliation they hold. Third, studying public policy in a framework of political phenomena and concepts gets us closer to our primary objective—getting a better understanding of American democracy. In short, if you want to get a fuller understanding of our democracy, you need to understand public policy making, and the best way to solidly interface with the field of public policy making is to think about it as the stuff of politics.

To these ends, this text examines the policy-making process—from identifying a problem through the analysis of the success or failure of the implementation of solutions—with a consistent focus on the political factors that influence each of these phases. This "policy as politics" approach highlights the nature of power in our democracy and features the struggle over ideas and values brought by a range of established and emerging players in the policy-making process, as well as those spawned by recent political, social, and economic changes.

Politics is generally thought of as a zero-sum game, meaning there are distinct winners and losers; the winners win absolutely and the losers are totally vanquished. If this sounds a great deal like the terms used in warfare, you are right, except that what are won and lost are not the typical spoils of war, such as natural resources or geographic territory. Instead, politics is about power over political institutions—such as the presidency, the courts, and Congress—and over the processes that these institutions carry out—such as law making and rendering decisions. Additionally, the means of battle are different. While no armies face off on battlefields using lances, swords, or rifles, political "warfare" does share many of the linguistic and conceptual items associated with a physical war. Candidates wage "campaigns" against their rivals. Some places are considered the "battleground" because the outcome of the election will be determined by winning the vote in that location. Parties "square off" to win a vote through maneuvering in a legislature. A Congress may try to defy a president over a war. Interest groups or social movements may use dramatic actions to push politicians to see it their way. Because so much "heat" is generated by political action, we are naturally attracted to the personalities and drama that permeate politics. After all, one of the most enduring of all plot scenarios going back to antiquity is the dramatic tension we see in a contest of wills. In short, that is the stuff of politics.

One of the most enduring definitions of politics was crafted by political scientist Harold Lasswell. He wrote that politics is "who gets what, when, and how."[1] It is a good starting point for a discussion of the relationship between politics and policy because it contains a good mixture of the two. This classic formulation may, at first look, seem trite or simplistic, but in reality it is a rich and meaningful way to think about politics because it asks us to think about actors (who), values and rewards (what), the time frame for action (when), and the means to gaining goals (how). We can also add the arena of conflict or action (where) to Lasswell's formula to make it more complete. One part of this formulation—the "what" aspect—is generally what comes to mind when people think about public policy, since policy is, in many cases, the outputs of governmental action. These outputs, such as a law or court decision, are for some political actors desirable outcomes because they provide material benefits (e.g., a change in the tax code that puts more money in a person's pocket) or more symbolic benefits that give people status in society or rights that are not solely material in nature (e.g., the recent laws creating same-sex marriage in some states).

The "what" part of Lasswell's formula—the outputs of the policy-making process—is very important in its own right, but just looking at a public law, regulation, or court decision is a bit like looking at or even eating a slice of pizza. Yes, knowing about the final product is worthwhile, but understanding the process of how the product was created—making the dough and sauce, shaping the crust, slicing the toppings—and the myriad of decisions and subtleties of choices that went into the results—what to put on the top, how long to cook the pie—can only deepen our appreciation of the outcome. Thinking about the process can help us answer questions about the outcomes while also getting us to think about what we do not yet know about the end results and, perhaps, how to improve both the process and its outputs in the future. So while there are plenty of examples of classic and contemporary policy outputs in this text, they are included as a means to illustrate aspects of the process and to spur your own questions about both the process and its outcomes.

A timely example may help to clarify the text's approach: at present, one of the real "hot-button" policy areas has to do with immigration. Both legal and illegal immigration are good topics to bring up if you want a heated exchange. Try striking up a conversation with a stranger in a grocery store on the subject or watching the debate over the state of immigration on the floor of the US Congress! Few people, especially elected politicians, react with disinterest about immigration. President Bush campaigned in 2004 on a pledge to create a program that he claimed would provide a way for people who are here illegally to stay in the country legally. The president's emphasis on this policy was often carefully meted out on the campaign trail because part of his natural base of support, social conservatives from many of the Sunbelt areas of the country, did not like the president's proposed program and, instead, called it "amnesty" for people who should be punished for breaking our immigration laws. Candidate Bush often avoided talking about this policy in places where it was sure to ruffle the feathers of potential voters. Members of the president's own Republican Party, either out of genuine dislike for the guest worker policy or because they knew their constituents were against it, were not at all receptive to the policy. Oddly enough, after the 2006 midterm election, it was the Democrats in Congress that rallied to the president's side on the issue. Some Republicans squawked that the president was caving in to special interests that enjoy an immigration

system that provides the plentiful and relatively inexpensive labor that they claim would flow from the president's program. For example, agriculture, the hospitality industry, and meat processors all benefit from cheaper labor because the often difficult, dangerous, and dreary jobs of picking fruits and vegetables, making beds, and slaughtering cattle are more easily filled by people who lack the education, skills, and legal status to find better paying jobs. By keeping the pay and benefits low, contended the president's critics, these industries would make more money; hence, in their opinion, the guest worker program was simply a fig leaf over an unscrupulous labor practice that shortchanged the American worker.

So what do we have here? Was President Bush's guest worker and immigration reform proposal just political payback to one of the president's constituencies or was it a thoughtful and reasoned attempt to craft a policy that would deal with a difficult set of problems? (The prospect also exists that it was both of these things, but that is not our concern at the present time.) If this division over the meaning and intent of the Bush White House's immigration policy seems like a familiar pattern of thinking in Washington and elsewhere, there is a good deal of truth to such an observation. When politicians and the news media bandy about politics and policy, there is often an all-or-nothing quality to the discussion. It is as though policies are merely vessels to contain the real power advancement goals of the policy maker, and any hint of political gain for a person or group is evidence that the policy itself is a sham. While all this line drawing about politics and policy may be very political itself—after all, there may be something to be gained by demon-izing an opponent's policy as being too "political"—it does point out a ten-dency on the part of political observers to sort the world of politics into two conceptual boxes. Even academics that study politics, government, and policy tend to do the same thing. For many years, and with some holdover today, it was assumed that there was a politics/administration dichotomy. Woodrow Wilson, a political scientist before he was elected president in 1912, advocated just such a division in his book *The Study of Administration* (1887) as a way to keep politics out of governing and assure a purer administration of policy without corruption or undue special influence.

While no one has seriously believed that elected officials and other policy makers are elevated to some special realm of pure governance and policy making after they slip the bonds of politics and gain office, there has been, and to a degree still exists, a feeling among the public and some policy makers that politics—usually an election or appointment to office—decides the conflict over who will make decisions. Once the players are seated to make decisions, then politics is over and governing can begin. Does this sound impossibly Pollyannaish? Maybe, but recall that not long ago, just after the election of Barack Obama in 2008, some commentators were specu-lating that we were entering a "post-partisan" era in which President Obama would, by virtue of his commanding victory and unique place in history, be able to govern with a mandate that transcended politics as usual. While Obama did enjoy a "honeymoon" of positive press coverage, mostly cordial relations with Congress, and support from the public, his major policy initia-tives, especially health care insurance reform, ran smack into a very tradi-tional set of political hurdles featuring strong opposition from Republicans in Congress, dissent among Democrats, and well mobilized counter pressure from interest groups. While reality intrudes into our wish for the "political struggle ends after the election" dream, we continue to hope for its real-ization. Much of our discontent with government and the policy-making process stems from the dissonance we get when we witness the clash of values and goals that make up the reality of policy making. Historically, the process of policy making and governing has, with few exceptions, been framed by politics. Even the halcyon days of the early years of the Republic, prior to the creation of formal political parties, featured conflicts over where to place the nation's capitol and a plan to have the federal government take over the debts incurred by the states during the fighting of the Revolution, to name two well-known examples. The Founding Fathers, including Thomas Jefferson, George Washington, and Alexander Hamilton, all engaged in poli-tics over these and other issues of policy. This brings up an important point: politics is not a dirty word if, by politics, we are talking about representation of constituents in the policy-making process. Certainly, the American public casts a cynical eye toward those who populate government. However, if we step back for a minute and think about politics as a process that allows for the expression of our particular interests in the course of decision making, we will realize that politics is, in many ways, just what the people want.

Elected officials in a republic are representatives of the people. (To what degree and in what fashion this takes place is an important debate for later.)

DEFINING PUBLIC POLICY

A timeworn practical joke is the snipe hunt. The snipe is a bird that really does exist, but the snipe hunt is a gag that asks the unwitting participant to try to catch one of these birds, usually at night in a location that probably has not been graced by the presence of a snipe in a good long while, if ever. The "hunter" sets off on the impossible mission and others laugh at his or her expense. It is common for many policy texts to offer up their own versions of the snipe hunt in their early chapters. They take a long path intended to nail down some meaning for public policy, but sometimes end with a concession that public policy can mean so many things that it cannot be adequately defined. This does not have to be the case.

Starting with the basics of the term itself, it is apparent that policy has a generic meaning of a "how-to" set of instructions or a "do not do" sign. Anyone who has applied for a driver's license or received a parking ticket knows these things firsthand. There are a whole range of things that can be considered "policies." Power is a necessary element of political, social, and economic order, and the decisions of those with power are commonplace forms of policy. A presidential executive order, a bill passed by Congress, a verdict rendered by a court, these are all familiar forms of policies to most Americans. However familiar these forms of policy are to you, it is wise to keep in mind at this point that policy is more than just what the government does or, just as importantly, what the government does not do. (A decision not to do something is still a policy. The decision to stay out of the direct fighting in World War II after the war began in Europe in the late 1930s was still a "policy" of the American government.) In a very interesting twist, two policy scholars once argued that policy making frequently takes place when governmental decision makers avoid dealing with a problem or an issue. Bachrach and Baratz called these instances nondecisions because they do not directly affirm or deny the need for government to tackle a problem or an issue, but they still map out a position taken by government.[2]

The "public" part of public policy is a bit less straightforward. Fraternities, sororities, clubs, and other organizations may have all sorts of policies about how to do things and what is and is not acceptable behavior, but these policies do not govern the actions of nonmembers. The "public" in public policy is far more sweeping than that. Such policies may not encompass every citizen at all times, but they are aimed at much larger portions of the population. For example, the federal government's recent creation of a prescription drug program for older Americans does not affect all citizens. The other aspect of the "public" side of public policy that needs to be addressed is the idea that what makes a policy public is that someone or something has the power to require compliance with the process or restrictions created by the policy.

To illustrate this point, if the leader of a campus club set a policy that only students with at least a 3.0 GPA could vote in US presidential elections, most students on campus—especially nonmembers of the club—would probably see this directive as silly and simply ignore it. Some club members might also think the directive was ridiculous and ignore it. However, the club could try to sanction members who voted in the election without the requisite GPA by kicking them out of the club or by other punishments. In this example, the campus club has limited power because its legitimacy and authority to impose restrictions is highly restricted. The federal government and state governments, however, have much more in the way of legitimacy and authority and, therefore, are able to impose restrictions on all manner of activities and behaviors, including voting.

One of the basic elements of American democracy rests on the notion that our representative form of democracy—our republic—is governed by decision makers populating institutions that have the legitimate ability to exercise authority over the rest of us. John Locke, a 17th century English political philosopher who greatly influenced the Founding Fathers here in America, was the main person who articulated the idea that governments gain legitimacy, and thus power, only through the consent of the governed. He argued that in legitimate political systems, the public is connected to the government by a contract in which the people give up some of their natural, inborn rights so that government can establish a well-ordered political, economic, and social system. If the government lives up to its end of the bargain by using its power wisely and judiciously, the public will continue to support the government by going along with its decisions. On the other hand, if the government abuses its power, it is in danger of losing legitimacy because the public has the right to break off its support. Our political system is far more entrenched, and the public has such a long history with the ideals of American democracy that exercising the right to terminate the contract with the government, in other words, call for a revolution, is not a likely option for most Americans. However, the idea behind Locke's "social contract theory," as it is often identified, is still valid and important for our discussion about the "public" part of public policy. In the hypothetical example with the campus club and voting, few students are likely to go along with the club's limitations for at least three reasons. First, the club's authority is limited to club members, and because of this, its potential impact is largely in the private and not in the public realm of life. Second, even if we set aside the points about authority and the nature of policy itself, the policy is still questionable because the way it was produced does not seem to be democratic and fair since the campus student body had no ability to influence the decision of the club. Third, even if the club had the authority to dictate the voting requirements for students on campus, the arbitrary nature of the decision undermines its legitimacy. After all, why is a 3.0 GPA the cutoff? This aspect of the policy does not make it any less public in its intent, but does point out that citizens must accept the legitimacy of the policy if it is to affect them in a meaningful way. For example, several states have adopted bans on the use of cell phones while driving, but these laws are routinely violated to such an extent that their impact may be negligible.[3]

Taking these points together, the "public" side of public policy can be summarized in the following way:

- Public policies affect a wide segment of citizens or other actors—such as corporations, the mass media, and the government itself—that directly impact the public. (Of course, for every rule there is probably some exception, and that is a danger of defining terms. For example, the US Congress passes private bills regarding specific individuals, usually for people who are seeking to gain citizenship in the United States but are unable to use the more common route to becoming citizens.)
- Public policies are made by decision makers who have the legitimate authority to set policy. (For a policy to be more than public in intent only, it must be accepted by enough of the public to confer legitimacy.)

POLITICS, AGAIN

While this chapter has already touched on the meaning of politics, it is worthwhile to revisit those ideas with an eye toward making explicit connections between public policy and politics. Given the way public policy is connected with power and the public, the lines between politics and policy should be fairly obvious, but in many discussions by academics and policy practitioners, they are not. If we stick with the definition borrowed from Harold Lasswell that politics is "who gets what, where, when, and how," then policies themselves—the laws, rules, and other forms of decisions and nondecisions by legitimate authorities—are the evidence of the process of policy making and the political power that fuels the process. The process is important for a number of reasons. First, it is worth knowing how things work when it comes to the nuts and bolts of, say, a legislature. The US Congress and a state's legislature are both complex and rule-driven institutions. Understanding the structure, historical evolution, and functions of such institutions evident in their processes is valuable, in and of itself. The process is also important because if we peel back a layer or so down from the process, the power—such as party control, elections, or the influence of a host of other actors including but not limited to the executive branch, the judiciary, the media, and the public—that shapes the process becomes more evident. Therefore, if we can keep the reason for studying the process in front of us, we can use it to know more about the politics that underlies the process. That is the promise of studying public policy as a means of knowing more about our political system; it can give us a context to understand politics that is sometimes absent when we just focus on what is usually considered "political," such as an election or the decision that comes from a contentious court case.

Politics is a word derived from *polis*, a term the ancient Greeks used for their key unit of government, the city-state, such as Athens. The term *polis*, in turn, is a word that has its roots in the expression for "the people" or "the public." Most conceptions of politics take these ideas into consideration and weave definitions of politics that are amalgams of the people, however they are defined, and some governmental structure or some other form of authoritative societal creation, such as an army. The result is a hefty assortment of definitions that underscore the meaning of politics as a relationship between the government (and other possible powerful actors, such as unions, corporations, interest groups, movements, and the media) and the governed. Sometimes the relationship is one where the public has great influence over the government. In most political systems that have the support of their citizens, the public likes to at least think that they have this upper hand on the decision makers. At other times and other places, the government and other political actors are in a position of dominance over the people. Milton Rokeach, a social scientist of great renown in the 1960s and 1970s, had a handy way of explaining the nature of government using the terms of political ideology. Nations, like the United States, with great freedom for the individual but with limited guarantees of equality—supposedly provided by governmental intervention— were classified as "capitalistic." Nations with little freedom for individuals but with supposedly high amounts of equality—again, created by governmental action—were classified as "communist." Rokeach used this format to map out the makeup of the other dominant ideologies of his present and fairly recent past, including fascism and socialism.

Rokeach's ideas are just one example of how politics has been conceptualized as a marriage between the public and government. It is tempting, when in a cynical mood, to think that is all there is to politics. Some people crave power, and the public lives in the transitional space around this struggle for power, sort of like living at the shoreline as the ocean does battle with the land for dominance. As Thucydides, an ancient Greek historian, wrote over two thousand years ago, "The strong do what they can; the weak suffer what they must." Certainly, there are those who engage in politics because they lust for power. However, the nature of politics is more complex than this simplistic rendering. People create institutions because they need a means for doing what they cannot do alone because of their lack of resources, expertise, time, and knowledge. If politics is the means of governing forces that people would like tamed and, perhaps, made better, then policy is the means to undertake these tasks.

PLAN FOR THE TEXT

This text examines the policy-making process—from identifying a problem to the evaluation of the success or failure of the implementation of solutions—with a consistent focus on the political factors that influence each of these phases. This "policy as politics" approach highlights the nature of power in our democracy and features the struggle over ideas and values brought by a range of established and emerging players in the policy-making process, as well as those spawned by recent political, social, and economic changes.

Each chapter examines fundamental aspects of policy making by first placing them within the context of the policy-making process. The process is then examined to highlight how the actual production of policy is a battle over the definition of problems, variations in possible solutions, and assessment of the efficacy of policies once they are implemented. While the commonly recognized political activities of democracy—such as campaigns and lobbying—are understood to be major influences on policy making, they are not the only instances where politics—the struggle over ideas and values—work to shape public policy. Each chapter of this text works to merge the basics of the policy-making process with a sharp-eyed focus on the apparent and not-so-obvious influences of the political world on policy making. By taking this approach, the reader will learn about the policy-making process and its implications for understanding the intricacy of democracy as it exists in the American political system.

Chapter 2 delves deeper into the exact nature of both politics and policy by commenting on how the two have intermingled over time and why this has taken place. The chapter also discusses why this move toward a more politicized form of policy making is an important development for those concerned with American government, politics, and democracy.

Chapter 3 presents a survey of the major scholarly approaches to public policy making. It begins by focusing on power, one of the building blocks of any understanding of the essence of politics. Power is then related to the ways in which policies can change the existing political, social, and economic relationships in the United States. The chapter concludes by offering a synopsis of the major scholarly models of policy making.

Chapter 4 establishes a frame of reference for how the policy-making process works by mapping out many of the major influences on past and contemporary public policies, including our political culture, changes in the nation's demographics, the revolution in communications technology, and trends within the nation's economy.

The main emphasis of Chapter 5 is the role that political actors outside the government (i.e., interests groups, social movements, corporations, and the media) have on the identification of policy problems and their placement on the policy-making agenda inside of government.

In Chapter 6, the policy-making process is placed in the context of the text's "policy as politics" approach by focusing on how policy makers inside the apparatus of government control or influence the formulation and implementation of policies.

Chapter 7 provides a discussion of policy evaluation. It offers a set of diverse examples designed to get the reader to think about evaluation as it relates to the concepts of success and failure and how the influence of politics shapes these most basic and universal benchmarks of policy assessment.

Chapter 8 ends the text with a set of ideas that challenge the reader to think about both the stable and the more changeable factors that shape the making of public policy. The chapter concludes with a challenge to the reader to use both of these factors as tools for their continued thinking about what policy making can tell them about American government, politics, and democracy.

SUMMARY

Oftentimes, public policy is viewed as something that is beyond politics. This introductory chapter sets the stage for the text's "policy as politics" approach which examines the public policy-making process and resulting policies as important to the understanding the nature of power and democracy in the American political system. The dominant way that public policy making is taught to students is to place the process within the framework of a set of steps. However, using this type of model to understand policy making can sometimes lead us to dismiss the reality that the process of pubic policy making is, first and foremost, a political process. While the process of policy making, from the point of identifying a problem to implementing solutions, is examined throughout this text, along the way, there is a focus on how the actual production of policy is a battle over the definition of problems, variations in possible solutions, and assessment of the efficacy of policies once they are implemented.

DISCUSSION QUESTIONS

1. Why are there so many definitions of public policy?
2. What is the difference between a private policy and a public policy? Why does this difference matter to our understanding of how politics and policy making interact?
3. Would it be possible to remove politics from public policy making? Would this be desirable? Why or why not?
4. How does understanding the politics behind a public policy provide us with a deeper understanding about the nature of the American political system?

NOTES

1. Lasswell, Harold Dwight. *Politics: Who Gets What, When, How*. New York: P. Smith, 1968.
2. Bachrach, Peter, and Morton Baratz. "Two Faces of Power." *The American Political Science Review* 56, no. 4 (1962): 947–952.
3. McCartt, A.T., and L.L. Gear. "Longer Term Effects of New York State's Law on Drivers' Handheld Cell Phone Use." *Injury Prevention* 10, no. 1 (2004): 11–15. http://injuryprevention.bmj.com/cgi/content/abstract/10/1/11 (accessed June 8, 2007).

Politics and Policy

J. Scott Applewhite/File/AP Images

CHAPTER OBJECTIVES

When you finish reading Chapter 2, you should be able to do the following:

- Define what the ancient Greeks meant by politics
- Distinguish between programs and policies
- Illustrate how politics and policy are thought to differ from one another

- Summarize the main factors that have contributed to a more politicized policy-making environment
- Relate the values of freedom and equality to idealized models of liberal and libertarian political ideologies

Sometimes it seems that the world is broken into two sects. One group loves all that is "political." By this we generally mean that people are either attracted to the competitive aspects of the pursuit of power and influence over the public realm of life or they are drawn to the interworkings of the policies themselves. In the lingo of Washington, DC, and other centers of policy making, the latter group is the policy "wonks." Aficionados of politics often disdain the supposedly dull world of policy, while the lovers of policy enjoy immersing themselves in the complexities of issues, problems, and solutions. When Tim Russert, the renowned host of NBC's Sunday morning news show *Meet the Press*, passed away in the summer of 2008, one of his fellow journalists noted that Mr. Russert was always focused on politics and disdained policy stories, even though he was always well versed in the "nuts and bolts" of the policies themselves. In the minds of many people, notably among the nation's premier journalists, policy often takes a backseat to politics because policy just does not seem as interesting. More recently, *Wall Street Journal* said of Rep. Paul Ryan, a major player in the GOP's budget battles with the Obama White House and Mitt Romney's running mate in 2012, that he was "routinely described as wonkish, a policy-detail guy short on political reality."[1] Such a viewpoint lays down clear markers between politics and policy that are more imaginary than real. In order to show how the whole policy-making process—from problem identification to the analysis of the effectiveness of the policies themselves—is really a form of politics, the terms *policy* and *politics* both need some attention.

Politics and policy are intellectually distinct concepts. Any dictionary can provide the notion that politics is about the struggle for power and policy is a course of action or inaction set by those in power. As distinct as they are in the abstraction of a dictionary, politics and policy are clearly fused at some point in reality. The approach taken in this text, what I call the "policy as politics" framework, argues that policy making is a really a political endeavor. Whereas politics, broadly conceived, is the struggle for power itself or is the means to gain control over the instruments used to make policy, policy making is the struggle over ideas and values.[2] This chapter discusses the many conceptual facets of both politics and policy making. It also makes the case that policy making, and at times policies themselves, are best viewed from a political perspective by discussing the underlying struggle over values and ideas. As the chapter illustrates, this struggle takes place throughout the policy-making process, from the promotion of policies to their implementation and evaluation.

After reading this chapter, you should have a good sense of why policy making is a form of political activity and how the amount and intensity of this activity has increased over time. By emphasizing their political nature, we can have a fuller, more complete, and—hopefully—more compelling view of both policies and policy making. In so doing, this "policy as politics" approach should give you a better understanding of the intricacy of democracy as it exists in the American political system.

POLITICS AND POLICY: WHAT IS THE DIFFERENCE?

The term politics comes loaded with emotion and meaning—often quite negative. For example, to say that politics was at play when the city council in your area decided to award a contract to one construction firm over another for some roadwork, is to assert that favoritism played a role in that decision. Maybe the construction firm's owner has been a contributor to the mayor's campaign fund, or maybe the firm has ties to the political party that forms the majority on the council. In either case, power in the form of undue influence is on display in this example and, if true, such an action is unethical and probably illegal. While these words cover ethically and legally sketchy behavior, the use of "political" and "politics" in this way places tension on the other meaning of the words by stretching the terms to fit a wide range of meanings. Like stretching an elastic cord over and over again, the thing itself tends to lose its basic properties from overuse; this is the case with the terms "political" and "politics." The meaning of politics is in reference to the *polis*, or the people, in the language of the ancient Greeks. Since we have settled on a republic or representative form of government for our political system, politics and things that are political are logically the outputs or the processes of what representatives do in the service of the public. This may sound somewhat naïve given the low opinions Americans have about politicians, but it is a wide-angle perspective that should be considered when thinking about the meaning of politics.

Clearly, some forms of activity have an easier fit with the American view of what constitutes politics. Elections are the most obvious form of purely political action in the United States. (As if to confirm that this is true, *Campaigns and Elections*, a magazine read by professional campaign consultants and crammed with ads for polling firms and new software to "microtarget" voters, changed its name to *Politics* before changing it back.) Elections embody so much of what we think about when we reflect on politics largely because they are zero-sum affairs based on competition and conflict. Almost all of our elections are for single-member districts (only one person wins the office up for grabs), and they are usually based on plurality rules for winning (the triumphant candidate need only win the largest chunk of votes in an election to capture the victory). Coming in second, even if it is only by a scant margin, does not win anything for the candidate.

The drama surrounding the outcome and what seems like high stakes at the time are fascinating aspects of elections, and the media often reinforces these elements of campaigns since they resonate with our desire for politics as a form of entertainment. This is not a new phenomenon in our country or elsewhere. Even lawmaking, something that seldom features absolute winners and losers, has a history of being used as a form of entertainment and social-status climbing. It used to be quite fashionable and common for the elite of Washington, DC, to view the proceedings of the US House and, more desirably, the Senate from the galleries. The gentlemen and ladies would dress in their finest clothes and hope to be seen by others and perhaps have their presence noted in the society pages of the newspapers. The representatives and senators would do their best to provide a suitably enriching or noteworthy presentation on the matters before their respective legislative bodies. However, for most of the twentieth and twenty-first centuries, the business of policy making has been seen, with a number of very notable exceptions, as a less interesting endeavor.

The passage of the Civil Rights Act in 1964, the overhaul of the federal system of welfare in the mid-1990s, the congressional authorization to allow President George W. Bush to use force to enforce United Nation's mandates in 2003, and the passage of the Affordable Care Act (health care insurance reform) in 2010 were dramatic moments of legislative policy making. It would be fairly easy to go on and provide a listing of many other "big moments" in policy making. While this would be a useful exercise, it would also work to obscure an important point: much of what happens in terms of public policy does not feature the drama of these "big moments." We might not even know about fundamental shifts in policy until sometime later. In 2002, President Bush signed a presidential order that allowed the nation's domestic intelligence agencies to wiretap the phones of US citizens without first getting a warrant from a court, something that many people from both the conservative and liberal sides of the ideological spectrum saw as a clear violation of the Constitution's Fourth Amendment regarding search and seizure. This program of domestic surveillance that the administration said was aimed at rooting out terrorist activity only came to light for the public when the news media got wind of its existence. In December of 2006, the *New York Times* ran a story entitled, "Bush Lets U.S. Spy on Callers Without Courts."[3] The reaction to the warrantless wiretapping program caused a major uproar in Washington and elsewhere, and Congress took action by at least looking into the program. However, after intensive lobbying by the White House, Congress relented and did little to curtail the program.[4] This is an example of a policy that affected many Americans and upset many more when it was publicized, yet we lived for quite a period of time without knowing that it was present. It is a dramatic set of events and ideas, but does not easily conform to the "political" framework of what we would expect from something like an election. Did President Bush use the policy to aggrandize the power of his office? Did he see the program as a way to get to the heart of the next terrorist threat to the country? Are both of these prospects a possibility? Who won and who lost?

Democrats and others—not all on the left—howled at the damage done to our civil liberties by this program and were repulsed by what they saw as a bold overreach of power by President Bush. However, there were voices that agreed with the president when he argued that the uncovering of the domestic surveillance program was the real tragedy here and that Americans without ties to terrorism need not worry about their government's actions in the first place. Certainly there is a conflict over what we ought to be doing as a nation and a debate over governmental power evident in this example. Given these characteristics, it is hard to see the policy in question and the response to its discovery as apolitical. What about a policy that is less controversial? Is a policy only "political" when it causes enough friction to ignite conflict? This often seems to be true, since much of the policy we pick up on via the news media is highlighted because of its quarrelsomeness. But we need to get beyond this formulation if we want to see the real picture of public policy making as a part of politics.

It is a bit strange, then, to view the "wonkish" side of public policy as somehow outside the realm of politics. What if we slice the world into those who are interested in the rough and tumble fight over politics and those who are content with the supposedly more cerebral world inhabited by policy wonks? We are probably assuming that wonks, much like the stereotypical computer "nerd" who can fix your computer when you have no clue about what to do, are adverse to the conflict inherent in so-called real politics. These "wonkish" folks must desire the logical order that may be the stuff of policy making. However, the truth of the matter is that unlike fixing a PC, or even a Mac, policy making is not always a well-ordered endeavor. In fact, it is best thought of as another venue for political struggle, with winners and losers grappling over ideas and values.

What is needed is a way to think about policy and policy making that recognizes the political aspects of both. Policy and the processes that form it are what come from human invention. Because of this, policy must show the tool marks of its creators. The beliefs, attitudes, values, opinions, and prejudices of those involved will show up in the policies themselves. Such an approach is useful because we have moved from an outlook in which government, especially at the federal level, saw its main responsibility as creating and carrying out programs, a largely reactive posture of program administration, to an approach that focuses on the making of policy: policy making is a far more proactive and politically charged set of actions and responsibilities that includes choosing problems for resolution, creating solutions, and carrying those solutions out. As the eminent political scientist Theodore Lowi has argued, "Yes, policies cause politics."[5] By this, Professor Lowi means that the substance of a policy can and does cause the degree and type of conflict that one will see over the policy-making process. Relatively noncontroversial policies that reflect established societal norms and goals seldom produce much political strife. But policy goals that do run against the established tide of acceptability or that conflict with the desires of well-established interests are the ones that will generate the most political friction.

A MORE POLITICIZED POLICY-MAKING PROCESS

We are living in a world where all the phases of policy making—from the identification of problems to the implementation of solutions and the evaluation of their efficacy—have seen increases in the amount and intensity of disagreement over the proper role of government, what policy goals to pursue, and the usefulness of the policies themselves. While there has always been disagreement over policy making—after all, such friction is built into our constitutional structure by the choice of the country's founders—anecdotal and empirical evidence indicates that we are living in an era of increased conflict. Insider accounts from policy makers reflecting on their tenures in office in Washington, DC, for example, hold a sustained note of sadness for how policy making has become increasingly partisan, petty, and vindictive.[6] Nostalgia for the "good old days," that might never have existed, can account for some of these pronouncements about the current state of policy making, but the data coming from our chief policy-making body, Congress, is harder to dismiss. The level of partisanship as measured by party-line voting has increased over the last twenty years.[7] The increased power of party leaders, especially the Speaker of the US House of Representatives, has allowed the parties to act in ways that offer demands rather than compromises about the substance of policies; the result is that fewer major bills are passed in the contemporary era of Congress.[8] (Of course, one could argue that this is a positive outcome.)

The evolution of the presidency into the focal point for the public's attention on policy matters, largely framed by the news media, has given rise to phenomenon of "going public," in which presidents confront Congress over policies by using public pressure as a means to move lawmakers in the president's direction. The expanded numbers, increased professionalization, and sophistication of interest groups have added to the policy mix a field of skilled and effective players advocating for their particular interests on policy matters. Additionally, some have argued that the nation is in the throes of a culture war that pits traditional culture against progressive culture in a no-holds-barred fight for control of our policies and the nation's future.[9] These examples of the increased sources and expanded arenas of conflict place policy making and policy makers in a new world, one that has been evolving for some time, but that has now become our reality. Where did it come from and how did it happen? In essence, why has policy making become so polarized and conflictual, what is more conventionally thought of as politicized?

THE TRANSITION FROM PROGRAMS TO POLICIES

In a report issued by the White House's National Goals Research Staff on July 4, 1970, Daniel Patrick Moynihan, then a counselor to President Nixon and later a Democratic US senator from New York, wrote of a fundamental transition underway in government, one that deepened the political character of the government itself. Moynihan, who held a PhD in political science, among other academic credentials, argued that a shift was taking place away from program-oriented government toward policy-oriented government. "Government," wrote Moynihan, "is, for the most part, a collection of programs." Programs are "activities of certain kinds which are their own justification." For example, a program to increase the size of the interstate highway system has the implicit policy goal of making travel easier for the driving public. These activities are "authorized or required by statute."[10] We would easily recognize these programs by the legislation or other actions that put them in place and keep them going. The Federal-Aid Highway Act of 1956 and subsequent reauthorizations to fund the act illustrate what Moynihan meant by "program." Policy is a bit more opaque in his conceptualization, but it is worth the effort to understand it in his terms because it makes a useful contribution to the meaning of public policy making as part of the political process.

For Moynihan, problems, solutions, and actors were best seen as part of a holistic system; if one part of the system was altered, then the rest of the system's components would be affected. As such, understanding policy making requires a much broader view of how the system works or should work. Programs are based on the inputs of the system such as the demands of the public or interest groups, and the assumption is that programs result in desired outputs of the system. For example, if the public clamors for more jobs, training programs for job seekers could result in higher levels of employment. (However, higher levels of employment could foster inflation in the nation's economy as too many dollars, now in the possession of the newly expanded workforce, seek too few goods and services. All programs may produce unintended results, such as inflation in the foregoing example.) Policies, on the other hand, are "primarily concerned with the 'outputs' of a given system. The key term here is...system."[11] Continuing on with the example of economic matters, during ordinary times, the nation's economic policy—the overarching economic goals for the nation—is likely one that seeks to foster high levels of employment (short of full employment) and low inflation, but the federal government must act within the political, economic, and social constraints of the system. (A program to have the federal government take ownership of bad debts held by banks and other financial institutions such as the Troubled Asset Relief Program (TARP) or to become a major owner in a carmaker like Chrysler or GM would be, in ordinary times, outside of what the system would allow. Yet, the last several years have not been ordinary times, and the system itself may have changed or contained enough flexibility to allow these things to happen, at least temporarily.)

Moynihan's ideas are clearly informed by the work of others. In 1965, political scientist David Easton published *A Systems Analysis of Political Life* in which he depicted the policy process as a network of players and processes that provide inputs, things like elections and lobbying, and produce outputs, the programs and other outputs of government. The systems analysis approach greatly influenced the study of public policy and continues to do so today. Moynihan assimilated many of these ideas and, yet, his interpretation of them is importantly unique because he used them to explain the bigger shifts in *what* government was doing and *why* it was acting, rather than focusing on *how* government was doing these things. Policy is aimed at goals, not so much the means to the ends, as is the case with programs. In his own words, Moynihan gets to the heart of the role of policy as the road map for understanding and attempting to control the system: "[T]he object of policy is to guide government activities in accordance with the properties of a system."[12] In essence, the policy maker's job is to understand the constraints and possibilities of the system and fashion goals that fit within the system. Specific programs may be the ways to meet policy goals. Moynihan's conclusion was that by design or by happenstance, government was evolving structurally and philosophically around the shift to a worldview based on government as the *principal agent of policy change* rather than simply as the actor that created or implemented programs. This was not just reflecting the promises of successful candidates for office and the like. Rather, the federal government was becoming or had become a sustained promoter of policies. Part of this could well be the result of the momentum of government as it grew in the 1930s and expanded again in the 1960s. But it is more than inertia. It may have had a liberal/progressive pedigree at the outset, but this evolutionary role as policy advocate is something taken up by many wearing the label of conservative. Beginning with the Reagan era in the early 1980s and continuing with the George W. Bush presidency in the first eight years of the twenty-first century, the pattern of governmental policy advocacy continued apace. The interest in Ron Paul's libertarian ideas during the 2012 presidential race and the rise of the Tea Party movement both illustrate a backlash to what has been derided as "big government conservatism."

This all may sound like a rather fine point, but there is a great deal of importance to this shift. By embracing a systemic approach to activity based on policy, the government was wading deeper into the world of politics and away from the shores of program administration by becoming a proactive policy advocate in its own right. (Note, too, that his ideas are different from Easton's *systems analysis*, an academic approach to explaining the policy process. Moynihan's argument is that government actually embraced a systemic approach or was being molded by a system into something new.) Because policy making is holistic, it necessarily involves the public and other nongovernmental players. Moynihan states that the move toward policy should bring with it at least two of the hallmarks of American democracy: participation by the public and accountability to the public.[13] Back in 1970, Moynihan was arguing that some force—perhaps cultural change—was transforming government. He contended that this transformation would mean an increased role for the public and others to influence the outputs of government and would require government to be more responsive and open to the people.

Think back to our attempts so far to define the meaning of public policy as a political phenomenon. You may be struck by how much Moynihan's perceptions about what was just emerging at that time—about forty years ago—fit with what we have been thinking about so far in this text.

THE GOVERNMENT AS A POLICY MAKER

Keeping in mind Moynihan's ideas about the transition toward the increasing policy role played by government, let us think about some moments of political significance in the last twenty to twenty-five years that predict a smaller a role for government in the future, and arguably, a diminution in the amount and scope of the policies made by government. (A mantra of many contemporary political conservatives and most libertarians is that more government results in an increase in policies, programs, and taxes—what they consider to be very undesirable things.)

The Size of Government

In a debate held in the Reagan Presidential Library during the 2008 Republican primary and caucus season, the candidates fought each other over which one of them was most like Ronald Reagan. Each candidate claimed the right to say he was more "Reagan-like" in his love of lower taxes, stronger national defense, and smaller government. The 2012 GOP nomination fight between Newt Gingrich and Mitt Romney repeated the tug-of-war over claiming the mantle of Reagan. About a decade prior to this in 1996, during his State of the Union Address, President Bill Clinton told a joint session of Congress and the nation that the era of big government was over. In the star-crossed presidential campaign of 2000, candidates George Bush and Al Gore each promised a smaller and more efficient federal government if they were elected. The idea of a smaller federal government is, apparently, an attractive one for many candidates, officials, and segments of the public. It is a fair question to ask then, has the federal government gotten smaller over time? If it has, the fewer resources and functions it has at its disposal would probably mean less in the way of federal programs and policies.

In the summer of 1990, the tipping point was reached for the demise of America's rival in international politics. The Soviet Union was beginning to unravel. Internal reforms, sectionalism, a failed war of occupation in Afghanistan, and general unrest among the population added gravity to the increasingly untenable economic and political systems within the USSR. As the Soviet system dissolved—right on television, in the case of the fall of the wall separating East and West Berlin—the United States began to stand alone as the globe's only superpower. With no other comparable rival, what need was there for the massive US military and its ancillary civilian supports that made up what President Eisenhower called the "military-industrial complex"? George Herbert Walker Bush, the president at the time, openly talked about a "peace dividend," or newly freed sources of funding for programs or tax breaks now that we no longer needed to fund the Cold War. It was thought at the time that government would shrink in size, in terms of employees, because the Department of Defense and every other Cold War oriented department, agency, and bureau in the federal government would need to do less. In the short term, this was an accurate prediction. The number of federal employees did shrink by about 2 million in the period from 1990 through 1999. By 2003, more than 1 million of those jobs had been added back.[14] Certainly, the terrorist attacks of September 11, 2001, were a reason for the increase in the size of the federal government as it worked to respond to new threats from abroad and at home. However, if we take out the true reductions in the wake of the end of the Cold War and add in the post-9/11 increases, the exact size of the federal government is still debatable. This is because both the Clinton and George W. Bush administrations practiced a bit of sleight of hand with the measurements of the federal workforce. The Clinton administration's Reinventing Government program aimed to reduce the size of the federal workforce and to show how the government could work better and more efficiently if it trimmed some unnecessary jobs. On paper, there were reductions in the number of federal workers. However, workers were often farmed out to other departments, agencies, and bureaus, or borrowed from other locations. This made the head-counting for employment measurements a bit tricky and, as critics of the program charged, showed that the administration was not really doing much to reduce the size of the federal workforce. Similar charges were leveled at the administration of George W. Bush, along with a new twist. Since federal employees are either "on-budget," meaning they are directly employed by the federal government (mostly in the military or as civil servants), or "off-budget," meaning they are contracted to do work as private sector employees. How these two groups are counted will give you different measures of the size of the federal workforce. (You may recall that some of the people in the State Department who snooped in the passport files of the major presidential contenders in 2008 were contract employees—people hired by private firms to work for the federal government. Some of these people were fired for their unethical behavior, but they were less likely to face the threat of legal penalties because they were not directly employed by the State Department.) In keeping with its conservative image that promotes smaller government, the Bush administration was a champion for the reduction in the size of the federal workforce. However, just as the Clinton administration was slammed for playing a "shell game" with federal workers, so too was the Bush administration taken to task for undercounting the size of the government by excluding "off-budget" workers from its tallies.[15]

Is the federal government smaller today than it was at the end of the Cold War? Without equivocating too much, the answer is no. In important measures, the federal government is as big or bigger than it was in 1990. Again, it depends on how the numbers are tallied. There are now fewer on-budget civil servants, although that number has been rising, but what some call the "hidden workforce" of those hired under contracts or grants swelled to nearly 11 million in 2006. Political scientist Paul Light has tracked the size of the federal government since the 1970s, and in 2006 he estimated the "true size" of the federal government—on-budget and off-budget—at 14.6 million, up from 12.1 million in 2002.[16] The addition of a new cabinet level department, Homeland Security—first fought against partly because it would increase the size of the federal government, and then embraced by the Bush administration—is obvious evidence of a structural expansion of the federal bureaucracy. And more recently, as the financial recession dragged on into the summer of 2009, President Obama called for the creation of the Consumer Financial Protection Bureau (CFPB) designed to help consumers avoid risky loans and to oversee the credit industry.[17] Amid a great many charges and countercharges over the need for and usefulness of the agency, the CFPB was created in 2010 as part of the Dodd-Frank Wall Street Reform and Consumer Protection Act. The agency's advocates see this new addition to the bureaucracy as a necessary "cop on the beat" that will protect the nation's borrowers, while its detractors are sure that it is just a new layer of regulatory bureaucracy that will only harm the business environment. There was such acrimony over the existence of the agency that, in early 2012, President Obama had to use a recess appointment to install a commissioner to run the bureau to avoid a showdown with the Senate that would have continued to cripple the functioning of the CFPB.[18]

Perhaps the more telling point is one gained by comparing the size of the federal government today with what it looked like in 1970, the year that Patrick Moynihan saw the coming shift in emphasis from programs to policy. It is not easy to make this comparison since there is little reliable data about the number of federal government employees, both on- and off-budget, prior to 1984. However, one of the recognized experts in the analysis of the size of the federal government, Paul C. Light, estimates that by the mid-1990s, civilian on-budget employment doubled since 1968 and the "shadow government" of off-budget workers skyrocketed.[19]

Two points are worth making. First, if we assume that a larger government—in terms of workers and other institutional components—means more capacity to engage in policy making and may add to the inertia that a larger government can create in maintaining and expanding existing programs, the political character of policy is likely to be more visible today than when government was smaller. Since policy making is a political process, it is logical to assume that more capacity for policy making will increase the importance of political forces. Second, the composition of this expanded government, especially the

Mesut Dogan/Shutterstock

workers themselves, are a potential source for an increase in the politicization of policy making and, perhaps, of the policies themselves. Excluding the military, people hired to work for the federal government "on-budget" generally have the label of "civil servant." They are hired because of their merit as demonstrated on exams and other forms of objective evaluation. They are not supposed to be hired or promoted because of their political connections, family ties, or other non-merit attributes. The whole point of the creation of a merit-based civil service was to remove the overtly political aspects of the federal government's dealings with policy and administration and provide a competent federal workforce. However, since the "off-budget" part of the federal government has grown so much in recent years, this expansion in contract and grant workers means that the vast majority of the federal workforce is not hired nor entirely managed by the civil service laws of the United States. If an "on-budget" civil servant does something to further a personal or partisan point of view in an overt way that undermines the operation or the goals of his or her department or agency, there are fairly clear rules and procedures to discipline and possibly remove that person from his or her job. What about contract employees? Can a civil servant in a managerial position effectively discipline such a suspected wrongdoer? Since the contract worker does not technically work directly for the federal government, the lines of authority are often blurry.

Who Works for an Expanding Government?
The Rise of the Contract Workforce

Just who is being hired to work via contracts and grants is an important question, too. The civil service system of hiring is based on a premise that partisanship and ideological leanings are not factors in the decision to hire; merit is the consideration used for initial employment, continuation, and promotion. Civil servants know this and are well versed in the laws that limit the political activities of federal employees in the course of their jobs. However, companies and organizations given contracts or grants to provide employees to the federal government are not required to abide by the same set of rules. Yes, they must stick with prohibitions against discrimination in hiring and other federal laws concerning the public workplace, but the hiring mechanisms in place for the federal government that seek to neutralize the influence of partisanship and ideology are not duplicated in the private sector hiring process. Is this a problem? Does it mean that the "off-budget" federal workforce is honeycombed with partisans and ideologues out to do the political bidding of some party or faction? That is a rather dark scenario and one that would be difficult to substantiate, even if it were true. The best evidence to date is often circumstantial.

There may not be an epidemic of such partisan or ideological behavior, and neither major political party's adherents are likely to be immune to such weaknesses, but such instances underline how the changed makeup of the federal workforce has the potential to politicize the policies and administrative functions of the federal government. A US inspector general's investigation concluded that a senior aide to Alberto Gonzales, the attorney general for much of George W. Bush's second term, admitted to using partisanship as a key factor in hiring career attorneys for the Department of Justice. The aide, Monica Goodling, was reported to have asked prospective employees why it would be an honor to serve President Bush and why they were Republicans, questions that are clearly out of bounds for the hiring of civil servants. Connected to the hiring scandal at the Department of Justice is the firing of several US attorneys who may have had their jobs terminated because they failed to prove their loyalty to the Republican Party. The allegations are that they did not vigorously prosecute the types of cases that would strike at Democratic Party constituencies—cases dealing with core party issues such as voting access and the prosecution of illegal immigrants.[20]

Outside of the shift to a reliance on the contract workforce, it is also worth noting that the federal government, especially the executive branch, has become more politically engaged. For example, the Executive Office of the President (EOP) was created by the 1939 Executive Reorganization Act to provide more support for the increasingly burdensome task faced by the somewhat archaic institutional presidency in attempting to carry out the flood of federal programs created by the New Deal. The EOP was there to give the presidency help with the implementation of policy and basic staffing requirements of the modernizing presidency, but it quickly morphed into a large organizational feature that presidents have used to create and then promote policy proposals. The present EOP employs about 1,600 people and has a budget over $100 million a year.[21] The Office of Management and Budget, the largest part of the EOP, has been used as the means for presidents to direct policy choices by way of the creation of executive budget proposals and manage implementation through review of departmental and agency proposals for new regulations. These sizeable levers over major aspects of the policy process in Washington have, arguably, become more politicized as presidents have increasingly staffed OMB with appointees rather than with presumably less politically motivated career civil servants.[22]

Policy Promotion and the Permanent Campaign

There is other evidence for increased politicization of the policy process within the federal government, especially the executive branch. In 1982, journalist Sidney Blumenthal first wrote of what he called the "permanent campaign," a utilization of campaign techniques by those engaged in governing. In other words, presidents and members of Congress were taking the practices of election campaigns—things like poll testing ideas for their viability with the public, using media advertisements to sell policies, attacking opponents in personal ways for failing to agree with positions on issues—and applying them to governing. Said another way, the campaign to elect the candidate did not stop when the office was won on Election Day, it just shifted into a never-ending operation to market the president or member of Congress and his or her policies. Blumenthal was greatly put off by this since he believed that governing should be and had been a process in which the struggle for power was over after the election and the time for honest debate and even compromise was at hand. However, the permanent campaign has little, if any, room for deliberation and conciliation. Governing is campaigning, and campaigning is war.

Blumenthal seems quite prescient as we look back and see what transpired in Washington and elsewhere since 1982. By most accounts, the level of friction over policy mushroomed in the 1980s and got even worse in the 1990s. Certainly, divided government during this time played a major role in the increase in hostilities between the White House and Capitol Hill. The so-called Republican Revolution of the mid-1990s brought the GOP to power in both houses of Congress for the first time since the 1940s, and the conservative wing of the party had reason to believe that their ideas and determination got them to that place. True believers in the Revolution, especially in the House, and thin margins for the Republicans in both houses ensured that a disciplined Republican Party would challenge the Democrats at every turn. The election of George W. Bush in 2000, and the brief return of the Democrats to the control of the Senate soon after, made for a contentious period in Washington. Even with the post-9/11 ascendency of the Republican brand, culminating in Bush's win in 2004, the divisive tone of governing that so neatly fit the mold of the permanent campaign did not dissipate. The president's drive toward policy initiatives was very much in keeping with what Blumenthal first identified nearly a quarter of a century ago. In early 2005, flush with a perceived injection of political capital from his victory over John Kerry, President Bush moved forward on a number of domestic policy fronts, but mainly a push to reform the Social Security system by creating private retirement accounts. These efforts had all the hallmarks of a campaign for office. The president's staff used polling to test language and word choices for the policy initiatives. For example, Social Security would not be privatized—a term that tested poorly with the public—but would be reworked to allow for more "opportunity" through the creation of "personal retirement accounts." As Republican pollster and language guru Frank Luntz put it, " 'Private' is exclusive. 'Private' is limiting.... 'Personal' is encompassing."[23] The president literally hit the campaign trail to gain media attention for these policies. He held town hall-type meetings with members of the public who were carefully selected on the basis of their preexisting support for the president's goals. Even the stage settings for these events were cautiously rendered, including backdrops with the message of the day repeated in cascades of print on a scrim or banner behind the president. As the battle over the president's reform plan ran into stiffer opposition, especially from senior citizens who would be particularly affected by the policy, the administration refined and narrowed the messages found on the stage sets from "Strengthening Social Security" to "Keeping Our Promise to Seniors."[24]

Of course, the president's efforts did not happen in a vacuum, and the role of interest groups is very important in this case, as it has been in all the struggles over major policy initiatives for at least the last generation. With the expansion of a larger federal government in the 1960s, the number of interest groups has greatly increased. The simple logic of the matter is that if the government is more active in the policy arena, then groups need direct involvement with policy making in order to bend policies and programs in ways that will advance their goals and values; the expansion of the size and activities of federal and the state governments resulted in a concomitant rise in the number and activism of interest groups.[25]

These groups are often well funded and highly sophisticated in terms of their ability to influence both policy makers and the public. We would be hard pressed to find an instance in which interest groups failed to support or attack a major or more middling policy initiative at the federal level. President Bush's attempt to reform Social Security was no different: groups, such as Progress for America, an organization with ties to the Republican Party, spent millions of dollars in support of the president's plan, as did a host of other organizations, most with connections to the GOP or the business community.[26] "As a spokesman for [Progress for America] said, it was applying the lessons it learned electing a president to selling a public policy."[27] Groups opposed to the president's plan were also quite animated. The American Association of Retired Persons (AARP), one of the largest member organizations in the country, claimed to have orchestrated the placing of 460,000 phone calls in opposition to the plan to members of Congress.[28]

In the end, President Bush failed to convince the public and Congress that his plan to overhaul Social Security was a worthwhile idea. Most participants and observers agreed that the nation's safety net for older Americans and other citizens who depend on Social Security for at least part of their well-being was not and still is not in great shape. Yet the president could not move the public and its representatives, even with a major effort by the White House and a sizeable coalition of interest groups helping along the way. George Edwards, one of the first scholars of the presidency to systematically investigate the presidency's relationship with the public in the modern era, argues that there are serious limits to the power of the permanent campaign mode of leadership. In George Bush's case, a number of major policy victories were won early on in his presidency in issue areas as diverse as education, prescription drugs for seniors, and the decision to go to war in Iraq. Edwards argues that these gains were won when there was little organized opposition by the Democrats or others to the plans, and when the public simply had more trust in George Bush. It may be, states Edwards, that the use of the techniques of the permanent campaign itself made the public skeptical of the president's ideas.[29] It was as though the public had seen this magic trick enough times to know how it was done, and they were put off at the notion that someone thought that it would work again.

The episode of George W. Bush and Social Security says a number of things about the nexus of politics and policy making. First, Bush is not alone in adopting the use of the permanent campaign as the main mode of his governing style. His predecessor, Bill Clinton, did it too and with much gusto. As two longtime observers of presidents and Congress noted in 2000, "In his eighth year in the White House, Clinton remains in full campaign mode."[30] Going back to the time of FDR, there are numerous examples of presidents attempting to measure and then move public opinion on behalf of their desired policies. What is noteworthy about Bush is that he used these techniques so consistently. (This is not to argue that some structural change in the political environment requires the intense reliance on the tools of the permanent campaign. Barack Obama has used them, too, but in the long run, the personal managerial and leadership style of future presidents will be the factors that determine how consistently these techniques are employed.) Second, presidents and other elected officials use these techniques of selling public policies because they believe they work, and they believe that if they don't use them, the opposition will. Third, the public may have or is developing a "baloney detector" that is triggered when public officials use permanent campaign-type techniques too often or go too far with them in the selling of policies. What may be acceptable during an election campaign may not always or even sometimes be suitable for the governing of policy matters. In 2004, when the Democratic Party's presidential nominee, John Kerry, had his service during the Vietnam War questioned in a process that has since become known as "Swiftboating," or when George W. Bush's arrest for drunken driving in the early 1970s was leaked to the press in the last few days before Election Day in 2000, many Americans probably said, "Ugh! Politics!" We claim to dislike such underhanded moves, but we tend to accept them as part of electoral politics. (In fact, our history is filled with rather scurrilous attacks on candidates. The election of 1800 is noteworthy for the nasty assaults on Thomas Jefferson.) Have we come to a point where governing—policy making and carrying out policy—is seen as more important than elections themselves? Certainly a strong streak of cynicism is marbled through the American public at the present time. We see our political parties as offering the choice between the lesser of two evils. Many of our problems, from racism to the environment, seem intractable or too costly to properly attack. We may be at a moment in time when the sparkly music of the permanent campaign rings hollow in our ears and we crave something more substantial. The poor performance of government in the aftermath of Hurricane Katrina, the failure to find weapons of mass destruction in Iraq and the bloody insurgency that followed the US invasion to remove the threat of those nonexistent weapons, the seemingly endless rounds of negations over trying to avoid the "fiscal cliff," and other shortcomings of what we were either promised or expected from our government could be leading us to a more hard-boiled view about policy and policy makers. As with all phenomena, the next tests of policy makers will provide the data points for measuring the expectations and reactions of the public.

The transition from a programmatic to a policy focus at the federal level, the expansion of government and potential politicization of its workforce through off-line jobs, the rise of the permanent campaign in governing, for all these reasons, the policy-making process and its extension into governing have become increasingly politicized. What may be less obvious, yet more fundamental, is that even without these developments—and they are evolutionary changes—public policy would still be political because of its human origin. You may be thinking, "Well, if that is the case and all human actions are in some way political, then artistic expression or what kind of car I drive are political, too."

The short answer to the implied question here is a qualified no. Are you writing a song that seeks to change or at least bring to light the power relationships you see in the world around you or do you just have an urge to put some words to a catchy melody? Do you choose to drive a hybrid car because you see it as an expression of your distaste for the nation's foreign policy or was it just one of the ones on the lot that fit your budget? The lines comprising overtly political statements get thinner and finer the farther away we get from the actions taken by those who have been given the power to make consequential decisions on the public's behalf in this republic. Social movement activists in the 1960s were fond of noting that the personal was political, meaning your lifestyle and personal actions had political consequences and overtones. While this is a great subject for debate, it is outside of the definitions of *public* policy we have already established. Individual-level actions and thoughts are important, but for the purposes of understanding the political character of public policy, they need to be understood mostly as collective factors.

HUMAN VALUES, IDEOLOGY, AND POLICY MAKING AS POLITICS

It has been said that making legislation, a form of policy, is akin to making sausage, since both are messy and create products that contain things that are, perhaps, best not thought about. As much as it is trendy to cast a cynical eye toward policy making, especially legislative policy making, such an approach tends to obscure the point that humans are responsible for the policy outcomes. Humans create the process by which the product is produced and are an essential part of what goes into the outputs of the process. While the parameters of a system shape the way policy is made, just as the machinery and procedures in a factory create a fairly uniform product, the results are often idiosyncratic and show the marks of the makers.

Taking a slightly different metaphorical track, the world of fine art offers a similar illustration of the importance of the human element—the essence of all that is political—in the character of policy. The world of fine art is plagued by forgeries. It is rather amazing to think that somewhere, sequestered in clandestine studios and workshops, very skillful men and women are busily toiling to create fake versions of paintings, sculptures, and other types of artwork that appear to come from the hands of recognized masters. Of course, when there is money to be made, the temptation to fool gullible buyers is strong. Experts in art appraisal and forgery detection are often required to rule a work in or out as a true creation rather than a well-executed fake. Even today, with powerful forensic tools available, many art experts can tell a phony from an original just because it does not seem "right." Something about the artist's way of leaving him or herself in the piece cannot be duplicated even with the right materials and tools. All art is wrought by human hands, and the intentions and even peculiarities of these humans are transmitted to and made part of the final product. Jackson Pollack's famous "splatter" pictures, in which paint was literally spilled and sprayed on a canvas, look easy to duplicate, but the trained eye can see the artist's hand in what may look like the aftermath of a paintball war to others.

Policies are not art nor are they sausages. They are, however, human creations based on ideas. Political scientist Deborah Stone states this in the following way:

> Ideas are a medium of exchange and a mode of influence even more powerful than money and votes and guns.... Ideas are at the center of all political conflict. Policy making, in turn, is a constant struggle over the criteria for classification, the boundaries of categories, and the definition of ideals that guide the way people behave.[31]

For Stone, the heart of policy making is how people interpret values such as equity, efficiency, security, and liberty and how they use these values in the identification of problems and possible solutions. For example, most people would agree that equality is a highly desirable goal for our society. Should we, therefore, guarantee an equal level of health care for all citizens? Or should the government simply offer the *opportunity* for health care through policies that help businesses hire more workers who might then receive some health care coverage through their employers? Our answers to such questions reflect our preferences about the role of government in our lives. They also reflect the influence exerted on us by the government, the media, and other organized interests.

In the early 1990s, debate about health care coverage for the roughly 40 million Americans who lacked insurance (today's numbers are even higher) took center stage. President Clinton presented a plan to provide health care coverage that mobilized both supporting and opposing forces. Some critics charged that the bill was done in by an oppressive and misleading lobbying campaign, led by the nation's health care and health insurance industries. The lobbying campaign featured TV ads voicing opposition to an overly complex policy that would ultimately hurt the average health care consumer and urging people to contact their government representatives. The ads worked wonderfully, and public support for Clinton's plan slipped drastically. Opinion polls taken at the time still showed strong support for the basic idea of insuring those who lacked coverage, but the Clinton plan was dead in the water.[32] Ultimately, Clinton's health care policy proposal died at the congressional committee stage.

This issue is difficult to fit into conventionally used ways of thinking about public policy such as the policy process or stages model. Using this model, we might say that the president put health care onto the nation's agenda but that it then failed to move successfully through the other phases of the process. This is a fairly accurate statement, but it tells us very little about what actually happened along the way. This is where ideas about how people view what is good and desirable in government and politics become important.

Let us look at two terms that are often found at the bull's-eye of debates about public policy, **freedom** and equality. Consider this familiar portion of the Declaration of Independence: "We hold these truths to be self-evident, that all men are created equal, that they are endowed by their Creator with certain unalienable Rights, that among these are Life, Liberty, and the pursuit of Happiness." This often-cited excerpt is the profession of a set of values that, presumably, makes us one people sharing core beliefs in equality and liberty. There is some truth in this statement: not many people in this country would openly denounce the ideas of freedom or equality.

These two values frame many of the policies proposed by our representatives or by those seeking governmental action. For example, President George W. Bush signed a bill into law that made it harder for people to declare bankruptcy and thus avoid repaying their debts. He praised the policy as an opportunity for lower-income Americans to get access to loans and other credit, indicating that banks and lenders would approve more loans because of the decreased possibility of failure to repay them. In other words, the president was praising the new policy as a way to equalize access to credit for all citizens. Critics of the bill charged that this change in the law would increase profits and reduce risks for the already powerful banks and other financial institutions by decreasing the freedom of those not in power, the down-on-their-luck defaulters, to get out of paying back what they owed. *Both* the president and his opponents spoke the language of freedom and equality.

Think about how the word *freedom* is used. President Bush used it twenty-seven times in his second inaugural address—in connection with proposals as different as his vision for a free Iraq and a plan he called the "ownership society," which would give each US citizen more control over his or her personal finances and economic future. Bush zeroed in on reform of the nation's Social Security system as the centerpiece for domestic policy in his second term in office. Social Security is the most important strand in the so-called safety net—created in the 1930s by FDR's New Deal and extended in the 1960s by LBJ's Great Society—which protects workers in their retirement years. Bush proposed that workers divert some of their Social Security taxes, which currently pay benefits to existing retirees, into individual investment accounts. Those accounts would earn or lose money like other private investments, such as stocks. According to the president, this change in policy would give workers the freedom to exercise more control over their finances in preparation for retirement.

Not everyone agreed with President Bush's use of the terms *equality* and *freedom* in conjunction with bankruptcy reform and the "ownership society." Critics of the bankruptcy bill said that ensuring equal access to credit was not really an issue, since banks are happy to give credit even to people with poor financial histories so that the banks can make money on late fees, high credit card interest rates, and other penalties that snare people who become financially overextended. These critics charged that the real purpose of the new law was to bar debtors from seeking bankruptcy so that creditors could keep making profits from them.[33] Bush's detractors saw the "ownership society" not as an advancement of personal freedom but as a way for the government to decrease its responsibilities to honest, hardworking citizens who have contributed to Social Security and count on it to ensure a comfortable retirement.

So who is right? How can people on one side see an advancement of equality or freedom when those on the other view the same actions as a retreat from these cherished values? One persuasive answer is that each side defines *freedom* and *equality* in different ways. A number of political thinkers have pondered this solution, and their ideas have much to say about the nature of public policy.

Freedom

In the "land of the free," we assume that we share the same meaning of liberty or freedom. If this is true, we should pursue policies that promote freedom, right? However, freedom is a complex idea, and not everyone defines it in the same way. Is freedom the ability to think, travel, and speak freely and associate with whomever you want? Or is it the limitation of other people meddling in your life? Of course, you can only think, travel, speak, and associate to the degree that you are limited by other people and outside forces. However, as Americans, we tend to group ourselves into two camps. Some say that freedom exists to the extent that we can do what we wish; others see freedom only in the absence of someone or some force limiting what we can do. The British political theorist Sir Isaiah Berlin called the first version *positive* liberty or freedom because people tend to express it as the ability to do something. Berlin labeled the second version *negative* liberty or freedom because the measure of freedom, usually expressed as the freedom from some outside force, is based on how few limits there are on its enjoyment.[34]

These two versions of freedom are connected closely to people's views of the role of government. If freedom is measured and defined by what you can do (positive freedom), whatever helps you extend this enjoyment of liberty must be a good thing. Students in a public university or college may see that government can create opportunities for a high-quality education that would otherwise not be available to them. Students in both private and public colleges and universities can experience the extension of freedom through the federal and some state governments' student loan programs, such as Pell Grants. Without this support, your freedom to learn and gain an advantage in the competition for good jobs and careers would be decreased. From this viewpoint, government creates freedom by expanding opportunity. However, a reasonable person could look at the same example and make the case that to provide a lower-cost, high-quality education to a wider segment of the population at a public college or university, the public must pay higher taxes. This person might view these increased taxes as an intrusion into his or her private life and a limitation on the freedom to use the money as he or she sees fit. If we look at it this way, government activity such as sponsorship of grants, loans, and funding of public colleges and universities causes a loss of personal freedom.

Let us revisit the example of President Bush's "ownership society." The president stressed individual freedom in a way that touched largely on negative freedom, increasing personal freedom by limiting government action. If the federal government controls the Social Security taxes used to fund the benefit system, this limits your enjoyment of personal freedom. A policy that frees up your earnings by diverting them away from the existing Social Security program and allowing you to choose how to invest that money creates more freedom for you.

People who see freedom in its positive form would likely take the perspective that the federal government's Social Security program does something that private accounts may not be able to do: provide retirement benefits that are resistant, if not immune, to the ups and downs of the financial markets. In this way, government lifts the burden of worry about the performance of stocks and other investments, freeing individuals to concentrate on other matters, which may include additional ways to save and invest for retirement.

The idea about personal or private accounts is one that may have had its greatest airing during the George W. Bush era, but it surfaced again on the 2012 presidential campaign trail, with Newt Gingrich touting many of the same arguments for their desirability.[35]

Equality

Like freedom, equality is highly valued by Americans. And like freedom, equality is divisible into two meanings that have powerful effects on public policy. The ideas of Alexis de Tocqueville, the French aristocrat and political thinker who traveled through the United States in the 1830s to study our version of democracy, persist today. He argued that Americans often hold conflicting interpretations of equality, especially if it means political equality or something broader, such as social or economic equality.[36] Later political thinkers have elaborated on Tocqueville's insights by asserting that there are two forms of this value, one based on the *equality of process* and the other based on the *equality of outcomes*.[37]

Deborah Stone illustrates the difference between these two concepts by asking us to do a mental exercise: divide a cake among a group of people. How, she asks, might we go about this task in a way that would ensure equality? One sure way to do this would be to do what happens at most birthday parties: you count the number of people who want cake and then divide the whole cake by that number. What matters here is that the final result is fair, as measured by who gets what. But there is an equally logical way to approach divvying up the cake that reflects another way of thinking about equality. What if the cake were placed in the center of a room and all who wanted some sat in a circle at an equal distance from it? Now everyone has an equal opportunity to get what they want—a messy proposition, especially if you're talking about kids, and particularly if some want more than others. And, of course, some may be faster or more ruthless in their pursuit of the cake. (Think again of the kids.) It is safe to assume that some party guests will get more cake than others. Stone calls this opportunity-based version of equality the *equality of process*.[38] But is this equality? If so, it is not the same kind of equality as an equal division based on the number who say that they want cake.

The cake example is likely to stick in your mind because of the absurdity of the exercise. We can easily imagine the slapstick results of an all-out mad dash for cake at a child's birthday party. But what if the desired object is not cake but health care, a well-paying job, or a sound education? Should we strive for the equality of outcomes and redistribute those outcomes from the haves to the have-nots? Or should we seek out and support solutions that provide opportunities to equalize competition? The answers to these questions rest on your view of equality. As with the concept of freedom, this view is closely connected to how you perceive the role of government. If you champion equality of outcomes, you will likely see the need for government action to create equal outcomes, because you see human beings as generally self-interested and unwilling to share their resources. Our nation's founders stated this eloquently in their writings, notably "Federalist No. 10". People who believe that equality prevails when the rules of the game are fair and open for participation (the equality of process) will view active governmental involvement less favorably. To them, government's role should be limited to setting and enforcing basic standards of fair play and access.

Political Ideology

These ideas about freedom and equality may sound more familiar when they are linked to political ideology. Table 2.1 shows that the ideas of someone who holds the *process* view of equality and the *negative* view of freedom have a strong resemblance to **classical liberalism**, an ideology of the eighteenth and nineteenth centuries that today we call libertarianism or a limited government version of **conservatism**. (Given the embrace of larger government and expanded government programs by the recent administration of George W. Bush, it is clear that the diversity of the modern conservative movement encompasses differing views about the appropriate size and scope of government. The 2012 campaign for the Republican Party's presidential nomination featured Ron Paul, a Republican congressman who makes much about his record of voting for very few spending bills and his desire to eliminate many of the departments of the federal government.) In many ways, this modern libertarian/limited government conservative view of politics is built on faith in the free market to regulate the economics of a society. Modern libertarians/ limited government conservatives see government's main role as setting basic policies to see that people have equal *opportunities*, but government's activity must stop there so that it does not limit personal liberty. In opposition to this present-day libertarian/limited government conservative ideology stands **modern liberalism**, or what is now often called **progressivism**. Liberals or progressives, who tend to favor equal *outcomes* and share faith in the *positive*

TABLE 2.1

Summarizing Notions of "Freedom" and "Equality"

	Positive Freedom ("Freedom to...")	Negative Freedom ("Freedom from...")
Equality of Process	Mixed ideology	Libertarian/Limited government conservative ideology
Equality of outcomes	Liberal ideology	Mixed ideology

version of freedom, favor a more activist government. They see government as a powerful force needed to overcome inequality and expand the amount of freedom available to all citizens.[39] Of course, these are models of pure ideologies, and most Americans have more mixed ideological orientations. Some analysts argue that the pragmatism of America's political culture comes from a mainstream, blended ideology that uses its views of these key values in different ways in different situations.

It is tempting to think that a process, the result of a systemic undertaking or a complex event or happening, is beyond the influence of human values and desires. We tend to think this way concerning matters great and small. Take for example the way we sometimes treat the music that we enjoy. Great musicians are often known for their signature "sound" and even give human names to their instruments, as though the guitar, violin, or trumpet had a voice of its own without the input of the performer. The great blues guitar player B.B. King has had a succession of very similar Gibson guitars he calls "Lucille." Rock legend Eric Clapton made many of his signature recordings with the Fender Stratocaster that he dubbed "Blackie." The late Jerry Garcia had a series of custom made guitars—"Wolf," "Tiger," "Rosebud," "Lighting Bolt," and "Top Hat"—crafted from exotic woods and other rare materials that made them stand as works of art beyond their playability and advanced electronics. (After his death in 1995, some of these guitars were auctioned off for at least $100,000 a piece, a sum well beyond what it would cost to have such instruments built from scratch.) A niche in the musical instrument industry has emerged to try to provide versions of famous guitars for the masses with the urge to rock like their heroes. Companies even tout effect boxes that they claim will give the player that "Clapton," "Hendrix," or whatever tone. Yet, in this era of YouTube, it is easy to find examples of these musicians jamming with borrowed instruments and sounding very much like themselves. Clearly, much of the signature sound of such iconic players is in their hands and their approach to playing. This point is applicable to policy as well; the process or policy environment may have less to do with the character of policy than the value orientations of the policy players themselves. The other parts matter, but in many cases they may be the colorations rather than what makes up the essential nature of the policies themselves.

CONCLUSION

Policy making has become increasingly politicized over the course of at least the last forty years. There is a great deal of evidence, both anecdotal and empirical, to support this observation. This trend may be permanent or only a set of points on the graph of our political history. It may signal the decline of the deliberative and representative soul of our republic or it could be evidence that these aspects of our democracy are alive and well, if a bit discomforting to witness from time to time.

No matter what position you may take on the contemporary state of policy making, it is worth noting at this point that policy making is a very human endeavor. We humans live with one another in communities tied together in varying degrees by many factors including culture, age, wealth, kinship, partisanship, gender, and ethnicity. The conflict that we see, while sometimes upsetting and frustrating, is the heart of politics in a democracy. As Deborah Stone states, "Policy making...is a constant struggle over the criteria for classification, the boundaries of categories, and the definition of ideals that guide the way people live."[40] We are, as Aristotle noted over two thousand years ago, "political animals," working and competing with one another over things that are of value and over the meaning of values themselves. Policy making has always been at the center of such struggles. That the struggles have intensified and, perhaps, are waged over higher stakes, means that we should pay even more attention, certainly not less, to policy making as part of the political process. Gaining more knowledge about how public policy is made gives us a greater grasp of contemporary politics in the United States and the present state of our democracy.

SUMMARY

The division between politics and policy is often overstated; policy making is a highly political process and much of politics—especially electoral politics—is framed in terms of the policies candidates say they will pursue once in office. Policy making has always been a political undertaking but it has become much more so in the last forty or more years.

Social and political changes occurring in the 1960s and 1970s have transformed government, especially the federal government, into more of a proactive policy advocate and less of a pragmatic administrator. This policy posture is largely a response to societal changes and an evolution in the expectations about what government can and should do—a trend that Pat Moynihan presciently noted at the beginning of the 1970s. These changes in expectations about the role for government helped to fuel an expansion in the institutional capabilities of government and in its size. Additionally, a governmental workforce more open to political influence has evolved as the use of "off-budget" contract workers has become more commonplace and as presidents have increasingly used the institution of the president to promote policy goals and to shape policy outcomes.

The layers of government in our federal system are increasingly ready and positioned to act as a policy advocates. This stance helps to explain the prevalence of the "permanent campaign" and a world of policy advocacy in Washington, DC, and elsewhere predicated on ideological divides over fundamental ideals, such as the meaning of freedom and equality in our democracy. These developments are troubling for many people who desire a less political form of policy making, one that seeks to find the greater good for all through compromise and deliberation. While there are real concerns about a policy-making system that is as politically underscored as ours, the system itself is a reflection our current society and our political system.

DISCUSSION QUESTIONS

1. When someone or something is deemed "political," why is it that this is considered a negative trait? What does the use of "political" as a pejorative term tell us about the way we view our political system in the United States? Do you agree? Why or why not?

2. In the early 1970s, Patrick Moynihan claimed that the United States was shifting from a government of programs to one of policies. What did he mean by this? In what ways does this shift reflect changes in our society and our political system? Are there any specific policies you see today that reflect this shift?

3. Would a smaller government be less susceptible to political influence? Would a downsized government lead us to an era of less politicized policy making, or have shifts in our political culture or other deeper changes in our political system erased such a possibility for good?

4. How do you fit into the idealized types of ideology presented toward the end of the chapter? Are you an ideal "liberal," more of an ideal "libertarian/limited government conservative," or are you somewhere in between, depending on what issue is up for consideration? Do you think that people should make decisions about which policies they favor by consciously using their ideological beliefs as a guide? Why or why not?

NOTES

1. Henninger, Daniel. "A Ronald Reagan Budget." *Wall Street Journal*. http://online.wsj.com/article/SB10001424052748704101604576246900648182340.html (accessed February 5, 2013).

2. My inspiration for this approach is Deborah Stone's wonderful book, *Policy Paradox: The Art of Political Decision Making*. New York: Norton, 1997. The phrase "the struggle over ideas" is hers, p. 11.

3. Risen, James, and Eric Lichtblau. "Bush Lets U.S. Spy on Callers Without Courts." *New York Times*. http://www.nytimes.com/2005/12/16/politics/16program.html (accessed February 5, 2013).

4. Warrick, Joby, and Ellen Nakashima. "Senate Votes to Expand Warrantless Surveillance; White House Applauds; Changes Are Temporary." *Washington Post*, August 4, 2007. A1.

5. Lowi, Theodore. "Foreward." In Tatalovich, Raymond, and Byron W. Daynes, eds. *Moral controversies in American politics*. 3rd ed. Armonk, NY: M.E. Sharpe, 2005. xxvi.

6. Eilperin, Juliet. *Fight club politics: how partisanship is poisoning the House of Representatives*. Lanham, MD: Rowman & Littlefield, 2006.

7. Sinclair, Barbara. "Chapter 1." In *Party wars: polarization and the politics of national policy making*. Norman, OK: University of Oklahoma Press, 2006.

8. Sinclair, 355–361.

9. Hunter, James Davison. *Culture wars: the struggle to define America*. New York: Basic Books, 1991.

10. Moynihan, Daniel P. "Counselor's Statement." In *Toward balanced growth: quantity with quality*. Washington: [For sale by the Supt. of Docs., U.S. Govt. Print. Off.], 1970. 5–6.

11. Moynihan, 6.

12. Moynihan, 6.

13. Moynihan, 8.

14. Light, Paul C. "Fact Sheet on the True Size of Government." Washington, DC: The Brookings Institute. http://www.brookings.edu/research/articles/2003/09/05politics-light.
15. Light, "Fact Sheet."
16. Lee, Christopher. "Big Government Gets Bigger." *Washington Post*, October 6, 2006. A21.
17. Andrews, Edmund L. "Banks Balk at Agency Meant to Aid Consumers." *New York Times*, July 1, 2009. B1.
18. Cooper, Helene, and Jennifer Steinhauer. "Bucking Senate, Obama Appoints Consumer Chief." *New York Times*, January 4, 2012. http://www.nytimes.com/2012/01/05/us/politics/richard-cordray-named-consumer-chief-in-recess-appointment.html?pagewanted=all (accessed February 5, 2013).
19. Light, "Fact Sheet."
20. CQ Midday Update. "Inspector General Sees Political Meddling by Former Top Justice Aide." *CQ Politics*. www.cqpolitics.com/wmspage.cfm?docID=cqmidday-000002927803 (July 28, 2008).
21. Ragsdale, Lyn. "Studying the Presidency." In Nelson, Michael, ed. *The Presidency and the political system*. Washington, DC: CQ Press, 1984.
22. Lewis, David E., and Terry M. Moe. "The Presidency and the Bureaucracy." In Nelson, Michael, ed. *The Presidency and the political system*. Washington, DC: CQ Press, 1984.
23. As quoted in Edwards, George C. *Governing by campaigning: the politics of the Bush presidency*. New York: Pearson Longman, 2007. 248.
24. Edwards, 250.
25. For a classic treatment of the rise of interest group politics, see Berry, Jeffrey M. *The interest group society*. 2nd ed. Boston: Little, Brown, 1989.
26. Edwards, 234–235.
27. Edwards, 235.
28. Edwards, 237.
29. Edwards, 283–284.
30. Ornstein, Norman J., and Thomas E. Mann. *The permanent campaign and its future*. Washington, DC: American Enterprise Institute and Brookings Institute, 2000. 219.
31. Stone, Deborah A. *Policy paradox: the art of political decision making*. New York: Norton, 2002. 11.
32. Skocpol, Theda. *Boomerang: health care reform and the turn against government*. New York: W.W. Norton & Co., 1997.
33. Brooks, Jennifer. "Senate Passes Bankruptcy Bill Making it Harder to Shed Debts." *USA Today*, March 1, 2005. 1.
34. Berlin, Isaiah. *Four essays on liberty*. London: Oxford University Press, 1969.
35. Associated Press. "Newt Gingrich calls for private retirement accounts." *Boston Herald*. bostonherald.com/news/us_politics/view/20111121newt_gingrich_calls_for_private_retirement_accounts (accessed November 21, 2011).
36. Tocqueville, Alexis de, Richard D. Heffner, and Vartan Gregorian. *Democracy in America*. New York: Signet Classics / New American Library, 2010.
37. Nozick, Robert. *Anarchy, state, and utopia*. New York: Basic Books, 1974.
38. Stone, 53.
39. This is an iteration of Milton Rokeach's "two-value" model of political ideology; see Rokeach, Milton. *The nature of human values*. New York: Free Press, 1973.
40. Stone, 11.

Approaches to the Study of Public Policy

CHAPTER OBJECTIVES

When you finish reading Chapter 3, you should be able to do the following:

- Identify the two main forms of power that shape policy making
- Describe how power creates the boundaries for the scholarly approaches to the study of public policy making discussed in the chapter
- Illustrate how polices can be categorized by their outputs

- Summarize the main approaches to the study of the policy-making process, including systems analysis, the stages model, the policy streams model, rational choice theory, punctuated-equilibrium, and the advocacy coalition framework
- Evaluate the need for policy-making theories and the limits of the models based on these theories

Shopping malls generally feature map kiosks or signboards that indicate "you are here" and lay out the geography of the stores and services nearby. A similar feature is offered in this chapter, in that what is to come here will provide a rundown of how scholars and some practitioners have studied public policy. At the outset, it is important to note that these approaches are really the building blocks for the "policy as politics" approach contained in this text. You should take care to understand them not because they completely explain the political nature of public policy making, but because they offer some fairly clear points at which the road ends and we can begin our explorations. They are also worth understanding because these approaches reflect fundamental, if incomplete, ways of studying and thinking about policy making.

As we begin our discussion of the approaches to understanding public policy, the two most elementary road markers visible at the outset are power and the degree of change brought on by a policy.

POWER

Reality programs have come to dominate much of American television. Networks like them because they are fairly cheap to produce and do not require actors or, so it is said, writers and scripts. Viewers probably like the voyeuristic aspects of these shows and the easy identification we have with the individuals we see on the screen. We may find ourselves saying, "Ha! I would have done that too!" or "Why did they do that? I never would have done that!" The other aspect of these shows that is a likely source for our attention is power. Human beings are fascinated by power. Whether it is the *American Idol* judges passing out verdicts on a singer or *Survivor* contestants plotting to set up a rival for elimination, the ability to influence or control what happens to others is a force that draws our notice. Power is a venerable topic with a long history of classic reflections and contemporary musings available to us for consideration. Certainly, those who have formal power such as the elected or appointed officials in the United States are of interest to us because they may use power in ways that actually affect us. In this way, our preoccupation with power is partly self-interested.

Formal and Informal Versions of Power

In a general way, even without the connection to self-interest, a strong curiosity about other forms of formal power is abundant. Consider the recent spate of popular books, movies, and television shows about the British aristocracy, both past and present. Why would this be so? Power, even if it does not seem to directly affect us, is a means of measuring standards and functions in a political, economic, or social system. Even if we are not individually aided or hurt by the use of formal power, we are judging if the execution of that power is valid, fair, or necessary. If we think it is so, then such a judgment reinforces the legitimacy of the actor who wielded the power and probably the legitimacy of the power itself. For example, the Supreme Court has recently allowed states to continue with the execution of inmates convicted of state laws. A fairly small percentage of Americans are on death row for state crimes and a larger, but still quite small, percentage of the population is directly affected by such a decision because of personal connections to these inmates. A still larger part of the public is opposed to capital punishment, yet most Americans are likely to accept the Supreme Court's exercise of power for two reasons.

First, the Court is seen as a legitimate user of formal power because of the status given to it by the Constitution and because of its history as a political actor. (After the *Bush v. Gore* decision in 2000 that ended the recount of the presidential election in Florida, many observers—at least one on the Court itself—wondered if the Court had seriously damaged its legitimacy by wading into overtly political waters. Most public opinion polls indicate that the Court's legitimacy has not been severely damaged or at least has rebounded.) Second, while certainly not transparent, the process used by the Court to go about its business is explainable and even predictable. Depending on the case, the procedures the Court follows include the review of lower court rulings, oral arguments, and conferences on opinions among the justices. Americans may or may not like the Court's exercise of power when it comes to a matter like capital punishment, but they are highly likely to go along with it if both of these conditions are met.

Informal sources of power and their use are important aspects of public policy, too. While not perceived by the public or other policy players in exactly the same ways, the ideas of legitimacy and procedure are similarly significant. If a company decides to lay off workers, just as US carmakers had to consider in the wake of the "Great Recession" of 2008–2009, this is something that has great impacts on a host of policy matters from school taxes to the environment. The former employees and everyone else certainly may not be pleased by this turn of events, but they will accept that the company's bad economic performance needs some action to try to improve profitability. (Of course, there are many factors that can account for layoffs, some from the labor side of the situation and some from the management side, too.) Unless there is a major dispute over the terms of the workers' contract, most employees will end up accepting that they can be terminated from their jobs because the company has the power to legitimately do so. How the company goes about doing this is also important. A phased set of layoffs with public announcements and consultations with the workers' union will probably be a far more acceptable procedure than a scenario in which workers are literally locked out of a quickly shuttered auto factory.

Power is legitimately used when those who use it are formally vested with that power, meaning that they have the right to use that power by law, ownership, past accepted use of that power, or by the expectation that they should use that power. The Supreme Court and a car manufacturer, like GM or Chrysler, have a mixture of these characteristics. Additionally, in the above examples, these policy players used their power in ways that followed patterns or procedures that were explainable and, perhaps, even predictable. Even though we may not like a decision of the Court or an action by a company to lay off workers, the power to do these things is far less questionable for many because of the legitimacy and the procedures underlying the power to carry out these actions.

The Degree of Concentration of Power

Of course, no one person or group holds all the political, social, or economic power in a system. A great and ongoing debate has sprung up precisely about the degree of power held by individuals or collectives in a society. Those perceiving an overabundance of power in the hands of a few regular players who generally dominate the outcomes of the system for their own benefit fit into the views espoused by the eminent sociologist C. Wright Mills, whose book, *The Power Elite*, set the standard in the 1950s for the discussion of elite theory. Mills was convinced that the many were ruled by the few and that what we viewed as "democracy" was largely an illusion used to hide the true exercise of power behind democratic stagecraft. Maybe the peons do get a bit of the goods of society or some symbolic acknowledgement by the powerful of their demands, but for the most part, the people are subordinate to the moneyed, connected, powerful class. Today, the idea of outsized elite influence or even elite dominance of politics and policy is alive and well in the works of scholars such as Michael Parenti[1] and Thomas Dye,[2] among others.

In a blunt refutation of the ideas about the existence of a power elite, pluralists see the political world in the United States as a permeable system that allows those of varying resources and status to shape the direction of government and policy.

Looking almost literally into his own backyard of the 1950s, political scientist Robert Dahl sought to discover the nature of power in the environs surrounding Yale University, his academic home at the time. New Haven, Connecticut, was and is today a city of contrasts. Home to Yale, one of the most prestigious and expensive institutions of higher education in the world, New Haven has had a strong blue-collar tradition that today, like many urban areas of the Northeast, has witnessed a loss of employment opportunities and a related increase in the problems of drug use and crime. In Dahl's era, however, the city was both the home to Yale and to neighborhoods that reflected the relative wealth of the people making up their population. The poorer sections were mostly enclaves for recently arrived or assimilated immigrant groups, whereas the richer sections featured populations of established order. Dahl's study of New Haven is fairly easy to summarize: he simply wanted to see if the richer, more socially resourceful segments of the population got what they wanted more than those from the parts of the city with fewer resources. If Mills and others in keeping with the major tenets of elite social theory were right, then the "have-nots" of New Haven would be on the losing end of most policy disputes. However, Dahl found a far more mixed picture of power in his city. Sure, the wealthier people got what they wanted from time to time, but so did those who were less economically endowed. Dahl explained that this diversity in power was largely a result of the open system of political power in New Haven. With elections as the means to select decision makers, the power of the voters—no matter how rich or poor—was quite real. The ability of individuals to band together in groups to voice their concerns to decision makers—something guaranteed by our Constitution—was also a form of power available to all. In many ways, argued Dahl, our system of politics and government was open and responsive to a variety of individuals and groups. That is to say, the sources of power were many or plural, rather than singular.

Both Mills and Dahl and each man's many scholarly progeny have been attacked for their ideas about power. Mills has often been taken to task for being too conspiratorial in his thinking and unwilling to see the potential power, if not the actual results, available to even the lowest social classes. Dahl's basic conceptualization of pluralism became the dominant viewpoint of the social sciences for about a generation after he first published his New Haven study, and this influence is still quite powerful. Pluralism certainly has taken a number of hits, too. One early and quite influential critique of pluralism came from Bachrach and Baratz who, in 1962, wrote about what they called nondecisions. What if, the two authors argued, power was not as obvious as who gets what they want when a choice is made by elected or appointed decision makers. For example, Dahl's book provides an example about the construction of metal houses in New Haven that he uses as an instance of people with fairly limited resources getting what they wanted. While not the poorest of the poor in New Haven, the residents of this neighborhood—mostly newly assimilated immigrants from Italy and Russia—were working class people with generally low levels of political involvement. They did not want prefabricated metal houses placed in their area, fearing that it would draw what they perceived as "undesirable" neighbors.[3] In this case, the choices are presented in a binary fashion: either a group wins or it loses. The outcomes are clear and they indicate the successful use of power at a given time. But what if power was not simply about making a decision about what, say, a city's government might do to meet the needs of a particular group? What if members of the city council on their own or spurred by influential groups or individuals in the community kept an issue from being discussed by decision makers? The ability to keep an idea or problem from reaching the decision-making process means that no decision on that idea or problem will be made. True enough, but does this mean no one made a decision? Bachrach and Baratz made the point that if this were to happen, then someone did make a type of decision, something they labeled as a nondecision. If we were applying Dahl's formulation of pluralism based on who wins when they want a particular outcome, a nondecision might not even register on our radar screen because it takes on an atypical form of power. It may be obvious, but for Bachrach and Baratz, the people who are best able to make or encourage nondecisions are those who have specific authority, meaning governmental officials, or those who are most influential on these decision makers, namely the wealthy and the politically and socially prominent people in a community.

What can we make of this debate about the nature of power in the United States? First of all, the striking point from the debate over elite theory and pluralism is that both viewpoints are probably correct, at least in some cases at some times. It is fairly easy to find cases where the wealthy and connected people get more than their fair share, just as it takes no great effort to find instances of regular folks winning the day in the face of adversity. In fact, these are common story lines that make up much of what we read, see, and hear in news coverage. The greater importance of this debate is that it should make us more sensitive to the idea that power is always a part of public policy and that power is inherently a political substance. While we are attuned to news stories about graft and corruption along with stories of the "good guys" beating the odds, it's useful to remember that power is more fluid than either of these polar extremes would suggest, and the study of public policy gives us a unique window that we can use to observe a larger vista of power in the United States than what we might perceive in a single news story.

Just as cartographers in the distant past recognized the need for both lines of longitude and latitude on a globe to establish a system for measurement and determining location, we need a second means of thinking about public policy. Knowledge of power in contemporary American government and politics is an essential element in the quest for understanding the political nature of public policy, but by itself it is insufficient.

THE DEGREE OF CHANGE

Related to but distinct from power is the degree of change made by policy. (Inherent in the concept of the degree of change is that larger changes require more power.) Some policies may vastly reorder the political, social, or economic world. When parts of the New Deal were enacted in the 1930s, the banking and financial investment industries in the United States were fundamentally modified by regulation. Bill Clinton's decision to support the Republicans in their drive to pass welfare reform truly did, in President Clinton's own words, "end welfare as we know it." In 2003, the decision to invade Iraq vastly transformed US foreign policy toward preemptive war making. These dramatic examples are, however, swamped in a sea of much smaller policy changes that are far more frequently the work of policy makers. While the exacting nature of writing the language in congressional legislation can literally mean that the addition or deletion of one word can immensely modify existing policy, for the most part, policy change at the federal level and below is minor. Students of public policy have coined terminology to identify the range of change found in the examples just described.

Minor adjustments to existing policies are usually labeled as "incremental," whereas major, sweeping change goes by a number of terms, including the unpoetic but accurate "non-incremental."

Non-Incremental Change

Non-incremental policy changes like those from the New Deal or something like a preemptive war are so dramatic and change so many of the existing relationships in the economic, political, and social order that they usually happen only in times of crisis. The Great Depression of the 1930s and repudiation of the Republican Party's stewardship of the economy and the nation led the public and the new Democratic administration under FDR to experiment with substantially different ways of approaching the federal management of the nation's economy. The shock of the 9/11 attacks and the Bush administration's insistence that Iraq posed a similarly great danger to the United States drew the nation into a war with a new rationale; it would be the first time that the United States waged a war to preempt the aggression of another nation. Even Bill Clinton's decision to do away with AFDC, the antipoverty program created in the 1930s, and adopt TANF, a program that gave much more discretion to the states about eligibility and welfare benefits, came out of a crisis of sorts. The loss of both the House and Senate in 1994 to the Republicans and the looming presidential election in 1996 probably looked like a political crisis to Bill Clinton at the time, and there was no shortage of words—some thoughtful and accurate and some vastly overblown—about the failures of AFDC and the crisis of welfare in the United States. These instances are referred to as triggering events, since they work like the trigger of a gun; once pulled, they cause the policy process to begin in earnest, just as pulling a gun's trigger causes a bullet to begin its race down the barrel of the weapon.

Non-incremental change is hard to come by because our system of government and policy making largely keeps it from taking place. Going back to the founding period of the Republic reveals the concern that James Madison and other framers of the Constitution had about the possible influence of organized factions and the general public over the affairs of government. In his justly famous "Federalist No. 10," Madison makes the case for the danger of faction and provides a partial sales pitch for how the Constitution can lessen this risk. By creating a larger republic that will be governed by the "republican principle," in part meaning majority rule in legislative decision making, Madison hoped to construct a policy structure that would thwart all but the most persistent majorities from getting their way. The true will of the people could be reflected through this system, but some fleeting whim or fancy would fail to surmount the complexities of a separated system of branches and the shared character of decision making established in the Constitution. As a device to hinder the power of factions, the constitutional order fathered by Madison works very well, but it does not work well as a system that can dramatically and swiftly provide solutions to problems. Again, the values of deliberation and the checking of faction trump quickness and responsiveness.

In such a system, the degree of policy change is likely to be narrow because larger change challenges the existing expectations about what government should or should not be doing. The machinery of policy making—an apt term for Madison's design based on a very mechanistic view of political engineering derived from Enlightenment thinkers such as Newton—is prone to inertia, staying at rest or moving in the same direction until a powerful force jolts it into action. A strain of conservative political thought has long championed the benefits of less government since a smaller government wields less influence over policy. However, even the most ardent small government conservative recognizes the need for some governmental activities, and crisis often widens the scope of what is acceptable. The limitations of Madison's system become visible when government needs to act to solve problems. Without some means of knitting together the disparate parts of the system—power strewn across branches and divided horizontally by federalism between the states and the federal government—the friction and stasis dominating the system will keep solutions from making their way to problems. In some ways, the policy-making system embodied in the Constitution is like a car's engine drained of its oil; without lubrication, the parts of the whole will overheat and fail. This tendency toward standstill became obvious early on in the operation of the nation under the Constitution. Thomas Jefferson—at one time an enemy of parties and later a creator of our first party, the Democratic-Republican Party—recognized the need for some way of overcoming the Constitution's tendency toward policy gridlock and offered partisanship and party organizations as the answer. Parties would recruit and nominate people with a shared view of both problems and solutions. Parties could discipline and order the actions of those who won office with their backing by using an assortment of political carrots and sticks. Under Jefferson's formulation, policy making could be more cohesive and change could be greater in its impact than that originally allowed for in the Constitution, which did not allow for the creation of parties and, in many respects, worked to impede their creation.

Even with the lubricating and centripetal forces of parties, the policy-making system is still often slow and limited in what it accomplishes. There are relatively few examples of sweeping policy change at the federal level because the power of parties to order the system is limited and party politics can be used to stymie policy making. FDR's famed first one hundred days in office stands as a time of some of the most non-incremental changes to national policy because it was a unique moment in our political history. The election of 1932 is one of the two elections that historians and political scientists agree upon as a realigning election. A realignment is like a political earthquake, with the election of the president forming the epicenter from which waves of change emanate. In 1932, control over both houses of Congress was won by the Democrats. State governorships and legislatures swung from Republican to Democratic hands in large numbers. Among the public, affiliation with the formerly dominant Republican Party atrophied as the electorate switched to the Democratic Party in droves. Macro shifts pushed the political system to the edge of realignment. The colossally bad economic circumstances of the Great Depression soured the public on the Hoover administration and his Republican cohorts in Congress. When federal troops under Hoover's orders violently dispersed World War I veterans assembled in Washington, DC, seeking delivery of payments owed to them by the federal government, the public was shocked by the president's actions. The election of 1932 reflected the major social, political, and economic disjunctures caused by the Depression and the public's lack of faith in President Hoover or his party to come to their aid.

Realignments are, in some ways, the *Moby Dick* of politics; they are often sought out because they are big, conclusive, and even exciting moments in our political history, and because they are rare. For Melville's Captain Ahab, a monstrous white whale was a prize that was worth everything to claim. While scholars and others fascinated by realignments are not as fanatical about them as Ahab was about his whale, the desire for the next realignment is real and is driven to a good degree by a longing for sizeable policy change. But the prospect of a realignment is dimmed by a number of factors, including the public's movement away from party affiliation and toward political independence and the parties' tendency to play up differences between themselves that work to activate their respective bases but that do little to clearly and diametrically map out how they differ over core policy issues.

Major policy change does take place without realignments. The tax policy overhaul and other Reagan-led changes of the early 1980s had scholars wondering if they needed to rework their definition of realignment to account for these big shifts in policy. Bill Clinton's legislative "batting average" with Congress in the 1990s was remarkably good, but few presidential scholars or even more casual observers of his time in office would likely argue that he was a powerful legislative leader. He was unable to achieve his major policy goal—reform of the nation's health care system—even during part of his first term in office when he enjoyed unified government with the Democrats in control of both houses of Congress. (After the Republicans gained the majority in the House and the Senate, Clinton's drive to pass major legislation seemed to bow to the reality of a partisan roadblock in Congress. For example, Clinton's 1996 State of the Union Address is a grab bag of fairly minor policy ideas, such as challenging public schools to require uniforms for students to instill discipline.)[4] The point of the matter is that we should take care not to confuse the degree of change with the number of changes made. Reagan's policy victories in the early 1980s were far more non-incremental than those of Clinton, although both have similar rates of success with Congress.[5] Short of a crisis or other macro change, the successes Congress or presidents are likely to have in changing the existing policy order is limited.

It is worth noting that there have been a few special policy areas in which non-incremental change takes place without the force of something on the order of a catastrophe or realignment. As Paul A. Schulman points out, the US manned space program is an example where there was a "demand for *comprehensive* rather than incremental decisions; synoptic rather than piecemeal outlooks and vision."[6] The space program had the special characteristic of being indivisible—that is, unlike most policy issues, this one could not be approached by having multiple interests and actors provide their contribution to the total policy in small doses. Because of its staggering complexity and cost, and the public's great desire for the policy goal, the manned space program required a wholesale and highly centralized shift from what had existed before.

In the summer of 2009, many polls showed the majority of Americans in favor of a major overhaul of our health care system to cover the millions of uninsured people. What should federal policy makers do? Why not a clean sweep and create a form of government-run health care for all Americans? Other nations have this form of medical coverage, why not us? If we had the data to show that such a program would provide the greatest coverage at the lowest cost, why not create such a program? There have been some advocates of decision-making models that do ask us to gather data and then use quantitative methods of analysis such as mathematical modeling to arrive at the "best" policy; in the 1960s there was a trend in the world of both public and private management of organizations toward "systems analysis" that focused on quantitatively driven decision making. (This systems analysis should not be confused with David Easton's use of the same label for his model of policy making.) The beauty of such an approach is that it should remove the fog from the decision-making process caused by disagreements over values and even from political pressure. In this form of decision making, non-incremental changes are more likely since any change is possible as long as it is objectively the most suitable choice. Systems analysis has fallen out of vogue, and even in its heyday it was never widely adopted by policy makers because it is not very applicable to complex policy problems. This has not kept policy scholars from taking the notion of these approaches to task. In 1959, Charles Lindblom wrote about what he called rational-comprehensive decision-making models such as systems analysis that, like the root of a tree, grow "from fundamentals anew each time, building on the past only as experience is embodied in a theory, and always prepared to start completely from the ground up."[7] It is implicit in Lindblom's critique that larger change is possible with the rational-comprehensive approach than with what he terms the "branch" or successive limited comparisons approach, in which decision makers require far less information and are limited by law or political pressures from choosing from more than a few alternatives.[8]

Incrementalism

Because of the limitations of the rational-comprehensive model in terms of time, resources, and support from political actors, theorists such as Lindblom argue that the rational model is too rigid to explain policy making or to help guide future policy makers. Without a push of considerable force from macro political, social, or economic forces, incrementalists see policy making as a process of limited steps away from existing policy choices. Some policies even have a sort of "autopilot" type of incrementalism built into them. A 1973 federal law set cost-of-living adjustments (COLAs) for recipients of Social Security payments to the changes in the nation's Consumer Price Index. Prior to this, Congress had to come up with a payment rate in each year's budget,

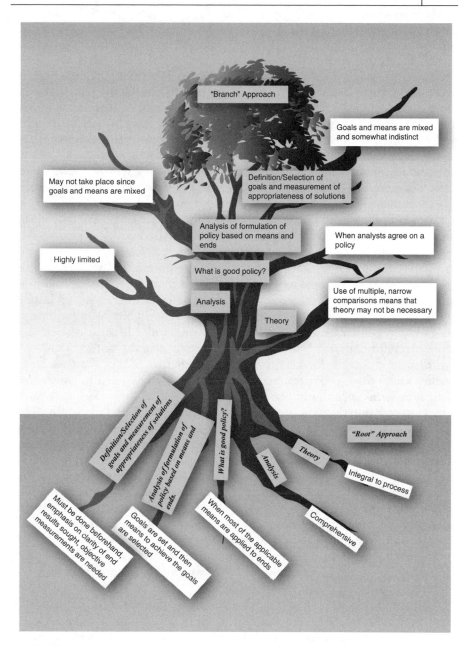

"Branch" Approach

Goals and means are mixed and somewhat indistinct

May not take place since goals and means are mixed

Definition/Selection of goals and measurement of appropriateness of solutions

Analysis of formulation of policy based on means and ends

When analysts agree on a policy

Highly limited

What is good policy?

Analysis

Theory

Use of multiple, narrow comparisons means that theory may not be necessary

Definition/Selection of goals and measurement of appropriateness of solutions

Analysis of formulation of policy based on means and ends.

What is good policy?

Analysis

Theory

"Root" Approach

Integral to process

Must be done beforehand, emphasis on clarity of end results sought, objective measurements are needed

Goals are set and then means to achieve the goals are selected

When most of the applicable means are applied to ends

Comprehensive

FIGURE 3.1
Lindblom's Two Approaches

but now the automatic COLA provides incremental increases or decreases for recipients. In 2009, the COLA increased by 5.8 percent. (The projection for 2010 was that there would be no increase.)[9] Notice what this instance of policy making did not do: there was no fundamental rethinking of the need for the Social Security system; there was no attempt to find all the potential alternatives for such assistance or to plot out all the possible outcomes from each alternative; and there was little, if any, desire to go against the well-entrenched and organized interests that represent senior citizens in this country. From the incrementalist perspective, in 2009, the small step upward in the benefits paid out by the federal government was quite in keeping with what we should expect in our policy-making system and, possibly, what we should desire.

In terms of fitting with what we see in the everyday press of action on Capitol Hill, incrementalism conforms to the reality of the demands placed on members of Congress and most other legislative bodies. Most members are experts in one or a few areas of policy—these specializations are often tied to their committee assignments—but only have general knowledge in other areas. Members often must rely on the advice of their staff, trusted colleagues in the House or Senate, their party leaders, prominent interest group leaders, and their own home districts or states for cues about which way to move on policy choices either because of a lack of information or because of a crush of too much information. These cross-cutting pressures and points of view make it difficult for decision makers to know just what is most or least useful for getting solutions to problems, and it makes it extremely hard to weigh costs against benefits since things like the loss of support of the voters back in the district may trump the gains made by a useful, but unpopular, program. What is a decision maker to do? Lindblom argues that they simply "muddle through" by looking at a small range of possible changes away from where policies presently stand, and in the absence of some compelling force, they move slightly away from that point, if at all. The tendency for decision makers is toward preservation not destruction of the status quo. In essence, incrementalism paints policy makers as conservative political actors who are risk-adverse. After all, if a program or policy is now on the books, then it has a certain level of legitimacy and acceptance within the policy-making community and among the public. Even if the program or policy is roundly criticized for being ineffective or wasteful, the "unknown" about other alternatives might entail such risks that they are seen as too precarious to even contemplate. Therefore, policy change is likely to be small. One can argue that this is actually a desirable thing since it provides a sense of stability concerning policy; we know what our goals are as a people or as a nation because of the consistency of our policies. Additionally, major mistakes and blunders are unlikely, because even if existing policies do not work very well at solving existing problems, they can be tweaked to work better, if not perfectly.

It is useful at this point to backtrack a bit and look at the two key concepts—power and the degree of change—discussed thus far in the chapter since they help to block some of the bigger theoretical spaces about policy as politics.

FIGURE 3.2

Forms of Power (the Number of Players) and the Degree of Change (Incremental and Non-Incremental)

	Non-incremental Change	Incremental Change
Pluralism (many actors)	Intense	Moderate
Elite Theory (few actors)	High, Moderate, or Low	Moderate to Low

Figure 3.2 is a means to try and merge the power and scope aspects of policy making. The amount of politics involved in policy making is in many ways dependent on the expression of power—elite dominance or the openness of pluralism—in a given case of policy making or in the policy-making system at large and the degree or scope of policy change that is produced—a non-incremental or incremental amount. Like all models, this one needs to be seen for what it is: a very oversimplified way of summing up far more complex ideas. You may have put together model cars or airplanes as a child, but even the most earnest imagination had to acknowledge that the car or the plane was only a representation of reality and not reality itself. The same is true with these models of policy. Even in this oversimplified state, the models tell us that not all instances of policy making are as linked with politics as others. For example, lining up pluralism with incremental change is most likely to feature moderate political forces. Why is this so? If we assume that the power element of a struggle over a particular issue such as global warming or handgun control is taking place in a political system that features access for many interests and policy players, the degree of political influence overall is likely to be limited by the clash of interests. Thinking back to the arguments of James Madison, the expansion of the nation into a large republic was a way of playing interests against other interests in order to limit the power of all interests. If the outcome of this struggle results in a fairly minor change away from what is now in place, say, a small reduction in greenhouse gasses or a limitation on the types of handguns that can be sold at gun shows, then there may be a great deal of political power on display, but it would pale in comparison to what would be in evidence if non-incremental change was achieved. For instance, if a 20 percent reduction of greenhouse gasses produced by US industry or a near-total ban on the sale of all handguns were to see the light of day, the amount of political influence necessary to overcome the inertia and entrenched interests defending the existing order of policy would be astronomical. And so the cell derived from pluralism and non-incremental change is labeled as "intense."

Elite theories of policy making and influence, like those of Mills', are less likely to provide evidence of power in action. This is not to say that no political power is involved, but since power may have multiple faces and can result in so-called nondecisions, measuring and comparing power in this guise is far more difficult than in a pluralist framework. Such difficulties show up in the wider range of possibilities found in the lower layer of the cells in the figure. If we take on the type of mindset developed by Mills in *The Power Elite*, then it is quite possible that a sparse collective of people called the shots on a particular policy, either using their outsized political influence to line up the rest of the policy-making apparatus, stifling the process by controlling the agenda, or by using some unilateral power to set the policy themselves. In each of these cases, it is fair to argue that an intense amount of political power is needed to pull off such actions, especially if the change is of a large magnitude. President Bush's unilateral power to declassify previously secret information about Iraq's nuclear program at a time when Vice President Cheney's chief of staff was implicated in an attempt to discredit a critic of the Bush administration's foreign policy is an example of unilateral decision making that comes from the formal powers of the presidency. The change, while not a fundamental shift in the nation's foreign policy, was still fairly sizeable given the circumstances under which it was taken, and the fact that this could only be done by the president because of his lock on the immediate declassification of classified documents.

Milder interpretations of elite-based theories of policy influence allow for further variations in political power. If we assume that most policy decisions are open to more than one source of influence and do not rest on unilateral actions, then competition between and among elites is likely. There are multitudes of examples to bring to bear in such a scenario. A historically poignant and, in retrospect, quite frightening case was that of the Cuban Missile Crisis in the fall of 1962. The main rival to US power at the time, the Soviet Union, placed nuclear missiles on Cuba, ninety miles from the US mainland, putting under target many parts of the whole country. While John Kennedy, the president at the time, had the final authority to decide how to react to this provocation from the Soviets as the constitutionally empowered commander in chief, the records of the conversations and debates of those tension-gripped days show a far more fluid give-and-take relationship between Kennedy and his advisors. Because of turf battles in the White House and the military and disagreements over the intensity of our response, some scholars even have gone so far as to suggest that Kennedy had to bargain with his advisors to reach consensus about what to do with the Cuban threat.[10]

In even less pressing cases of policy making, the theoretical framework of elite theory tends to portray a world where there can be a great intensity of power in use, but conflict with other powerful actors is limited or hidden. Therefore, the level of politics involved in elite-theory formats is more dependent on the scope of change than in the pluralist setting.

The picture that emerges from the four cells in the figure is one that is suitably complex since it is an attempt to capture two very big aspects of the political side of public policy. Inside this framework are the details of what public policy looks like and how scholars have gone about trying to study what is inside this perimeter. An illustration may be useful at this point: Now in what seems like perpetual reruns on PBS, Bob Ross's painting program, *The Joy of Painting*, drew the viewer into a half hour in which the late artist knocked out a finished painting—usually a landscape filled with "happy little trees"—in what appeared to be finely executed detail. Crags on mountains and subtle highlights on tree trunks looked as though the artist painstakingly used a very fine brush to bring them to life. In reality, Bob Ross was a master of using broad techniques—big brushes dabbed here and there with multiple hues, artist's knives loaded with paint and streaked across the canvas—to create the illusion of detail with astonishing speed. In many of the same ways, scholars of public policy often employ broad techniques or heuristics to try to capture the intense subtlety of the real policy world. This is not done for trickery; like a painter, the choice is to use approaches that may oversimplify and, perhaps, misdirect us somewhat in order to gain a timely and mostly accurate representation of the real world. To do otherwise would risk the use of approaches that may get the details right, but at the cost of undue labor and a skewed focus on the parts rather than the whole of the picture. Rather than invent a new approach to understanding public policy for each existing or emerging policy issue, from immigration to the potential risks from genetically modified foods, the traditionally used modes of public policy scholarship have tended to rest on two main pillars: the typology of public policies and public policy as a process.

PUBLIC POLICY TYPOLOGIES BASED ON OUTPUTS

The most intuitive way to categorize public policies is by placing them in issue areas. We can look at all of the attempts to solve problems in a particular issue area, for example, a broad category such as the environment, which contains the problems of preserving old-growth forests and reducing air pollution. Organizing policies by issue areas helps us make sense of the broad contours of both the problems and their possible solutions. But it is a rather blunt instrument for studying existing policies and figuring out how to devise new ones.

A more sophisticated approach to studying public policy involves creating categories that classify what policies do and how they do it. Theodore Lowi created a classic formulation of policy types by breaking down the basic functions of government into **distribution, regulation,** and **redistribution.**[11] By looking at the functions of government, Lowi argued that we could see such actions as ways of engaging in the three forms of policy with three different intentions. Notice that Lowi's formulation is dependent on government action, and because of this, it is an approach to defining public policy that is narrower than what we have been using so far.

According to Lowi, a government *distributes* a society's resources, such as wealth, services, or other things of value, when it gives benefits to specific groups in that society. (When undertaken by a legislature, such distribution is often given the negative label "pork barrel" spending, since it seems designed to bring credit to the congressperson who proposed it.)

Dudarev Mikhail/Shutterstock

Regulation takes place when a government uses legislative, military, or judicial power to stop an action by a person, organization, or group or when it mandates other behaviors or actions. For example, because of the actions of citizens like Rachel Carson, a pioneer of the early phase of the environmental movement, today's energy producers must meet federal regulations designed to limit air pollution. If an electric plant does not meet these requirements, its owners can be fined or punished in other ways.

Redistribution resembles distribution in many ways, but instead of a specific group benefiting from the actions of government, a much larger segment of society receives goods or services. Of course, redistributive policies mean that resources are taken from one part of society and given to another. An example of a redistributive policy is taxing workers to fund social welfare programs for the poor. Because redistributive policies usually pit one social class against another, they are generally the most difficult policies to enact and implement.

Because all government policies can be placed in one of these three categories, this approach allows us to see the way governments operate. Categorizing policies by the nature of their benefits is also useful. Policies themselves can either produce tangible benefits for the public or merely symbolic benefits.[12] A tangible benefit, like the federal government's policy of assistance for victims of hurricanes and other natural disasters, is something that the recipients will experience in a material way—say, truckloads of clean drinking water and dry ice to preserve food. A symbolic benefit does not offer concrete, material results; it provides a theoretical solution to a problem. For example, the independent commission that investigated the intelligence failures leading up to the 9/11 terrorist attacks could not directly change the US government's antiterrorism policy, nor could it restore life to the almost 3,000 people who perished in the attacks, and a number of its suggestions have not been adopted by the federal government. Still, the actions of the commission did communicate to the public that the government was working to solve this very difficult problem. The benefit—the feeling of security we may get from knowing that intelligent and dedicated people are trying to make us safer—may not help put food on the table, but it is still a benefit.

Lowi's classification of policy into three slots is a useful, albeit limited, approach to studying public policy. This is so for a few reasons. First, it is a way of thinking about policy that is based on the actions of government, first and foremost. Since politics is not solely a governmental function, any dependence on seeing policy as always or primarily influenced or shaped by a government leaves out too much of what we ought to know about public policy. Second, some policy scholars such as James Q. Wilson point out that the three categories established by Lowi are hard to use in actual practice. Think about this: Many states have raised their taxes on cigarettes; is this a way of redistributing money from smokers to the funds for the general public or is it a way of regulating the behavior of a segment of the population? After all, many states have proclaimed that a major reason for increased cigarette taxes is to curb smoking. The point is that the increase in cigarette taxes could reasonably fit into one or both of these categories. Because of this weakness in Lowi's typology, Wilson thinks it is more accurate to categorize policies by costs and benefits. Some policies will be very costly in terms of money, time, or other disruptions to the existing social, political, and economic order, whereas other policies will not be very disruptive at all. Large segments of the public may feel the effects of a policy, yet other policies may influence only a handful of the population.

PUBLIC POLICY AS THE RESULT OF A PROCESS

While Lowi and Wilson are in obvious opposition about how we should categorize public policies, they are in league with one another on one fundamental point; policy is best understood as an outcome or product of the interaction of government and society. Like any product, there must be a means of production or a process that creates the end result. Among policy scholars, a fixation on the process of policy making took hold starting in the 1940s when Fuller and Myers' work on social problems set out a framework of stages consisting of awareness about a problem, formulating a policy to provide a solution, and carrying that policy into being.[13]

Systems Analysis

David Easton's work on policy making dating from the 1960s is, in key aspects, an elaboration on that of Fuller and Myers', in that Easton, too, saw policy making as a product of a process, but the process was far more complex than

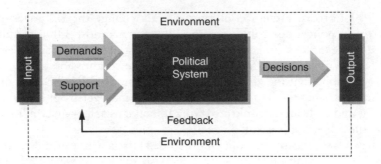

FIGURE 3.3

Easton's Model

Source: David Easton. A Systems Model of Political Life. New York: John Wiley. 1965.

that suggested by earlier scholars.[14] Easton's systems analysis model is based on the notion that the political system reacts to other systems such as the economic system or social system of a nation or state. Within the larger environment that contains the systems, all systems are in touch with and react in some way with one another. Actors and other forces place demands (the inputs of the system) on the policy making parts of the political system, which, in turn, produces policies in response to some of the demands (the outputs of the system). Easton supplies a feedback loop for his model to indicate that satisfaction or disapproval of policies will work to shape new demands and help drive the policy-making process forward.

The "Textbook" Approach: The Stages or Phases Model

The basic approach of a process-oriented approach broken into discrete phases or stages came to dominate much of public policy scholarship until the 1980s when this viewpoint began to take on a good deal of criticism for its lack of fit with the real world of policy making. (In 1987, Robert Nakamura used the phrase "the textbook approach" to encapsulate the degree of dissatisfaction with the model along with its penetration into the pedagogical arsenal for teachers.)[15] Today, the process or stages model is a heuristic that still forms the basic parts of many policy textbooks—including this one—and undergraduate policy courses. Although there are serious limitations to the stages model, it does provide a workable conceptual package for understanding many of the fundamental concepts of policy making, and it provides a solid jumping-off point for inquiries into the ideas that the model omits or fails to account for adequately.[16]

While scholars in the field of public policy disagree over some details, the major parts of the policy process model are generally thought to consist of the following steps: identifying the problem, placing the problem on an agenda, formulating a solution in the form of a policy, adopting a policy, implementing the policy, and evaluating or analyzing the effectiveness of the policy.

Process implies separate actions that lead to a final goal. This view of policy making is faulty, however, because in many cases the steps in the process do not directly flow one from the other. (Because of this, we can say that the policy process model is not truly *linear*, with all parts flowing in one direction. Nor is it truly *cyclical*, with each part necessarily following from the preceding part and forming a never-ending loop.) In the policy process, such disjunctures are not necessarily disasters; they may not be the best way to make policy, but what the policy process model does well is tell us how policy was made—well, poorly, or indifferently. The fact that making public policy is a highly political endeavor—open to and resulting from the activity of political actors—helps explain why the model does not always reveal a nice, neat set of predictable steps. Political actors can affect the process at every stage, and sometimes they cause an unexpected progression of phases or the elimination of phases. As political scientist Deborah Stone states, "Much of the political science literature in this genre [policy making] is devoted to understanding where and how good policy gets derailed in the process of production.... The production model fails to capture what I see as the essence of policy making in political communities: the struggle over ideas."[17] For Stone, much of the struggle over which policies ought to be made, how they are made, and judgments about their effectiveness are based on the *values* of the policy makers, the public, and society at large, and this struggle is not well explained by the stages model.

OTHER VIEWS OF PUBLIC POLICY MAKING

The "textbook approach" featuring the policy process model does some things quite well but falls short in other ways. The model is valuable as a way to map out the typical progression of policy making, especially the tried-and-true formula of "how a bill becomes a law." Scholars who study public policy have documented considerable variations that offer a level of detail missing from the stages model we have outlined so far. Augmented versions of the model ask us to realize that, like real life, the making of policy is messy or at least far more complex than what can be captured by the model. Other approaches to theorizing about policy making, especially rational choice–based theories, provide neater models, but they are not necessarily more explanatory or predictive.

Presently, there is a good amount of debate over where policy theory is going: What questions should we be asking about policy making? (Do we want to know more about why some policies get made in the first place, how they are made, or why some are effective and others fail?) Should the models created by theorists seek to explain as much as possible about the entirety of policy making, or should the models focus on small chunks of the process?[18] While these are important questions for all students of public policy, no one is in a position to answer them with any certainty at the present time.

The theories and their attendant models that follow are a summation of the some of the major works and ideas that bring us up to the present crossroads in policy theory.

Garbage Cans and Policy Streams

March and Olsen approach policy making by using the **"garbage can" model**, which depicts problems, solutions, actors, and other parts of the policy-making universe jumbled together, much as trash builds up in a garbage can.[19] In this model, no clear order of steps dictates what happens first or next. Solutions can exist without problems, just as easily as problems can exist without solutions.

For example, in the 1990s, when the nation seemed flush with low-priced oil and gasoline, there were people (whom some called **policy entrepreneurs**)[20] pushing for policies that would support the development of hybrid cars. The entrepreneurs were advocating a solution to a problem that did not yet exist or could only be glimpsed on the horizon. In the garbage can model, all the elements of public policy float together, and the solving of problems, if it happens at all, is often based on the unintended mix of ideas and players, not on a set of linear steps.

A refinement of the garbage can approach involves what the political scientist John Kingdon describes as policy windows and streams. He envisions problems, solutions, and political factors (such as elections and interest group campaigns) as three separate streams that flow at the same time but often do not merge with one another. Like the garbage can model, these streams are not linear steps or cyclical phases but rather factors that exist at the same time. When the three streams can be brought together in the proper combination, the policy process goes to work. But to bring the streams together, an

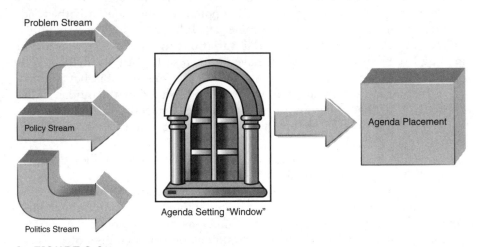

FIGURE 3.4
Kingdon's Multiple Streams Model

Source: Based on John W. Kingdon, Agendas, Alternatives, and Public Policies. New York: Harper & Row, 1984.

opportunity or "policy window" must open or be opened.[21] A national crisis is one such policy window. The 2001 terrorist attacks opened the window for Congress to pass a sweeping set of measures, known as the USA PATRIOT Act, which raised the permissible level of government surveillance of the public considerably. Without the events of 9/11, it is highly unlikely that Congress would have considered such a dramatic policy shift.

Kingdon's multiple streams model has an important place in the evolution of thinking about policy making. One of the most basic goals of anyone creating a model is to simplify reality so that it helps to explain an event or phenomenon that was previously poorly understood; Kingdon's model does a very good job of explaining the seemingly haphazard interplay of issues, ideas, and actors in the real world of policy making. Rather than throwing up our hands and saying "Eh, there is no way to make sense of how policy is made—it is too variable and unique to each case!"—the multiple streams approach provides a framework that allows for a wide degree of variation in the raw material of policy making and how these variations work to shape the process in distinctive but not random ways. Additionally, the model offers us a way to explain the degree of change taking place, from incremental to more sweeping change. A policy-making window, thrown open by an entrepreneur or an event or by both, can usher in major policy changes when the three policy-making streams are correctly combined. For example, the economic recession that welcomed the Obama administration propped open a window for the new president to attempt non-incremental policy changes to the nation's health insurance system. Of course, the tricky part of success—when viewed from the perspective of Kingdon's model—is for policy players to weave the streams together or ride them at their confluence through the open policy window.

Rational Choice Theory

A number of policy-making models are based on rational choice (sometimes referred to as public choice or social choice), a theory about human behavior derived from the study of economics. Anthony Downs is the progenitor of much of the contemporary work now being done on rational choice. (William H. Riker is considered to be the "father" of rational choice theory as a formal approach. His first major work, *The Theory of Political Coalitions* [1962] was published several years after Downs' *An Economic Theory of Democracy* [1957].) In very basic terms, rational choice theory argues that humans make decisions based on cost-benefit analysis; if you conclude that the costs outweigh the benefits, you do not take the action, but if the benefits are larger than the costs, then you do. In order to undertake such an analysis, we need a great deal of information, ideally all the information about the costs and the potential results, including the benefits but also potential consequences.

Another important aspect of the rational choice approach is the belief that our individual cost-benefit analysis is based on our own self-interest. The notion of self-interest is not new, since James Madison clearly made it a primary component of his understanding of human nature and how the Constitution would work against the dangers of self-interest. Certainly many of the classic studies in political science, such as Morris Fiorina's *Congress: Keystone of the Washington Establishment,* argue that a major driver for the behavior of policy makers is the desire for reelection and other self-preserving or aggrandizing goals. The key with rational choice theory is that the basic unit of analysis is the individual; all individuals are thought to be acting in a rational way based on their self-interest that does not have to be congruent with the interests of a group or culture. For example, Fiorina's application of rational choice for congressional behavior is largely an argument about how each member acts in accordance with his or her self-interest, not the interest of a party or of Congress as an institution. More generally, rational choice approaches see the overall will of the public as the cumulative interests of individuals.

Rational choice approaches to studying policy making have a great number of adherents in the world of policy scholarship, especially in terms of how the rules of institutions such as the US Congress and executive branch agencies shape their policy-making functions.[22] The basic premise of these models is intuitively satisfying, in that they provide a clear and highly measurable path between the goals and actions of players. Measuring and accounting for factors such as beliefs and values are more difficult than other more quantifiable variables such as the costs of products and services. However, there are many critics of rational choice theory, and they point out at least two difficulties that are inherent in the approach.[23] First, the demands concerning information placed on us by the rational choice approach are potentially beyond what we can do. How can we get all the pertinent information we need? How do we know we have all of it? Could we really make good use of such a mass of information and data if we were able to get all of it? Bounded rationality is an attempt to answer some of these questions. James March and Herbert Simon argued that the core element of rationality in decision making is a valid aspiration, but the limitations imposed on decision makers—such as deadlines, finite budgets, number of personnel, and levels of expertise—mean that the full-blown version of rational decision making is not a realistic goal.[24] In other words, rational decision making in the form of cost-benefit analysis or other quantitative approaches is possible but must bow to the realities imposed by the limits of the real world.

A broader, but sharper criticism of the rational approach is offered by Deborah Stone, who argues that what she calls the "rationality project" undertaken by many policy scholars just does not fit with reality. For Stone, the decision making that goes into policy making is not a neat, orderly series of steps in which the policy maker uses cost-benefit analysis to arrive at the "best" decision. Nor is our society much like a marketplace where relatively autonomous actors rationally compete with one another to get the best policy "deals." Instead, policy is made by humans who are "psychologically and materially dependent, [and] are connected through emotional bonds, traditions, and social groups."[25] Because of this, Stone asks us to see policy making from the perspective of the *polis*—her version of political society based on the struggle over ideas and the meaning of values—rather than from that of the logic of the marketplace.

Punctuated-Equilibrium

If we assume that policy making in the United States is largely as pluralism suggests that it is—a fairly stable and incremental process involving the interplay of groups seeking policy goals—then sudden, non-incremental change will require an additional explanation. Baumgartner and Jones' theory of punctuated-equilibrium is a model of policy making that seeks to explain how and why large and possibly sudden changes in the scope and substance of policies take place.[26] The model's name is quite descriptive of the theory in its own right; the typical state of affairs or the state of equilibrium of the policy-making process features incrementalism and groups. These groups often become so entrenched in their roles in the process that they form policy monopolies. (Iron triangles, the mutually beneficial and reinforcing relationships among interest groups, executive branch agencies, and congressional committees or subcommittees sharing a policy goal are an example of a policy monopoly at work. For example, an interest group representing defense contractors, the Department of Defense, and a House subcommittee with control over appropriations for new weapons systems could compose an iron triangle sharing the same goal of an increase in spending on new armaments.) Such groups and policy relationships may be the norm, but there are times when this equilibrium is disrupted or punctuated. Baumgartner and Jones see these changes as akin to what can happen in the world of biological evolution; occasionally, a major change takes place such as a jump in the development of a species that seems to leap over an intervening step or the disappearance of a species altogether. Some factor must be responsible for, say, the eradication of the dinosaurs. In the policy-making world, the theory of punctuated-equilibrium sees the media and other groups as playing the role of the agents of change, something like a comet hitting the earth might have been for the dinosaurs. Critical coverage of the news media about the cozy relationship found among the players in a policy monopoly or new or newly energized groups could exert enough influence to cause a substantive shift in existing policies. As in the natural world, once the new order has established itself, the stability of the policy-making system will return.

The theory of punctuated-equilibrium has won a good number of supporters because of its ability to fit with the widely accepted pluralistic view of stable policy making while also incorporating large-scale policy change as a feature of the same system.

Advocacy Coalition Framework (ACF)

Perhaps the most sophisticated of the recent models of policy making is Sabatier and Jenkins-Smith's work with the Advocacy Coalition Framework (ACF). In ways similar to the role of groups in the theory of punctuated-equilibrium, in ACF the focus is on "the interaction of advocacy coalitions—each consisting of actors from a variety of institutions who share a set of beliefs within a policy subsystem."[27] The coalitions could be as tightly bound and limited to a few participants as iron triangles or as open and populous as what Hugh Heclo termed issue networks, loose constellations of participants that come and go around an issue area.[28] Coalitions compete with one another within a subsystem over what the system will produce as policy. This conflict will involve what Sabatier calls policy brokers, "whose principal concern is to find some reasonable compromise that will reduce intense conflict. The end result is one or more governmental programs, which in turn produce policy outputs."[29]

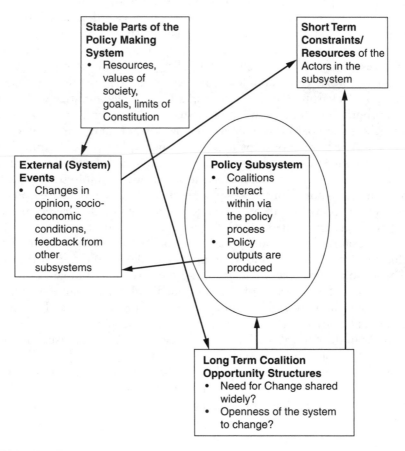

FIGURE 3.5
AFC Model

Source: Based on Paul A. Sabatier and Christopher M. Weible, "The Advocacy Coalition Framework: Innovations and Clarifications," in Theories of the Policy Process, 2nd ed. Paul A. Sabatier, editor. Boulder, CO: Westview Press, 2007, p. 202.

The actions of policy brokers are quite important to the process, but other factors are at least as significant in the model. The "stable parameters" of the process such as the basic values of society and the rules set up by the US Constitution work to shape the range of actions by the players. These points of stability form the base around which external events, including socioeconomic changes and the impact of other policies, flow and influence the actions of the coalitions and brokers in the policy subsystem.

Compared to previous models of policy making, ACF includes an extensive number of players and an ability to capture the dynamics of policy making by suggesting how the stable and changeable influences on the process form a framework for these policy players. The complexity of ACF is largely because it is a comprehensive theory, meaning that it is an attempt to explain a great deal about the policy-making process in one model, rather than taking on one narrower aspect of the process, such as agenda setting or implementation. As you are now well aware, the range of influences on the policy process are great, and the trend toward comprehensive theories means that complex models like ACF are likely to dominate the landscape of policy scholarship for the foreseeable future.

CONCLUSION

The models of policy making presented in this chapter provide us with sophisticated and rightfully complex views of policy and the policy-making process. They are, without a doubt, more elaborate and inclusive of political factors than the textbook approach featuring the stages or process model. The study of policy theory and the construction of models based on theories are highly useful for a number of reasons. Models and their attendant theories help guide research about policy making and help us to ask useful questions about the process. In essence, the models help us test the validity of the theories by allowing us to see how well they explain what has happened and maybe even predict what will occur. Yet, not all theories are created equal. As Kenneth Meier points out, testing the quality of the proliferation of theories—as you can see there are a lot of them—is not easy because "the theories themselves have different purposes and different scopes. Some theories want to explain why policies work or do not work (microeconomic approaches, institutional rational choice), others are concerned with why policies are adopted (advocacy coalition framework, policy diffusion), or why key events shape policy discourse (punctuated equilibrium theory), or perhaps how all this fits into an ideological process of governing (social construction)."[30] Meier's main point is not that policy theory is useless—far from it—but that it has become cluttered with many refinements and permutations of existing theories. He would like to see policy scholars redefine what it is that motivates their research. In other words, what is it that we want to know about policy and why do we want to know this?

Right now it is probably enough for you to know that these discussions about policy theory are taking place so that you understand that, like policy itself, the study of policy is not static. While there are "classic" readings and generally accepted approaches to the study of public policy, the position public policy holds at the fulcrum between the public and the institutions of government, coupled with the evolving nature of problems themselves, means that the study of public policy will always be developing.

SUMMARY

There are many different approaches to the study of public policy. Each of the various approaches has distinct advantages and limitations that enhance and detract from understanding the full story behind the making of public policy.

Theories about power and influence in the American political system and the degree of change achieved by public policies are essential to understanding the political nature of public policy. While both elite and pluralist theories of power can help to guide our understanding about the political nature of individual public policies, analysis of the degree of change that is brought about by public policies is also an important component to the politics of public policy. The amount of politics involved in policy making is in many ways dependent on the expression of power in a given case of policy making or in the policy-making system at large and the degree or scope of policy change that is produced.

There are several models or theories for understanding policy making that are employed by policy scholars. These models range in complexity from simple issue-area policy studies to more comprehensive models. Policy theories that are most concerned with understanding the outcomes or outputs of policy making include issue-area studies; Lowi's classic formulation of policy types into the categories of distribution, regulation, and redistribution; and James Q. Wilson's costs and benefits categories. Policy theories that are more concerned with the process of policy making include David Easton's systems analysis and the "textbook" approach which breaks down the study of policy making into distinct phases of the process. Other versions of the process model, such as the garbage can and policy streams models take into account the "messy" and more complex realities of the process than is possible using the textbook or phases approach. Rational choice theory, a theory about human behavior derived from the study of economics, utilizes a cost-benefit approach to understanding policy-making outcomes. The theory of punctuated-equilibrium is a model of policy making that seeks to explain how and why non-incremental policy changes take place. A more recent model, the Advocacy Coalition Framework (ACF), focuses on the interaction and competition of advocacy coalitions in the formulation of policies.

It is important for students of public policy to understand that, like policy itself, the study of public policy is not static. There are classic readings and generally accepted approaches that continue to inform our understanding of policy making and public policies, but because of the very political nature of the subject itself, policy studies are always evolving.

DISCUSSION QUESTIONS

1. Describe elite and pluralist theories of power. How do these theories of power and influence in the United States inform scholarly approaches to the study of public policy making?
2. Why is most policy change incremental? How does this type of policy making reflect our political system? What are the benefits and negative aspects of incremental policy making? What are some of the main causes of non-incremental policy change?
3. What is the difference between output-based models and policy-making and process-based models? What are the limitations of each type of model? What are the benefits to each type of model?
4. Discuss the main approaches to the study of the policy-making process described in this chapter. What do they tell us about policy making in the United States? Are there any models that you see as better reflections of your own views of how policy making really does work?
5. The trend in policy-making scholarship is to create more complex, holistic models. What are some of the main factors that make the policy-making process hard to explain with simplistic models?

NOTES

1. Parenti, Michael. *Democracy for the few*. 2nd ed. New York: St. Martin's Press, 1977.
2. Dye, Thomas R. *Top down policymaking*. New York: Chatham House Publishers, 2001.
3. See Dahl, Robert Alan. In *Who governs? Democracy and power in an American city*. New Haven: Yale University Press, 1961. 192–197.
4. Clinton, William J. "State of the Union Address." Washington, DC, January 23, 1996.
5. There are many disputes over the validity of "box scores" and other measures of presidential success with Congress. While imperfect, they do provide a baseline for comparison. See Shull, Steven A. *Presidential-congressional relations: Policy and time approaches*. Ann Arbor: University of Michigan Press, 1997. 84.
6. Schulman, Paul A. "Nonincremental Policy Making." *American Political Science Review* 69 (1975): 1354–1370. In Theodoulou, Stella Z., and Matthew Alan Cahn. *Public policy: The essential readings*. Englewood Cliffs, NJ: Prentice Hall, 1995. 129. Emphasis in the original.
7. Lindblom, Charles. "The Science of 'Muddling Through'." *Public Administration Review* 19, no. 2 (1959): 79–88. In Theodoulou, Stella Z., and Matthew Alan Cahn. *Public policy: The essential readings*. Englewood Cliffs, NJ: Prentice Hall, 1995. 115.
8. Lindblom, p. 114.
9. Pear, Robert. "Social Security Benefits Not Expected to Rise in '10." *New York Times*, May 3, 2009. A2.
10. Bernstein, Barton. "Understanding Decisionmaking, U.S. Foreign Policy, and the Cuban Missile Crisis: A Review Essay." *International Security* 25, no. 1 (2000): 158–160.

11. Lowi, Theodore J. "American Business, Public Policy Case Studies, and Political Theory." *World Politics* 16 (1965): 677–715.

12. Edelman, Murray J. "Chapter 2." In *The symbolic uses of politics*. Urbana: University of Illinois Press, 1964.

13. Fuller, Richard, and Richard Myers. "Conflict of Values and the Stages of a Social Problem." In *The study of social problems: Five perspectives*. New York: Oxford University Press, 1971.

14. Easton, David. *A systems analysis of political life*. New York: Wiley, 1965.

15. Nakamura, Robert. "The Textbook Policy Process and Implementation Research." *Policy Studies Review* 7, no. 1 (1987): 142–154.

16. Hank C. Jenkins-Smith and Paul A. Sabatier provide a thorough evaluation of the limits of the textbook approach in Sabatier, Paul A., and Hank C. Jenkins-Smith. "Chapter 1." In *Policy change and learning: An advocacy coalition approach*. Boulder, CO: Westview Press, 1993.

17. Stone, Deborah A. *Policy paradox: The art of political decision making*. New York: Norton, 2002. 10–11.

18. For a lively rundown on the state of policy theory, see Meier, Kenneth J. "Policy Theory, Policy Theory Everywhere: Ravings of Deranged Policy Scholar." *The Policy Studies Journal* 37, no. 1 (2009): 5–11.

19. Cohen, Michael D., James G. March, and Johan P. Olsen. "A Garbage Can Model of Organizational Choice." *Administrative Science Quarterly* 17 (1972): 1–25.

20. Kingdon, John W. *Agendas, alternatives, and public policies*. Boston: Little, Brown, 1984. 129–130.

21. Kingdon, Chapter 8.

22. For example, see Moe, Terry. "The New Economics of Organization." *American Journal of Political Science* 28 (1984): 739–777. Or Shepsle, Kenneth. "Studying Institutions: Some Lessons from the Rational Choice Approach." *Journal of Theoretical Politics* 1 (1989): 131–147.

23. Green, Donald P., and Ian Shapiro. *Pathologies of rational choice theory: A critique of applications in political science*. New Haven: Yale University Press, 1996.

24. March, James G., and Herbert A. Simon. *Organizations*. New York: Wiley, 1958.

25. Stone, 10.

26. Baumgartner, Frank R., and Bryan D. Jones. *Agendas and instability in American politics*. Chicago: University of Chicago Press, 1993.

27. Sabatier, Paul A. "The Need for Better Theories." In *Theories of the policy process*. Boulder, CO: Westview Press, 1999. 9.

28. Anderson, James E. *Public policymaking an introduction*. 3rd ed. Boston, MA: Houghton Mifflin, 1997. 83.

29. Sabatier, Paul A. "Policy Change over a Decade or More." In *Theories of the policy process*. Boulder, CO: Westview Press, 1999. 19.

30. Meier, Kenneth J., 6.

The Policy Environment

J. Scott Applewhite/File/AP Images

CHAPTER OBJECTIVES

When you finish reading Chapter 4, you should be able to do the following:

- Know the historical and theoretical backgrounds for the existence of the separation of powers and federalism as hallmarks of the policy-making system in the United States
- Understand the debates over the degree of polarization in American culture

- Have a better sense of how demographic changes influence the policy-making process
- See the connections between emerging technologies and the ways that issues are added to the policy agenda
- Be aware of how determinative economic conditions are for any discussion of the policy-making process

The policy environment is the framework of forces that shapes policy making. A framework provides structure, and structure creates the opportunity for some actions and limits or precludes other actions. For example, a tree's structure allows it to carry out photosynthesis and to sway in the wind without damaging its branches or trunk. This same structure that is so useful to the production of energy for the tree and that allows it to tolerate a good deal of punishment from the physical world, limits the tree in essential ways. Trees may be seriously injured and even killed when their leaves are stripped during an infestation of caterpillars or other leaf eaters. While a tree can bend in a strong wind, it is unable to move beyond the place where its root system has established its presence. In sum, it is important to remember at the outset of this chapter that while the framework of the policy environment is changeable and even evolutionary, the system as we are likely to perceive it at any one time is stable and may appear to us as fixed.

If we were to think about the physical environment for a moment, we would easily begin to compile a list of its component parts. The ground beneath our feet, air and water, sunshine, and the plants and animals would probably make it to such a list in fairly short order. Other items, such as the earth's magnetic fields, its ozone layer, and molten core may come to us with a bit of thinking. There is little doubt that given enough time we could list a highly detailed index of earthly components and forces. Some of these items are so obvious that we may fail to list them and other ones may be so esoteric that we are unaware of them or do not think they are worthy of inclusion. In many of the same ways, the policy environment contains both broad and fairly obvious elements along with some others that are rather obscure. The goal of this chapter is to map out many of the key components of the policy environment, some self-evident in their importance and others of a significant but lesser known quality.

THE STRUCTURE OF US POLICY MAKING

Looking at the US political system and government from a distance, the most easily seen feature of both is federalism, the division of power and responsibilities between the states and the federal government.

Federalism

The fallout over health care reform legislation passed in 2010, or more accurately, over the Patient Protection and Affordable Care Act, has been contentious. State governors and their attorneys general objected to the federal policy as an undue burden on state citizens and an overstepping of the federal government into the realm of state power. The Patient Protection and Affordable Care Act requires citizens to have coverage—either through their employer or purchased on an individual basis—or they are subject to tax penalties by the federal government. This individual mandate to carry health insurance was the cornerstone of the drive to reform health care in 2009–2010. Insurance companies lobbied for its inclusion in a final bill. (After all, they would reap the benefits of an influx of new paying customers.) Health care reform advocates championed the mandate, too, as a way to ensure coverage for the tens of millions of Americans without coverage. Those with an eye toward the nation's budget saw benefits in the reforms as well, believing that the changes would stabilize the growth in medical costs and help to trim federal outlays for programs like Medicare and Medicaid. But critics were quick to question whether or not the federal government could mandate the purchase of a product by individual citizens. The states had traditionally regulated the actions of the health care insurance companies within their borders. Was the new federal law an unconstitutional preemption of state regulatory power?[1] Twenty-six states joined together to ask the federal courts to strike down the law on these grounds. The validity of the Patient Protection and Affordable Care Act went before the Supreme Court; it was a decision that centered on the power of the federal government to regulate health insurance and the on the power of the states to resist the actions of the federal government in this area. In its much anticipated summer 2012 decision, the Court found that the Congress did, indeed, have the power to require individuals to have health care insurance, but also found limitations on other aspects of the law that blunted the reach of the federal government in this issue area.

Federalism is much like the high tide line on a beach; it clearly demarks the zones occupied by the ocean and the shore, but that line is not permanent and the zones of the sea and the land can and do expand and contract over time. Presently, there is a renewed impulse of populism in the United States, a belief that the common person is not getting fair treatment by those perceived to hold more power, such as economic and political elites. The Tea Party movement—a loose amalgam of groups and not an actual political party, at least as of yet—sees itself as the champion of the common person against the power of government, especially the federal government, in terms of tax and regulatory policies. In fact, the "Tea" in Tea Party is an acronym from the phrase "Taxed Enough Already." Along with the high media profile positions of the Tea Party movement, other voices calling for greater federal government action have also been part of the nation's conversation about federalism. The Occupy movement is, in many ways, the liberal/progressive answer to the Tea Party movement. Occupy protesters decry what they see as a gross inequality of wealth in the United States, with the richest 1 percent in conflict with the remaining 99 percent of the nation's people. (Unlike the Tea Party, Occupy quickly faded and is now a ghost of its former self.) In the aftermath of the financial meltdown and the recession that hit full force in 2008–2009, there were new calls for greater regulation of the financial services industry and Wall Street. In the disturbing and downright depressing days and months that followed the ecologically catastrophic oil spill from the BP's deepwater drilling operation in the Gulf of Mexico, the federal government's responsibilities for directing the cleanup were called in question. (BP used to be known as British Petroleum, but changed its name and corporate logo to an earth-friendlier flower as way of showing that it was not just an oil company, but an *energy* company that cares about the environment.) Should the company answerable for the spill—BP, along with its contracted partners, Halliburton, and Transocean Ltd.—shoulder the responsibility and liability for the cleanup or should the federal government jump in and take over the operation? What role should the state governments play? In a somewhat curious twist, some people who had recently denounced federal action on health care insurance reform as the federal government overreaching its authority, such as Louisiana Governor Bobby Jindal, demanded more action from the federal government when it came to the BP spill.[2]

While some areas, such as the issues of immigration and oil spill clean-ups, seem to straddle the line between state and federal powers and responsibilities, some aspects of federalism are clear-cut. Control over the coining of money and the declaration of war with another nation are, without any serious debates to the contrary, within the sole province of federal power. The federal Constitution's Article I, section 8 enumerates these powers for the federal government and preempts (blocks) the states from having control over these items. Some policy matters, such as the creation or elimination of geopolitical units like cities and towns are under the exclusive direction of states or municipal governments within the states. In the language of constitutional scholarship, the powers that are clearly listed by the Constitution as belonging to the federal government or that are precluded to the states are known as enumerated powers. Article VI of the Constitution provides for the supremacy of federal law and action over that of the states when their goals conflict. Given this actuality, the federal government would seem to be in a vastly superior position to that of the states when it comes to policy making. (The need for a stronger central government was a major reason for scrapping the Articles of Confederation, the nation's governing plan for the years from the end of the Revolution to the adoption of the Constitution in 1789. The confederal system created by the Articles placed sovereignty over economic and political affairs largely in the hands of the states, as there was only a weak and ineffectual central Congress at the time. The many weaknesses of the Articles led to the call for the constitutional convention.) However, as with today's small government conservatives, libertarians, and others, concerns of giving too much power to a government at a greater distance—physically and in terms of representation—from the people concerned both the framers of the

Constitution and critics of the proposed plan for a new form of government. These critics coalesced into a group calling itself the Anti-Federalists, a name chosen in opposition to the proponents of the Constitution's ratification, the Federalists. One of the chief concerns of the Anti-Federalists was that the enumerated powers for the national government found in the proposed Constitution, coupled with the supremacy clause found in Article IV, would cause the states to wither and die. Added to this distrust of the drastically altered power arrangements in the proposed document was the lack of a bill of rights, such as the one contained in Virginia's state constitution. In many ways, a bill of rights is a set of limitations on what a government can do to its people. Without a bill of rights and with the vast increase in federal power, the Anti-Federalists saw the proposed Constitution as serious threat to liberty. Given this backlash, key Federalists, such as James Madison, promised future fixes to the Constitution once it was ratified. The first ten amendments to the Constitution provide a bill of rights for the people as well as language that carves out power for the states. The Tenth Amendment declares that power not given to the federal government (enumerated power) or denied to the states, is left to the states or to the people. This leftover power, sometimes referred to as residual power, goes a long way toward guaranteeing that a system of federalism would be established and maintained.

While federalism is a constant part of the policy-making system in the United States, what it means at a given time has been and will continue to be open to debate. The period from the Constitution's ratification until the Civil War was one of testing the meaning of federalism, culminating in a bloody war that dramatically illustrated the extent of federal power over the states. From the end of the Civil War until the latter 1930s, the theory of dual federalism, with separate and immoveable spheres of state and federal power, often held sway. Even into the 1960s, the idea lived on that policies enforcing racial segregation were up to the states because of "states' rights." Starting in earnest in the 1930s with the New Deal and again with a massive spasm of federal growth and activity with the 1960s Great Society programs, the federal government took on more responsibilities and grew in size and complexity. By the late 1970s, the nation's conservative movement had found an adversary that, in their distrust and dislike, rivaled Communism: that enemy was government, more specially the federal government. Ronald Reagan's victory in the 1980 presidential election was, in many ways, the culmination of a debate about federalism. His candidacy was based on the notion that government is the problem, not the solution. Reagan used to get strong positive reactions to his joke that the ten most feared words in America are "I'm from the federal government and I'm here to help." While the size of the federal government has not been reduced much, if at all, since the Reagan administration's days (Reagan's budgets on defense and other programs actually greatly increased the size of the federal government) the idea that the federal government is not the appropriate actor to solve problems or that its actions are actually the cause of problems is one that holds sway with many Americans.

The line between federal and state power may seem like it is a dull notion, something akin to a boundary line on a faded map on the wall of a classroom of bygone days. But if we think about the historical flashpoints in our history—from the Civil War to the civil rights movement—and reflect on the contemporary debates about immigration, environmental protection, and health care reform, the seemingly constant, yet changeable nature of federalism is at the heart of much of what will form the core of future policy making.

Separation of Powers

Federalism divides power horizontally, between the federal government and the states. Within these strata, power is further split by the vertical separation of powers that defines the legislative, executive, and judicial branches at both the federal and the state levels. This division is such a commonplace feature of our governmental system that most of us probably do not give its origins much thought beyond a faith in the idea that the separation produces "checks and balances" and that checking and balancing is a good and maybe even a required feature of a democracy. If we look at other western democracies, such as Great Britain, we see something quite different. Their system fuses the executive and legislative aspects of government by drawing the chief executive, the Prime Minister, from the Parliament, their legislative body. While not like our own, the British system is a democracy by most objective applications of that term. If separate branches are not requisite for democracy, why do we have them? James Madison's main fear for the new republic was that a majority of the public would coalesce around an issue based on the group's self-interest. Madison termed these collectives "factions." The issue might be political, religious, or of some other origin, but would most likely come from the unequal distribution of wealth in society. In essence, the "have nots," being more numerous, would see the advantage of banding together to increase their power over the less numerous "haves" in order to capture parts of the government and turn policies to their favor.[3] By dividing power among three branches, Madison hoped to limit the ability of majorities to easily take control of the government. In order to control the policy-making process, a faction would need to have its people win a majority of the seats in the House of Representatives, manage to get a majority of the states' legislatures to select supporters to the US Senate (the Seventeenth Amendment, passed in 1913, provides for the direct election of US senators by the people of each state), see that a majority of the votes in the Electoral College went to its choice for president, and find a way to ensure their policy views would endure a Senate-approved federal judiciary that would eventually develop the use of judicial review as a means of stopping the actions of the other two branches. In short, the plan for thwarting the danger of faction found in Madison's framework for the federal Constitution is a masterpiece of controlling power. Add to this complex and sophisticated governmental structure a set of political parties unwanted and largely unforeseen by the framers, and what results is a system that tends toward inaction because of the friction produced by the separations of power and, at times, added partisan antagonisms. As Madison writes in "Federalist No. 51," "ambition must be made to counteract ambition." The net effect of the separation of powers produces a limitation on the ambition of one branch over another since each branch is given discrete and fairly substantial powers that cannot be taken away by the other branches. (This is the essence of "checks and balances": each branch can use its power to thwart or "check" the actions of the other two, thus creating a rough balance of power among all three.)

Perhaps more prosaically, the idea behind a separation of powers is also derived from a belief of the framers that good governance revolved around three basic functions: the making of law or policy; its execution; and possible adjudication of issues that would arise from the making of the policy, its implementation, or from both. In this way, form follows function.

Like federalism, the concept of the separation of powers is one that seems fixed and not all that open to change or interpretation. However, as with federalism, many of our greatest episodes in political history come from circumstances that have tested, defined, and even shifted our understanding of the separation of powers. Was a president beyond the reach of the law because, as Richard Nixon once infamously stated, if the president does it, it cannot be illegal? Can Congress, as it did in the 1990s, give the presidency the power to veto parts but not the entirety of spending bills? In both cases, the Supreme Court said no and in doing so clarified the lines that mark the separation of powers at the federal level. (The separation of powers is no less an ongoing debate at the state level. As the states face increasingly difficult economic choices, governors, state legislatures, and state courts have routinely squared off over how to run their states. For example, in 2010, when New York State's Governor David Patterson attempted to furlough state workers to save money, a state court ruled that the governor did not have the power to do so.)

Policy advocates at both the state and federal level face a complex and somewhat malleable structure of institutions that compose the policy-making universe in the United States The complexity of the system is quickly apparent if one just thinks about where to start. Will the issue or problem have the best shot at getting attention or possible resolution in the legislative, executive, or judicial arena? Will a combination of some or all these venues prove most effective? Will political factors such as turnover in personnel due to elections, or change in public opinion about issues or problems augment the ways that each branch may relate to a problem? For example, prior to the Democrats gaining control of the House and Senate in 2006, environmental interest groups looking for changes in regulatory policies dealing with issues such as water and air quality did not find a great deal of enthusiastic support for their ideas among the Republican majority. This circumstance led many groups to undertake or continue with policy strategies focusing on the use of litigation through the courts as a means of trying to shape policies more to their liking. When the Democrats regained control of both houses of Congress, these groups pivoted and began investing their energies in a legislatively based strategy.[4]

Federalism and the separation of powers form a sizeable part of the structure of policy making in the United States; their origins and meaning have been discussed here in some detail, but a number of other factors—not always so apparent—shape how and if policy is made. The reminder of the chapter focuses on several of these factors and how they influence the policy-making process.

Political Culture

"There is a religious war going on in our country for the soul of America. It is a cultural war, as critical to the kind of nation we will one day be as was the Cold War itself."

—Patrick Buchanan in a speech to the 1992 Republican National Convention

America is at war with itself. We are divided down the middle, a 50/50 nation. Some states are blue, while others are red. Liberals and conservatives are at one another's throats in this highly polarized nation, or so we often hear. If this is the case, then the political environment for policy making and the implementation of policy is largely shaped by a strong division between two competing cultural factions. In fact, sociologist James Davidson Hunter is credited with first claiming the existence of a culture war in the United States in which those of a traditional or orthodox cultural perspective battled with those of a liberal or progressive cultural description.[5] Hunter's work has taken on a life of its own, and in the 2000 election we saw the news media adopt the view that two cultural armies were doing battle with one another. The media even gave us a shorthand way to think about this divide in geographic terms; on their election coverage maps, Republican states were colored red and Democratic states were filled in with blue. Looking at such a map does help make some sense out of why the policy environment seems to be so confrontational and filled with conflict. If the Democrats, playing the role of the liberal cultural warriors, and the Republicans, taking on the part of the conservatives, are so evenly divided, then it is no wonder that we see a policy process that seems unable to respond in adequate fashion to the public's needs. Gridlock and inaction on problem solving is the likely result of such a stalemate. (The level of responsiveness of the government to the public's wants is an important topic for later. For the time being, let us assume that the public really is not getting what it needs from government and that we, the people, are accurately doling out our displeasure, such as the 86% of the public polled in 2012 that disapproved of the way Congress was doing its job.)[6] No one will be happy because no one will get all or even part of what they want since the opposition will dig in its heels and refuse to compromise or collaborate in any way. Of course, the 50 percent of the public on each side of this cultural divide will have to level most of the blame for inaction on the other side. "Blue staters" will curse "red staters," and red-state residents will malign their neighbors in the blue states.

How much evidence is there that such a culture war exists and that it shapes the policy environment in the ways described? Electoral outcomes provide a good deal of data about the existence of such a split. Many of our recent presidential elections have been very close and have, in fact, featured some victors who garnered less than 50 percent of the vote (i.e., Bill Clinton in 1992 and 1996) and one so-called wrong winner, George W. Bush, who did not win the popular vote in 2000. To some political observers, such narrow outcomes must mean an intensely divided electorate. (Obama's 53% to 46% victory over McCain is impressively large by comparison, but nothing close to the 22 point popular vote margin that Lyndon Johnson held over Barry Goldwater or the 23 point spread of Nixon over McGovern in 1972.) The Congress of the United States has had more frequent changes in party control in the last few decades. Even when one party has managed to hang onto both houses of Congress, as the Republicans did from 1994 until 2001, and then again from 2002 until 2006, the majority for the dominant party has been paper thin. The addition of twenty-one House seats and eight Senate seats for the Democrats in 2008 did expand the party's majority, but it did not produce the supermajorities that some had predicted. (The Senate's unique rules often require at least sixty votes for action to proceed, and the Democrats cobbled this margin together with the addition of two unaligned senators, until the death of Edward Kennedy and the special election victory of Republican Scott Brown in 2010.) The surge by the Republican Party in the 2010 midterm elections brought divided government back to Washington; the GOP picked up a massive sixty-three seats in the House to regain the majority in that chamber, and they came within shouting distance of a majority in the Senate with the addition of six new seats. The Democrats came back again in 2012, gaining ground in the House, holding the Senate, and reelecting President Obama.

Adding more weight to the culture war argument is that once inside the halls of Congress, its members are now more likely to vote along party lines than in the past. As political scientist Barbara Sinclair thoroughly catalogues, the ideological divide between the members of the two parties is impossible to miss. Even the Senate, the body that George Washington first argued was a place for the cooling of passions and reasoned deliberation, has become unmistakably polarized.[7] This polarization is, at least in part, a product of the narrow majorities held by the party in power, but it may also be a reflection of the strength of the cultural divide between red and blue America. If, as the argument goes, Congress is a representative body of the people, the actions of its members are a mirror of their collective will. Therefore, as the public coalesces into distinct conservative and liberal blocs, each camp will vote for people like themselves; Congress will be inhabited by staunchly liberal Democrats and equally conservative Republicans. If we just look at who is in Congress and what they are doing in terms of policy making, it is tempting to fall into line with such thinking about the ideological leanings of the American public. Without a doubt, the Congress is far more polarized today than it was twenty years ago. The empirical evidence, such as the increase in party-line voting, is quite compelling in this regard. Anecdotally, the Congress is said to be a very different place than it was in the past. More than the House, the Senate was once a sort of "gentleman's club," in which men—yes, even with the inroads made by women and minorities, the Congress is still far out of sync with all manner of measures of American demographics—were respectful toward their colleagues and often formed friendships that crossed party lines. Even the House, with its more boisterous history and lower expectations about the social breeding and behavior of its members, was, until fairly recently in the life of the institution, a rather genteel place. A classic study from the 1950s by Matthews argued that the folkways or the informal social norms of Congress, the Senate in particular, encouraged deference to senior colleagues, a reverence for the institution, and the need to serve a sort of apprenticeship in the job for a time before taking on a policy leadership role.[8] Others have noted that Washington, DC, used to have more of a community feel to it, and members of the House and Senate would often socialize with one another in houses of worship, softball leagues, and other forms of neighborly interaction. For many students of Congress, including the members themselves, DC is no longer like this. As a longtime Washington insider observes,

> Thirty years ago, new members were more likely to move their families to DC after an election. They were eager to become part of the capi-tol's social scene and wanted their spouses and children near to where they spent most of their week. Families often socialized with each other regardless of party, and these personal ties curbed members' tendency to demonize one another.[9]

Starting in the early 1970s, in a period scholars refer to as the post-reform era, a new generation of members worked for changes that decreased the power of party leaders and committee chairs. This power was redistributed among less senior members, mostly by giving them the chairmanships of a host of newly created subcommittees. The people who were part of this reform era and its aftermath, along with members who are more recent additions, are accustomed to the idea that their institution should change to meet the needs of their con-stituents and their own needs. This change in attitude about Congress has led its members to be less collegial with each other and less patient with their own branch and the other two. The vessel for focusing this aggressiveness has gen-erally been the parties in Congress. Reinforcing this relationship have been extensive periods of divided government (1969–1977, 1981–1993, 2001–2002, 2007–2008, 2011 to the present) during which the level of partisan conflict increased within the Congress and among the branches. In this charged atmo-sphere, rank and file members from both parties have seen advantages in chal-lenging the actions and decisions of the party controlling each of the legislative chambers on Capitol Hill. The template for such confrontations was aptly laid down by Newt Gingrich, a member of the House from Georgia who gained notoriety from the public and loyalty from fellow GOP House members for going after the Democratic leadership of the House, President Clinton, and, in some instances, members of his own party who did not see things his way. As a Republican House Whip, Gingrich stoked a confrontational feeling among his fellow members and worked energetically to add seats to the GOP's numbers. He recruited new candidates, raised money on their behalf, and even helped coach them in the art of campaigning for office. By 1994, the Democratic majorities in the House and the Senate were in trouble. A few years prior, the House had been rocked by a check "kiting" incident in which members frequently drew money from the House bank against the money they were to be paid in the future—something that most working Americans cannot do. While not all the offenders were Democrats, the impression left with many in the public was that the Democratically-controlled House was playing too fast and loose with what was, ultimately, the people's money and allowing its members to enjoy an elite perk unavailable to the rest of us.

Bill Clinton's election in 1992 raised hopes among Democrats and their supporters that unified government would jolt the policy-making system back into action after years of inaction and gridlock on key issues such as health care reform. At the time, about 43 million citizens lacked health care insurance, and candidate Clinton had stressed this policy problem as a one of his top priorities. As president, Clinton made an interesting tactical move in his bid to reform health care. Rather than give Congress the lead on formulating a legislative solution to the problem of uninsured Americans lacking decent medical care, he kept this part of policy making within his purview by creating a taskforce to propose a health care reform plan for Congress. The taskforce, headed by then-First Lady, Hillary Clinton, was criticized by Democrats in Congress as moving too slowly and without adequate input from Congress, the same Congress that would have to shepherd any administration proposal through the tortuous legislative process. With the 1994 midterm elections looming in the not-too-distant future, the bill was introduced later in the legislative session than Democratic leaders would have liked. Members of the president's own party even introduced competing versions of health care reform. The health care insurance industry and others with a vested interest in the status quo spent freely to persuade the public that the Clinton plan was bad for the country. The end result was that the president's plan was in trouble from the day of its introduction and failed to get reported out of committee, let alone pass both house of Congress. Rightly or wrongly, the failure to pass health care reform tainted both Bill Clinton's presidency and the Democratic-controlled Congress. For many voters, the 1994 midterm congressional elections were an opportunity to express their dissatisfaction with the performance of federal policy making and governance. The Republicans added seventy-three new members to their rolls in the House and took control of the Senate as well. The Democrats, out of power in both houses of Congress for the first time since 1954, were perplexed and angry. The Republicans felt vindicated and none too conciliatory toward the Democrats, whom they asserted abused their power and bullied the GOP. The anger and resentment that had been kept in place by the seemingly invincible hold of the Democrats on Congress spilled over.

Democrats chafed at their new minority status and, fairly or unfairly, some reacted angrily about how they were being treated by the GOP majority. The news media saw this frustration as a highly dramatic story line and gave it a good deal of attention. Interest groups with long associations with the Democratic Party realigned themselves with the new Republican majority, and new conservatively oriented interest groups sprang up to enjoy the more hospitable environment in Washington. Republicans and their supporters created the K-Street Strategy, a reference to the street that houses the offices of many of the nation's major lobbying associations. This strategy was an overt attempt by leaders in Congress, especially Tom DeLay, then the House Majority Whip, to coerce lobbyists into employing Republicans in their firms. In many ways, the strategy worked, prompting one observer to call the new order on K Street a part of the GOP's political machine.[10] With a new majority on Capitol Hill and new power in the lobbying trenches, the money for the reelection coffers then flowed toward the Republicans and away from Democrats. The atmosphere in Washington was highly charged with partisanship, ill will, and distrust. About twenty years later, the partisan divide in Washington may be greater than ever. A book written about partisanship choking off the ability of the government to do much of anything to solve the nation's problems captured the current zeitgeist in its title: *It's Even Worse Than it Looks.*[11]

But has all this disharmony come from us, the public? Certainly, a highly polarized public could be getting what it asks for, that is, a Congress that looks like the public and one that creates an all-or-nothing policy environment. An alternative explanation is also available. Morris Fiorina argues that a polarized public is mostly a myth.[12] While there are, indeed, partisan and ideological differences among the American public, they are fairly minor and have been generally consistent over time. If the source of the polarization seen in Congress was driven by an equally divided electorate, we would need to see such a division now and have the ability to look back and chart its increase over time. Neither of these factors is in place. Here is the puzzle: how can we explain the polarization in Washington without fixing it directly to the will of the public? Fiorina explains that some of the supposed indicators of a heated culture war—the closeness of elections for the presidency and the narrow majorities in Congress—might reflect an electorate that is narrowly rather than deeply divided. A deep division along party and ideological lines with hardly anyone in the middle would result in close elections and narrow majorities, but so would an electorate that had more of its numbers parked at or near the center of a left–right political continuum. Think of two figures or graphs: In one, a parabola forms a cup toward the center; here, the public is deeply divided. In the other, the curve creates a hill or a bell shape; here, the public is narrowly divided. Fiorina argues that the United States is much more like the second figure than the first. In other words, we may be far more moderate and centrist than polarized. The key for Fiorina is including the candidates and officeholders in the picture. If we are not segregated into warring blue and red states or districts, but are instead part of a mosaic of shades running from blue to red with a high amount of mixing toward purple, then the importance of the candidates and officeholders themselves becomes paramount.

Fiorina's arguments fit with a picture of politicians as self-starters who get into electoral politics because of some motivating factor, often an ideological fervor coupled with an intense feeling about one or more issues, rather than generalized motivations about service to one's constituency or country. This new breed of politician finds support in the world of powerful political action committees and other well-off political organizations and finds easy access to the nomination of a party by way of the system of open primaries in the United States. The result is that our *choices* for office have become more partisan and ideologically extreme, but we have not. This helps establish a feedback loop; more zealous officeholders taking increasingly extreme positions on key policies produces an image of politics as a type of blood sport, rather than a civic duty or just a public sector career choice. People who might have thought about running for office may shy away from it because of the harshness of the contemporary battlefield. Only the "true believers" and other hardy or foolhardy souls are willing to join such a fray.

Because the candidates have changed, the resulting batch of elected officials has changed as well. As these officials and the political class surrounding them—the "inside the beltway" collection of media, pundits, lobbyists, and think-tank experts—tend to focus on one another, the result is an overly intensified sense that whoever occupies the seats of power in DC and elsewhere must be the mirror image of the public. As Fiorina's data and persuasive arguments attest, this does not seem to be the case. There is little doubt that elite polarization powerfully shapes the policy-making environment. However, the source of that polarization is fundamentally important if we are concerned about its longevity and ability to continue to form the framework for how policy is made.

Demographic Changes

In 2006, Hispanics, Latinos, and many other people who simply disliked what they saw as an anti-immigrant mindset and associated policies took to the streets across the United States. In Los Angeles on March 25, 2006, about 500,000 people jammed the streets in a march aimed at securing the rights of immigrants and protesting against policies working their way though Congress that were deemed anti-immigrant, specifically H.R. 4437, the Border Protection, Antiterrorism, and Illegal Immigration Control Act of 2005. Los Angeles was not alone in witnessing such protests. Throughout the spring of 2006, other cities including Dallas, Phoenix, Chicago, and New York all had major protest marches.

In many ways the Border Protection, Antiterrorism, and Illegal Immigration Control Act of 2005 was a response to a policy proposed by President Bush in January of 2004. The president proposed a new policy to augment our existing immigration regulations that would allow the citizens of other countries, mostly from Mexico, to enter the United States, work for a period of time, and then return to their countries of origin. President Bush called this a guest worker program, and he proposed it at least in partial recognition of the important role foreign-born workers—a sizeable number here illegally—play in the nation's economy. The president's Republican Party has traditionally enjoyed the support of the nation's business community and the guest worker program would have legally funneled workers into jobs that, according to President Bush, most Americans do not want to do, such as working in slaughterhouses, picking vegetables, or cleaning hotel rooms. It would be logical to think that the owners of large meat processing plants, farms, and hotel chains would like to have a steady supply of workers who are in the country legally, and many such owners did cheer for the president's plan. However, other parts of the president's party, and an ample number of non-Republicans, loudly denounced the guest worker proposal as "amnesty"—one of the worst epithets that can be hurled at a policy proposal in the world of those who see immigration, especially illegal immigration, as one of the nation's major policy problems. Television pundit Lou Dobbs made a career out of his disdain for any moves that would make it easier for most people to enter this country and consistently calls for tighter borders and harsher policies on illegal immigrants now here. Dobbs' voice was just one of many that blasted the president's guest worker plan. These critics saw the policy proposal as a backdoor to allow illegal immigrants to receive amnesty from punishment under our laws and allow them to continue to live and work here and even go on to become citizens, much like what happened after major immigration reform was enacted in 1986. What drives the more stridently nativist elements of the anti-immigration forces is open to question, but it is reasonable to assume that some of the motivation for this bloc comes from a fear or dislike of immigrants. The United States has a long history of racial antagonism, with the dominant whites using their superior numbers to suppress the wishes and rights of minority populations. If even a modicum of the heat over immigration policy comes from the friction among racial and ethnic blocs, what will our policy environment look like in forty years when "no single racial group will be a majority"?[13] Indeed, the share of Hispanics in the nation's demographic makeup has already exceeded that of African-Americans, making Hispanics the largest minority group in the United States and an emerging political powerhouse. Hispanic voters were a major part of the coalition that helped Barack Obama return to the White House in 2012. In fact, Republican candidate Mitt Romney did less well with Hispanic voters than did George Bush in his last bid for the presidency in 2004, a result that has Republican Party supporters concerned about the ability of the party to win future presidential elections.[14]

Communications

We live in a mass society of about 305 million people spread out over the landmass of major parts of North America. We are citizens of our nation and citizens of a world brought together by a true revolution in communications. There is virtually nowhere on the face of the globe that is beyond the reach of our network of communications devices. Whether by landline phone, cell, or satellite phone, or some form of Internet-based communication, we are amazingly interconnected. We take it for granted that we can interact with nearly anyone at anytime and find information about most anything, day or night. Just twenty to twenty-five years ago, the world was a very different place. The Internet had not been turned into a publicly accessible information conduit. Cell phones were coming into use, but were large and unwieldy and users had very limited service areas. CDs and DVDs were still a novelty to many people at this time. Home computers were no longer mostly in the hands of hobbyists or people who used them in home businesses, but only about 15–20 percent of homes had one, compared with nearly 90 percent today.[15] In 1980, CNN was on the air, but news programming delivered by satellite and cable TV took a backseat in viewership to the nightly broadcast news programs offered by ABC, CBS, and NBC. How we gathered information and most of the ways we communicated with each other were done with timeworn technology. Of course, the wave of change was beginning to break, but the communication environment in the late 1980s had a great deal in common with that of the previous generation, and—to some extent—longer ago than that. These changes have had far-reaching implications for how players in the policy process interact with one another and on the existence and substance of policies themselves.

Historically, the limitations of the communication environment have shaped our policy environment and the very nation and its political system. In 1787, the framers' plan embodied in the US Constitution was one predicated on the control of factions. As James Madison explained in "Federalist No. 10," a faction is a group brought into being by the self-interest of it members. The danger of a faction is that the goals it seeks are likely to harm the rest of the citizenry. Factions amounting to less than a majority are unlikely to cause much of a problem in a system of policy making based on "majority rules" practices, but majority factions are exceedingly dangerous. They may use their superior numbers to take control of the levers of government and seek unwise and even dangerous policies for all. Part of Madison's means of thwarting the potential tyranny of the majority was to split power into different layers, producing federalism and branches within the federal layer, as embodied in the separation of powers among the legislative, executive, and judicial departments of power. Madison also made an interesting defense of the new large republic created by the federal Constitution by arguing that it would help to frustrate the creation of a majority faction. First, the larger size of the new republic—in contrast to the nation under the Articles of Confederation which really was an amalgam of thirteen mostly sovereign, individual, small republics—would dilute the existing factions or the basis for factions by forcing an increased number of interests to compete with one another. This watering down of faction by mixing many factions together was a major selling point when debate over the ratification of the Constitution was in full swing. The other imperative part of Madison's call for a physically large republic was that it would work to geographically isolate pockets of faction. A nascent faction in New Hampshire may share sentiments about taxes, the role of religion in politics, or any other issue, with others in Virginia or South Carolina. It is possible that these discrete pockets of mutually shared interest may compose a majority of the population, but their geographic isolation will keep them from knowing of each other and banding together. This line of argumentation and logical reasoning was brilliant for Madison's time, but today it sounds a bit quaint. With cell phones, instant messaging, and powerhouse social networking capabilities on the Internet, the ability of the nation's citizens to know of one another's interests and to organize and act based on those mutually shared views is stunning when compared to Madison's distinctly late eighteenth century views. Our contemporary interconnections are not simply regional or even national; they are global.

Changes in the nature of communication have greatly altered the policy-making environment. The formation of groups and movements, the rapidity of the dissemination of information, the reconfiguring of who comprises the keepers of information and the "truth," all channel what issues are considered in the policy-making process and how those issues that are taken up are treated by policy makers.

There are abundant examples of how the new information environment pulls at the fabric of what is truth and what is fiction. On September 11, 2001, nineteen men—most from Saudi Arabia—boarded planes at airports in the northeast. At 8:46 a.m. one of these planes was flown into the North Tower of the World Trade Center in New York City. Less than twenty minutes later, a second plane hit the South Tower. This terribly dark and bitter day for the United States was the work of terrorists loyal to Osama bin Laden. For most of us, these are the basic facts that encompass our understanding of what our collective consciousness knows as "September 11th." However, there is a small but persistent part of the nation's population that does not believe in the truth of this narrative. Calling themselves by names such as the 9/11 Truth movement, they see the attacks on New York, Washington, and the doomed flight that crashed in Pennsylvania as part of a conspiracy. Their reasoning is often complex, but most versions of the "alternate" truth argue that someone—often the Bush administration or some secret cabal inside or outside the government—had much to gain by either turning a blind eye to the impending attacks or that the attacks were really the work of the government itself. By allowing or carrying out these attacks, the United States was given the provocation to expand its power into the Middle East and to limit freedoms here at home. A number of films—mostly available on the Internet rather than released as typical productions first shown in movie theaters—purport to show that the destruction of the Twin Towers in New York was actually a controlled demolition caused by explosives planted in the buildings rather than the impacts and effects of the crashed planes.

The movement's members have been largely focused on "getting the truth out" to the rest of the public. Yet, there is a part of the movement that calls for protest and seeks to gain the ear of policy makers to either own up to their roles in the conspiracy or to investigate 9/11 in order to weaken what they see as a despotic grip on the truth by the government. If the conspiracy of 9/11 is real, then these goals are serious expressions of a drive to restore our democracy to a state of honesty and openness that truly empowers the people. As some have argued, however, if the movement is based on a conspiratorial misreading of the facts, then there is some danger that the movement devalues the lives lost on that day and afterward. This is because the cause of their deaths is being misdirected in order to prove a point about abuse of power that may not have happened. In essence, argue these critics, those lives lost are being exploited by the movement for its own goals.[16]

No matter what one believes, the fact that such a movement exists and can disseminate its views with ease is something that is largely attributable to our present communications situation. In James Madison's era of limited newspaper publication and communication largely by way of hand-carried letters, such a movement would have been unthinkable. Because of the immediacy and openness of our newly emerging system of mass communications—think about how easy it is to view and even post video clips to YouTube and other sites—a feedback loop has been added to our policy-making environment. Ideas and allegations can sprout up from anywhere and can "go viral," meaning they are rapidly disseminated by the new communications environment so that a vast slice of the public comes in contact with them in a short amount of time. There are positive and negative aspects to such developments in how we communicate. On the positive side, conditions that are undesirable may be seen as problems more rapidly. Since there is a tipping point after which the public and policy makers start to address circumstances as genuine problems, the ability to speedily place the troubling conditions before policy actors changes the structure of the policy environment. When once it took a great deal of time and persistence to raise alarm about a looming issue, there is now the potential to rapidly awaken the attention of policy players.

One of the thornier environmental and public health problems of the last fifty years has been the impact of chemicals, especially pesticides, on the natural world and on human health. One of the first people to sound the alarm about pesticides was Rachel Carson, a biologist who noted the reduction in songbirds during the springtime. In the late 1950s, Carson began looking at the possible causes of what were, in some cases, massive die-offs of birds and other animals. What she found was a link between commonly used agricultural and residential pesticides, especially the insecticide DDT, and the death of many species of animals. Carson rightly figured that if these chemicals were harmful to animals, they had the potential to injure human health. Her first contacts with the federal government over her concerns were not overly encouraging. After all, this was a time when the mere existence a female scientist was still rather exotic and the major chemical companies were foursquare against any attempts to undermine the safety of their highly lucrative products. Carson's early attempts to bring attention to her findings about the connections among pesticides, the natural world, and human health were at first ignored and then scoffed at by some of her scientific colleagues. She was persistent and eventually published *Silent Spring* in 1962, a book that has become a classic study of how to introduce the public and policy makers to the emergence of a problem that is presently unrecognized. Carson was an indispensable component in the fight to start action on a new policy issue, but her efforts—and the efforts of others like her—took time to produce results. Today it is fairly easy to think of how some of the things Carson witnessed or was told about, such as the mass deaths of birds in freshly sprayed farm fields, could be posted on the web in a matter of moments and possibly grab the attention of the news media, the public, and policy makers in less time than it would have taken Rachel Carson to write about the event on her old manual typewriter. For example, *Kony 2012*, a short film available about the atrocities committed in Uganda, gained a nearly instantaneous recognition of the situation by a worldwide audience.

Certainly there is something akin to a mantra in American culture that faster is better. Waiting means wasted time and inconvenience, and who wants that? It does make sense that we should benefit from the earlier detection of troubling circumstances and the greater ability to bring together consensus on the existence of problems. However, there are risks in speeding up the process of problem identification. We live in a postmodern culture, one with less patience for deliberation and one that is fueled by rapid change. Our news programs contain "sound bites" that have been getting shorter over time. Our television programs often utilize an editing format of very quick cuts from shot to shot and scene to scene. Becoming accustomed to change as the norm limits our ability to focus on circumstances that need more than a quick glance in order to understand the issue. Even when a sizeable number of people become aware of a potential problem, there may be a tendency to say, "Yes, that is too bad, but look at this other issue that is even more attention-getting here and now." The increasing volume of information and the rapidity of our change in focus from one idea or issue to the next makes it all the more difficult for circumstances in the pre-problem stage to gain a foothold in the minds of the public and policy makers alike.

Some problems need to come to maturation before they are ready for action. It may be that we do not grasp the seriousness of the circumstances at the outset, or we assume that it will go away or somehow be solved, or that it does not affect us either personally or in a way that connects to our lives in a meaningful way. A truncated attention span on our part exacerbates these tendencies to ignore or otherwise downplay the existence of problems.

While it is possible for the advocates for action on a potential problem to use the new communication environment to their advantage, the environment itself and our attitudes toward it set loose forces that work against the power of these new information avenues, making them unlikely to reach us in more than a superficial way.

The Economy

James Madison's "Federalist No. 10" notes that one of the perennial factors that leads to the creation of factions is the unequal distribution of wealth in a society. Madison was not writing this as a call to action against injustice but as a recognized fact that our economic system was and would continue to be based on the private ownership of wealth. In other words, capitalism— unfettered exchange of goods and services or private ownership as opposed to governmental ownership of the means of production—was here to stay. There really was not a serious debate about the continuation of capitalism during the founding period of our nation, even though there were historical examples and theories about other economic systems that the framers could have drawn upon. Our status as a colony had undoubtedly formed a national mindset that equated economic liberty with political freedom. Both of these values were thought of as individual rights rather than collective or shared goods, meaning that little regulation or control by government was needed or even desirable. This laissez-faire view of economic matters (what is also known as traditional liberalism) had an easy fit with our political culture's emphasis on personal and political liberty, and in the ensuing centuries the basic impulse that formed our nation's embrace of capitalism has changed but has not disappeared. In fact, this predilection has formed a major part of our policy-making environment over time. It has precluded some policy solutions as unworkable or undesirable. For example, plans to create some form of national health care have been discussed at least as long ago as the 1930s, but these policies have often been derided as "socialized medicine" and antithetical to our free market system of medicine. For its detractors, some form of national health care for the roughly 47 million Americans without adequate, or in many cases, any health care coverage, is a violation of a basic component of our economic system. That phrase, "socialized medicine," and what it seems to entail—for many of us—is enough to end the debate about how to fix the nation's health care problems.

Historically, the nation has lurched away from the absolutes implied by the term "free market capitalism" during times of crisis or societal change, such as the Great Depression and during the mid to late 1960s. The wave of regulations in the 1930s and the mushrooming of governmental programs in the 1960s are evidence that the nation is not absolutist about the nature of capitalism. Yet, absent a crisis or other form of strong leverage, attempts to tinker with what are perceived as fundamentals of the free market can spark a crisis on their own. The battle over the recharter of the second Bank of the United States in the 1830s is a classic example of how the nature of our economic system forms what we think is right, let alone useful. President Jackson's veto of the recharter can be seen as the forces of the free market winning out over those who would unwisely fiddle with the nation's economic system. The economic crisis that began in 2008 holds elements of this tension over the power of our belief in the free market to shape our policy choices. Should the federal government have moved to free up the credit markets and calm investors? Should the automakers get a bailout from the government? Should homeowners struggling to stay in their homes get relief for their mortgages? All of these questions revolve around the basic belief that forms this part of the policy environment; there is a nearly mythological adherence to the idea that government activity in the area of economic policy is somehow unnatural. Such a widely shared belief is often at the crossroads of politics and policy.

Our economic system is hardly one of free market capitalism, although this notion is often presented as an accurate depiction of reality rather than a romanticized wish. The US economy is and has been typified by governmental regulation for much of our history as a nation. For example, the use of tariffs and the creation of the Bank of the United States often dominated our economic policy debates in the early years and frequently drove our politics. The expansion of the economic regulatory power of the federal government was at the very heart of the campaign of 1932. Would the Republicans continue to hold

▶ THE RECENT FINANCIAL CRISIS

The Issue

What are the causes of the economic problems stemming from the "Great Recession," such as the failure of major lending institutions and the wave of defaults on home mortgages? Who is responsible for trying to fix these problems? Is our system of economic regulatory policy working or does the federal government need to exert more control over private economic activity?

The Story

"The fundamentals of the economy are strong." When John McCain uttered that statement on the campaign trail toward the end of the 2008 presidential election, there was a sense of grateful disbelief in the Obama campaign. Senator McCain had just provided them with a powerful weapon to use against his presidential aspirations. As Obama's communications director cried out, "Shut up! He [McCain] said what?"[i] After all, many economic indicators were showing signs of trouble for the economy, and the presidential election was increasingly driven by the public's fears about a recession—or something worse. A presidential candidate that seemed to underplay the magnitude of the nation's economic crisis did so at his own peril. McCain was not alone in believing that the basics of the nation's economic system were probably strong enough to withstand even a harsh blow, but his timing was unfortunate. Events would quickly make it seem that he did not understand the weaknesses of the economy. (His campaign did not defend this point and backtracked into an awkward position, stating that the senator was referring to American workers when he used the term "fundamentals." McCain then attempted to portray Obama as less supportive of working people because he ridiculed McCain for his initial statement about the strength of the economy.) Only days later, the fallout from the bursting of the housing bubble and the ensuing tightening in the nation's credit sectors blew into Wall Street, unnerving investors in a way not seen since the market crash of 1987. On October 15, the Dow Jones Industrial Average dropped 7.8 percent and the nation watched a near-panic unfold on TV, on-line at home or work, or with updates on their cell phones as the market dropped and kept falling. Many people who had been in the workforce for years cringed as their retirement accounts, often in the form of 401(k) plans that are directly tied to the performance of the stock market, lost huge percentages of their worth. For many Americans, the financial crisis of 2008 was something that took them by surprise. Certainly, the news media provided extensive reporting on the difficulties with the nation's housing and mortgage problems, often referred to as the "mortgage meltdown" or other evocatively sinister sounding terms. It was easy to find example after example of people who could not make the monthly payments on homes that had been bought for unrealistically inflated prices at the height of the housing boom. Overpriced homes required equally inflated mortgages that proved too much for many people to cover each month; often the mortgages themselves contained mechanisms that boosted monthly payments into the stratosphere once a far lower "teaser" rate ended. The bursting of the housing bubble with its inflated home prices, housing shortages, new building boom, and speculators buying houses in order to make a profit by quickly "flipping" them to a new buyer caused a set of problems that became a crisis with time and the collective weight of so many people with so many troubles. The staggering number of people who have lost or will lose their homes and ruin their credit ratings is one part of the crisis and another is the punch taken by the housing industry as orders for new homes dried up. Contractors, construction workers, and suppliers of building materials were all negatively impacted. So too were real-estate agents and others who make their living on the sale of existing and new homes. Of course, the banks and other lending institutions who loaned money to home buyers were affected by this crisis. Some of these institutions were hurt in the way that intuitively makes sense; they suffered because they made loans to people who could not pay them back. Other financial institutions suffered not because they originated the loans but because they bought into ways to spread the risk to others in case loans went bad. These complex plans to limit the risk any one bank or mortgage company has for its loans—the most talked about of these is the credit default swap—can either be thought of as a form of insurance for those with risk or a game of chance for those daring enough to buy a bit of the jeopardy in return for big payouts when the risk was past. In some versions of this risk diversification, investors could bet that the risk would be realized and make money when loans went bad, and in other formulations, investors could simply place bets on whether or not the risk would pass without ever holding any of the risk itself! This is akin to betting on a sporting event without owning any stake in either team. All of these activities were legal and the product of a major wave of financial deregulation during the first term and a half of the Bush administration.

Major financial organizations got burned by the mortgage meltdown either because of their own poorly thought-out investments and loans or because they were tied to other players who made poor choices. Banks and other lenders started to feel the effects of these circumstances. Credit that had once been plentiful—especially the short-term loans that banks lend to each other to keep money flowing at lower rates and increase the profitability for the lenders—was suddenly scarce. Lenders were sitting on their money hoping for better financial weather or simply did not have it to loan. Long-standing financial houses such as Lehman Brothers and major insurance companies like AIG began to go under. As the whirlpool of financial turmoil claimed more victims, the federal government began to act by loaning money to some of the imperiled companies. What started as a set of stories about trouble in the nation's housing sector on the inside pages of the business section of many newspapers now boiled over into a drama that dominated the nation's thoughts, spurred policy makers into action, and even threatened to derail a part of the presidential election when Senator McCain indicated that he might not participate in one of the debates with Obama, owing to the seriousness of the crisis.

There is an old adage in baseball that if we pitched as hard and as well as we did to get out of trouble, we would not have gotten into trouble in the first place. No doubt, there were many Americans, including policy makers, who were thinking something very much along the lines of this statement about baseball. After all, the economic crisis that started in late 2008 didn't really start in late 2008. The antecedents of crisis were with us for years. The ability to offer risky, unwise loans was made more likely when the federal government deregulated parts of the financial and lending industry in the early 2000s. The monetary policy of the Federal Reserve has been to stave off inflation—classically defined as too many dollars chasing too few goods and services—by cutting the prime rate, the rate banks use to loan money to each other, to businesses, and to individual consumers. Keeping inflation low with "loose money," meaning easy credit, surely made it easier for Americans to secure loans for cars, houses, consumer goods, and student loans, for instance. Without inflation to worry about, the economic policies of the federal government worked to stoke the economy so that we experienced low unemployment, expansion in home ownership, and what seemed like an endless spending spree by the public on consumer electronics and new cars. In the days after 9/11, President Bush urged the nation to go to shopping malls and other stores and spend as a way of economically strengthening the nation in the wake of the terrorist attacks. And spend we did! However, our level of personal debt rose and our savings rate, never very high as compared to other western democracies, went down. It is tempting to place the blame squarely with one actor in this crisis—the policy makers in DC or the profligate American public are handy punching bags—but the truth of the matter goes back to a basic concept that underlies most policy problems; public problems occur at the intersection of governmental authority and public behavior. If the banks didn't feel emboldened to make easy loans to risky borrowers through nifty forms of laying off risk in a deregulated industry, then there would not have been a mortgage crisis that helped bring on the wider economic crisis. If the public was more astute about the terms of loans or more circumspect about handling so much debt, then there would not have been a credit crisis that helped bring on the wider economic crisis. If the federal government did not deregulate key aspects of our financial system, call for consumer spending to ward off the blow of 9/11, and drive our latest spree with the Fed's low interest rates, then we would not have all the precursors that helped bring on the wider economic crisis. These are convenient and drastically simplistic ways to encapsulate the economic crisis, but they do hold at least a grain of truth about the economic aspects of the environment of policy making.

The Questions

- What role do campaigns play in shaping of the nation's policies?
- Should consumers simply abide by the age-old advice that the buyer must beware or is it proper for the government to provide guidance and safeguards against the potentially unwise actions taken by consumers?

- Are some companies really such a major part of the operation of the nation's economy that they are "too big to fail" and require extraordinary governmental assistance in times of crisis?
- Should the Federal Reserve use monetary policy to try to regulate the economy or should the business cycle play itself out so that weaker economic players are eliminated from competition?

See for Yourself

Watch *Meltdown* at the following link to see the players and the tension of the political and economic environments in the United States as the immensity of the financial crisis became apparent. http://www.pbs.org/wgbh/pages/frontline/meltdown/view/

[i]Nagoruney, Adam, Jim Rutenberg, and Jeff Zeleny. "Near-Flawless Run Is Credited in Victory." *New York Times.* http://www.nytimes.com/2008/11/05/us/politics/05recon.html (accessed February 11, 2013).

power in Washington and keep the nation's economic policies unchanged while waiting for the markets to correct themselves? Or would Roosevelt win the day with his vague promises about doing whatever he could with the power of the federal government to turn the nation back from the brink of economic ruin and, perhaps, even political revolution? The victory of FDR in 1932 and the impact of the New Deal on the regulation of the nation's banks, stock markets, and labor force were deep and nearly indelible. Even years of devolution—the return or devolving of power back to the states—under Republicans and, to a lesser degree, Democrats in Washington has not undone the basic premise that governs our nation's economic policy: regulation is necessary and the free market is simply too dangerous or unwieldy for a profitable business climate. The need or desire to regulate can expand and contract. There is no objective force that pulls or relaxes these impulses or requirements. The tension that comes from wanting to allow a freer hand for the economy playing against a need for more control is one of the most powerful and persistent forces in the environment of public policy. It is much like the tides of the ocean as the moon pulls at the water on the surface of the earth: the force is tremendous, yet its cause is not always obvious; its effects can range from the predictable and mild to the surprising and catastrophic.

CONCLUSION

The environment of policy making is far more complex that what we might assume from a simple schematic view of "how an idea becomes a policy." Social, political, economic, and technological factors interact in ways that are hard to predict and equally hard to see once they have interacted. The environment is constantly changing and, perhaps, even evolving into new types of social, political, economic, or technological elements. While such change is potentially daunting to those of us who study policy making, there are a number of long-lasting aspects to this environment that may help give us some needed perspective on the changes taking place.

Our system of federalism, the separation of powers, and other institutional characteristics of the US political system and our government provide a structural background upon which change can be seen and understood in context. The policy-making environment is far from static, but it has enough permanence to allow us to make sense of change and to see how actors operate within this environment. This is where we will turn in the next chapter.

SUMMARY

The policy environment is made of numerous and varied factors and forces. Some are obvious and quite durable, whereas others are less apparent and more malleable. Overall, the diversity that structures the policy-making environment helps to explain the very complex and politically driven nature of our policy-making system.

Federalism, the division of power and responsibility between the federal and state governments, is a major structural facet in American policy making and one that can appear to be static, but federalism is actually an evolutionary part of the policy-making system. The dividing line between federal and state power has shifted over our history and, presently, there is a great deal of political conflict over just how much power the federal government or the states should have over a wide range of policy issue areas including immigration, health care, and the environment. In a similar way, the separation of powers may appear to be fixed by the Constitution at the federal level, but the struggle for power over policy making among the three branches has featured periods of ascendency or decline for all three at various times.

Other aspects of the policy-making environment are even less fixed than are federalism and the separation of powers and, therefore, may be less noticeable to observers of the policy-making process. This does not mean, however, that such factors are unimportant or less a part of the politics of policy making. In fact, these factors may be even more likely to feature battles over key economic, political, and social values—the essence of politics itself. The existence of a culture war, if true, helps to explain the contentiousness of contemporary policy making. The importance of emerging and declining demographic blocs adds to the variation of how policy making is undertaken in the United States, with some groupings exerting increased political muscle while other blocs struggle with how to integrate or protect their policy goals with or from these changes. The lightening-quick changes that have taken place and continue to define our communications systems add exciting and, perhaps, troubling possibilities to how problems are identified and how they are treated in the policy-making process. Our economy, as all too clearly illustrated by the recent "Great Recession," is a major driver of the policy-making process. Even with sizeable amounts of regulation, our free market system is hardly a static factor in policy making. The same political impulses that spur policy making in other issue areas, especially as embodied in the ongoing debate over the proper role of the federal government, are front and center in the policy issues associated with the economy.

DISCUSSION QUESTIONS

1. Other nations lack the more durable divisions of power that structure policy making in the United States. For example, the British do not have our separation of powers, and power is centralized at the national level. Is our policy-making system too prone to breakdown because of all the checks and balances produced by our system? Would our policy-making system be better if we had a more centralized system, like the British? ("Better" is a debatable concept; how do you define it in the context of policy making?)
2. Are we really a nation of warring red and blue states? What evidence, if any, do you see in current instances of policy making that support the existence of a culture war? What evidence, if any, do you see in current instances of policy making that support the idea that we more a more moderate, "purple" nation? Overall, how much does political culture matter for the policy-making process?
3. Projections are that, in about a generation, the United States will be a nation with no majority ethnic or racial bloc. How important do you think ethnicity and race are to the current policy-making process? How might the policy-making process change, if it does change, when the nation no longer has a majority ethnic or racial bloc?
4. The use of communications technology has revolutionized the policy-making process. How do these changes influence what we see as problematic and how solutions are crafted to solve problems? In particular, do you think our "always-connected" world of social media makes it easier or harder to solve problems? Why?
5. Is the economy the dominant factor in policy making? Should other noneconomic factors, based on morality, cultural norms, accepted practices, etc., take a backseat to economic factors when policy makers make decisions about what to do and how to do it? Why or why not?

NOTES

1. As Joseph Zimmerman argued in the early 1990s, the rise of federal preemption over state policy making was nothing short of a "revolution." See Zimmerman, Joseph Francis. *Federal preemption: The silent revolution.* Ames, IA: Iowa State University Press, 1991.
2. Shear, Michael D., Steven Mufson, and William Branigin. "La. Gov. Jindal demands U.S. government, BP uphold pledges to avert environmental disaster." *Washington Post*, April 30, 2010. http://www.washingtonpost.com/wp-dyn/content/article/2010/04/30/AR2010043001044.html

3. See "Federalist No. 10," Madison's justly noteworthy tract in the *Federalist Papers*. A good collection of these crucial documents is Rossiter, Clinton L., ed. *The Federalist Papers: Alexander Hamilton, James Madison, John Jay*. New York: Mentor, 1999.

4. Burkhalter, Sarah K. "Green groups react to the election of Barack Obama." *Grist*. http://www.grist.org/article/enviro-reax (November 5, 2008).

5. Hunter, James Davison. *Culture wars: The struggle to define America*. New York: Basic Books, 1991.

6. Jones, Jeffrey M. "Congressional Approval Recovers Slightly, Now 17%." *Gallup Politics* (April 19, 2012). http://www.gallup.com/poll/153968/Congressional-Approval-Recovers-Slightly.aspx

7. Sinclair, Barbara. *Party wars: Polarization and the politics of national policy making*. Norman, OK: University of Oklahoma Press, 2006. 3–13.

8. Matthews, Donald R. *U.S. Senators and their world*. Chapel Hill, NC: University of North Carolina Press, 1960.

9. Eilperin, Juliet. *Fight club politics: How partisanship is poisoning the House of Representatives*. Lanham, MD: Rowman & Littlefield, 2006. 32.

10. Confessore, Nicholas. "Welcome to the Machine." *Washington Monthly* July/August (2003).

11. Mann, Thomas E., and Norman J. Ornstein. *It's even worse than it looks: How the American constitutional system collided with the new politics of extremism*. New York: Basic Books, 2012.

12. Fiorina, Morris P., Samuel J. Abrams, and Jeremy Pope. *Culture war? The myth of a polarized America*. 2nd ed. New York: Pearson Longman, 2005.

13. "Changing U.S. Electorate: Are demographic trends reshaping U.S. politics?" *CQ Researcher* 18, no. 20 (2008): 460.

14. Kopicki, Allison, and Will Irving. "Assessing How Pivotal the Hispanic Vote Was to Obama's Victory." *New York Times*, November 20, 2012. http://thecaucus.blogs.nytimes.com/2012/11/20/assessing-how-pivotal-the-hispanic-vote-was-to-obamas-victory/

15. "A gadget's life: From gee-whiz to junk." *Washington Post*. http://www.washingtonpost.com/wp-srv/special/business/a-gadgets-life/

16. For a timely journalistic investigation of the "truther movement," see Kay, Jonathan. *Among the truthers: A journey through America's growing conspiracist underground*. New York: Harper, 2011.

Agenda Setting and Massing of Interests—Actors Outside Government

Joel Sartore/National Geographic Image Collection/Glow Images

CHAPTER OBJECTIVES

When you finish reading Chapter 5, you should be able to do the following:

- Describe the differences between circumstances and problems
- Distinguish between institutional and systemic agendas

- Identify the three parts of the multiple streams model of agenda setting
- Summarize the factors that allow issues to stay on the agenda
- Illustrate how the key players in agenda setting use their resources to influence the agenda

The summer of 2010 featured a set of disturbing images from the Gulf of Mexico and the states of the Gulf Coast. Oil from the ruptured BP well about one mile below the surface of the ocean befouled the beaches and caused a massive ecological disaster for the region and, perhaps, for a sizeable part of the world's ecosystem. Few of us seeing the images of the chocolate-colored gunk covering birds and sea creatures could argue that a problem did not exist. In fact, it was evident early on in the BP spill that serious environmental and economic problems were present and were likely to continue. The people who fished the Gulf and those who made their livelihoods from the natural beauty of the area through tourism and recreation were clearly in peril. So too were those in the oil and gas industry whose future employment was made uncertain by the questionable future for expanded energy extraction in the deeper waters of the Gulf and elsewhere. Even people who did not make their living from the oil-polluted sea and coastline were threatened by the possibility of air and groundwater contamination and an economic chain reaction that would flow from those directly impacted.

Politically, elected and appointed officials at all levels of government were feeling pressure from their constituents to do something to stop the flow of oil and to clean up the mess. Congress held hearings to try to uncover solutions to the spilled oil, and everything from giant underwater balloons to capture the oil from the wellhead to large sponges made from human hair for soaking up the spilled oil were presented by inventors and other would-be saviors.[1] President Obama traveled to the Gulf on numerous occasions and gave his first Oval Office address to the nation about the spill and cleanup efforts.

Some problems, such as those stemming from the BP spill in the summer of 2010, are so obvious and of such a colossal magnitude that policy makers automatically swing into action in their roles as potential problem solvers or crisis managers. Fortunately for us, most problems are not of a self-evident nature like the BP spill.

While it is intellectually convenient to explain things that we like—such as a healthy ecosystem—or things that we do not care for—such as overly lax regulation of the energy extraction industry—as the sole product of politicians and other policy makers, it is not that simple. The reality of our circumstances is influenced by many factors, and some—like environmental disasters—are immensely complex and involve the actions and behaviors of governments, corporations, and individual consumers around the globe.

At the outset of this text, it was argued that policy making is political and that politics is more than just what government does and does not do. Policy making is influenced by other actions and actors that we accept as "political," such as elections and lobbying campaigns. Policy making itself is a political process with all the tugs of interests and differences in power among the players. In this chapter, the notion that we must look beyond government in order to understand the politics of public policy making is front and center. One of the clearest points to see this in the policy process is during problem identification and agenda setting. As you will read, influencing what is seen as problematic and taking action on these issues says a great deal about which actors have power within our political system.

One of the major debates over the very nature of our democracy has to do with the amount of power held by the public at large versus the concentration of power held by smaller groups. Quite succinctly, political scientist Robert Dahl asked this key question in the title of his landmark book, *Who Governs?*[2] Is it the common person, individually or collectively, who has the greatest influence over what problems are placed before decision makers for action (the viewpoint of those calling themselves pluralists), or is it those who have greater wealth and position in society who get the greatest amount of attention for their issues (the position of those subscribing to elite views of democracy)?[3] Much of what is political about public policy making comes down to this division.

It is because of this that a discussion of agenda setting, or how problems become items for action by decision makers, is best undertaken by looking at how various players can exert influence over this first phase of the policy process. If the definition of just what constitutes a problem and the urgency of that problem are affected by a large collection of players—some with resources like money and social or political prominence, but with many more lacking these resources—then our policy-making system looks more pluralistic. If most of the agenda's items more often reflect the wishes and desires of a small and powerful subset of the population, then elite theory best describes our policy-making system and our democracy.

It will emerge that some players, especially large corporations and the mass media, have gained power in recent years. How and why these changes have taken place will form a large part of what is to come, along with some ideas about what these changes may mean for public policy making and for you as a citizen. After all, as you will soon read and as you probably already know, you are one of the players in the politics of public policy making, too.

PROBLEM IDENTIFICATION

Oddly enough, actually agreeing that a problem exists is often a highly contentious and political endeavor. While some negative circumstances, such as those caused by natural disasters or man-made ones like the oil spill in the Gulf, are almost universally agreed to comprise predicaments needing action, other situations are less able to garner the label of "problem." Because a problem logically requires some attention, if not an outright solution, policy actors are often divided on labeling something as a problem, especially if it might be costly in money, time, or political clout. For example, New York's Hudson River was long the legal dumping ground for PCBs, a chemical compound used in making electrical transformers. General Electric dumped massive amounts of PCBs into the Hudson for years until it was discovered that PCBs are carcinogenic. The federal Environmental Protection Agency (EPA) studied the deposits of PCBs in the river and concluded that their presence was problematic. In response to the EPA's plan to dredge the river bottom to remove the cancer-causing PCBs from the river, two opposing camps sprang up. GE, some local governments, and many citizens living along the river did not want dredging. This camp believed GE's position: the river was cleaning itself, and dredging would increase the presence of PCBs in the water. These people did not doubt the presence of PCBs in the river; after all, GE itself had documented their presence. Nor were there many who argued about the cancer-causing potential of PCBs. But rather than seeing a problem requiring action, this coalition saw a circumstance in which inaction was the best choice.[4] In the opposite camp were people who saw the presence of PCBs as a problem that needed action.

Think about the dilemma that this situation poses for a government official in charge. Do you side with the local governments, with a huge multinational corporation that employs thousands of people in the area of the contaminated river, and with the residents who live along its banks and see only a condition or a circumstance, not a problem? Or do you side with the residents, local governments, and environmental interest groups that are equally adamant that a problem exists, requiring action for resolution?

There is no easy answer, which is true of many of the issues that confront policy makers. Scholars of public policy have supplied some guidelines for identifying problems, but these guidelines are often problematic because, as the policy scholar Aaron Wildavsky essayed, "policy problems are man-made in that we choose among infinite possibilities to attach one sort of difficulty rather than another."[5] Whether an issue is a problem depends for the most part on who is advocating each position. Well-organized groups with the resources of money, larger memberships, and connections are more likely to gain access to decision makers to persuade them to see things their way. Disorganized collections of people, even those representing very large segments of the population, may not sway decision makers simply because their message is not as well focused.

Without a doubt, some problems simply cry out for action. Terrorism on American soil, for example, crystallized in an unforgettable display of violence and brutality on September 11, 2001. Such events, including many of far lower magnitude, are known as focusing events because they bring a problem to the attention of both the public and policy makers. At least at first, there is no debate about the existence of a problem, and the event serves as a trigger mechanism—a means of propelling an established problem on to the next stage of the policy process, setting an agenda. (But deciding who is responsible or best equipped for solving the problem is another matter.)

WHAT IS THE PROBLEM? OIL SCARCITY, POLLUTION, AND THE PROMISE OF HYBRID CARS

The Issue

If a problem is identified, should the public (by way of the government) or the private sector (meaning businesses, industries, interest groups, and individual citizens) attempt to provide a solution? Entrepreneurs may push for governmental policy action on a problem or circumstance when public demands are low or not fully formed or when private sector actors are in a position to best solve the problem and stand to gain concrete or symbolic rewards (e.g., money or contracts for goods or services in the case of the former or status or recognition for policy advocacy with important groups or the general public in the latter). Just what should be done about the interrelated problems of the overconsumption of fossil fuels and vehicle exhaust pollution is a debate that involves the goals and actions of both entrepreneurs and governmental decision makers.

The Story

In 1973, the United States experienced its first major oil "shock," caused by an embargo of oil shipments from the Middle East by the countries that made up the Organization of Arab Petroleum Exporting Countries. OAPEC said that it was using the embargo as a way to punish the backers of Israel in the Yom Kippur War, also known as the Six-Day War of 1973.[i] The mid-1970s also featured action by Congress designed to improve the overall mileage of the cars sold in the United States by setting corporate average fuel economy (CAFE) standards.

A second oil shock in 1979, following a revolution in Iran and lower oil output from that nation, caused Americans more "pain at the pump" and left policy makers, consumers, and the auto industry wondering where to turn in a new era of politically and environmentally questionable and often costly fossil fuel supplies. Should the nation move toward renewable sources such as wind and hydroelectric power or sources such as coal and nuclear power that have sizeable environmental risks as well as potential benefits? What should we do about our major source of transportation, the personally owned automobile? Starting in the 1970s, California, a state whose major population centers often experience intense air pollution from auto traffic, mandated that auto manufacturers offer a percentage of zero emission cars in the state, causing several major manufacturers to offer "EV" or electric vehicle cars and trucks. By the 1990s, GM, Ford, and Toyota were all leasing EV vehicles in California and several other states. The state invested in electric charging stations for these vehicles and considered the use of these cars and trucks an important part of their efforts to fight air pollution. Yet a relatively short time later in 2003, the state board that set requirements for auto emissions removed its backing for the sale of electric cars in the state and, instead, advocated the sale of hydrogen-powered fuel cell vehicles.[ii]

The existence of hybrid vehicles—touted by entrepreneurs in transportation and environmental communities as a way to increase fuel economy while lowering the polluting emissions from automobiles—is now taken for granted as an option for the power trains of many new vehicles. They do seem to help alleviate both the problems of resource depletion and air pollution. Yet the rise of hybrids and ultra-fuel stingy cars is a fairly recent development in the automobile marketplace, with the first widely available hybrid coming from Toyota in 1997. Their development is but one attempt to take on energy consumption and vehicle exhaust pollution. Without the help of federal efforts that spurred research into their creation, the availability of hybrids might be very different today. The Electric and Hybrid Vehicle Research, Development, and Demonstration Act of 1976 provided grants to help the auto industry work towards the realization of new vehicle technologies. (Japanese automakers were likely concerned that US manufacturers would gain a major technological advantage with the help of federal funding for hybrid research, and so Japanese automakers began their work on hybrids in earnest.)[iii]

Hybrid cars are everywhere today, and a good deal of their ubiquity comes from policy makers incentivizing their purchase. For example, until 2009 the purchase of a Honda Civic hybrid was subsidized with a federal tax credit. Other car manufacturers have had similar credits for vehicles in their lines.[iv] Most of the current versions of hybrids use gasoline engines to produce electricity that goes to a series of batteries that are then used to power the car when the gas engine is not needed. The next generation of hybrids will likely feature a plug-in charging option so that the car owner can use his or her home's electrical connection to charge the car, much in the way that the all-electric cars have been configured.[v] The Obama administration hopes that by 2015 these plug-in hybrids will comprise about 1 million of our vehicles.[vi]

The summer of 2008 ushered in the era of $4 a gallon gasoline, but since then the price of gas has gone up and down. The reasons for the spike in gas prices are not easy to pin down, but actions by those who trade based on what might happen to the price of oil, a practice known as speculation, along with production and refining problems within the oil industry seem to explain at least the bulk of the steep increases in 2008. Given the volatility of oil and gas prices, the uncertainty of our energy future is about all we can safely predict. When it comes to the options we will have for transportation choices, the role of policy makers and entrepreneurs is equally open to conjecture.

The Questions

- Should the market and consumer tastes determine our choice of transportation?
- Should environmentalists, industry players, and other policy entrepreneurs drive the decisions made by policy makers?
- Is there really a problem with the source of our transportation energy that necessitates governmental action as a remedy?

- Should the government provide funding and other incentives for policy solutions pushed by entrepreneurs for problems that are not yet pressing or that are not truly seen as public?
- Should the government involve itself in matters that might best be solved by private funding and entrepreneurship?

See for Yourself

Check out the following link for more information about the evolution of low- and no-emission vehicles: http://www.pbs.org/now/shows/223/electric-car-timeline.html.

[i]Burr, William. "The October War and U.S. Policy." The George Washington University. http://www.gwu.edu/~nsarchiv/NSAEBB/NSAEBB98/index.htm (accessed February 11, 2013).

[ii]I base much of this section on the film, *Who Killed the Electric Car?* DVD. Directed by Chris Paine. Sony Pictures, 2006.

[iii]Kiley, David. "Chrysler's Jim Press and Toyota Differ on Prius Narrative." *Businessweek*. www.businessweek.com/autos/autobeat/archives/2008/04/chryslers_jim_p_1.html (accessed February 11, 2013).

[iv]Billitteri, Thomas J. "Reducing Your Carbon Footprint." *CQ Researcher* 18, no. 42 (2008): 985–1008.

[v]Romero, Francis. "A Brief History Of the Electric Car." *Time*. http://www.time.com/time/business/article/0,8599,1871282,00.html (accessed February 11, 2013).

[vi]Billitteri, Thomas J. "Reducing Your Carbon Footprint." *CQ Researcher* 18, no. 42 (2008): 985–1008.

SETTING AN AGENDA

As with problem identification, the setting of an agenda may seem nearly automatic and beyond politics; identified problems need to have their day before policy experts and political decision makers so that they can be solved. However, as has been intently studied, just getting a problem to "have its day" may be one of the most fertile areas for the observation of raw political power. Many groups and organizations use rules that exclude or severely limit any action on—or even discussion of—items not listed on the agenda. The ability to exclude an item from the agenda, for whatever reason, is a powerful way to control what government does. Peter Bachrach and Morton S. Baratz coined the term "nondecision" to refer to this form of power, what they called the "second face" of power. The "first face" of power is commonly thought of as the ability of one actor to get another to do what he or she would not normally want to do. The second face of power also features the control of one actor over another, but by shaping the scope of what is under consideration, rather than by using authority or coercion.[6] A stark and troubling example from

American politics helps illustrate how power is exercised by controlling the agenda. In the 1950s and 1960s, one of the Senate's most powerful members, Georgia's Richard Russell, was instrumental in keeping civil rights policy off the nation's agenda by declaring that there was no problem with racial segregation because segregation worked! Russell claimed that both whites and blacks preferred to live in a segregated society and that it was only because of outside agitation by civil rights activists that any unrest was taking place.[7] Russell's position in the Senate allowed him to shape the agenda on civil rights through a nondecision by refusing to consider segregation as problem.

The process of crafting a solution even to shockingly obvious problems, such as the racial segregation of the 1950s, cannot begin until formal decision makers, generally those who hold positions of governmental authority, actually place the problem on the nation's formal or institutional agenda.[8] For example, the flood of legislation introduced in Congress after 9/11 gave tangible proof that our national legislators now believed the problem of terrorism to be urgent enough to require an immediate solution. There had been terrorism on US soil before 9/11. The underground parking garage of the World Trade Center was bombed in 1993 (luckily with little loss of life). Yet, awareness and concern do not always transport a problem onto the institutional agenda. Often, a focusing event is needed to provide this push. Think of the issue of global warming today. Many scientists and citizens are deeply concerned about it, yet no focusing event seems to have occurred—so far.

As with a number of the examples presented so far, the existence of negative circumstances or some situation that is troubling to someone does not automatically elevate that circumstance to the level of a problem, let alone a problem that requires a solution in the form of a public policy. Negative or troubling circumstances are constantly around us. A trip to the grocery store can produce a flood of them that form questions in our minds: How safe is our food supply? Why has the cost of some staple items gone up so much? Who should play the lead role in helping to curb the nation's trend toward obesity? Problems are created largely through social construction, a process in which our values, norms, and attitudes work to frame the circumstances and events around us. Some of these circumstances will fall within an outline that we see as defining something that is problematic, while others will be left out. The criteria for inclusion within this framework are inexact and they are likely to shift. How many like-minded individuals are needed in order to create the tipping point that will move a circumstance into the realm of agreed-upon problem? One could argue that a majority must be in agreement on the existence of a problem, but then the question follows as to what constitutes a majority? Do we mean all the people in the nation, state, or locality? Is it just the part of the population that is affected by the circumstance or that has the potential to be negatively affected? As those espousing elite theoretical approaches would argue, it may also be the case that powerful minority groups—those with extraordinary political or social standing—may have the resources or clout to have their wishes count for more with decision makers. As E. E. Schattschneider once wrote in a critique of the pluralist position that power was widely dispersed in our democracy, "The flaw with the pluralist heaven is that the heavenly chorus sings with a strong upper-class accent."[9] Raw numbers will not tell us when a circumstance or a set of circumstances has reached the level of acceptance by the public that bestows the label of public "problem" since power can enlarge the impact that some have on problem recognition.

Even when that rather elusive line is crossed and there is a general agreement that a problem exists, there is no requirement for action by decision makers. Problems that have not been formally taken up by decision makers exist on the systemic agenda, a status in which some problems will linger for years or longer until some change either eliminates the problem or thrusts it onto the institutional or decision-making agenda. (Problems do not need to incubate on the systemic agenda; they may spring, fully formed, onto the decision-making agenda, usually by way of crisis.) Perhaps the most influential work on agenda setting comes from John Kingdon. His work on agenda setting theory envisions three streams—one of problems, the other of policies, and the third of politics—that must be combined in order for a problem to find its way to the decision-making agenda.[10] The three streams are brought together in Kingdon's model when a policy window, often pushed open by a crisis, brings the three into concert. Some policy actors that Kingdon calls entrepreneurs, found both in and outside of government, push for the recognition of the problem or for the usefulness of possible solutions. This model of agenda setting fits well with the messiness of the policy process in the real world because it depicts the somewhat unpredictable ways in which problems make their way onto the agenda while highlighting the importance that power and politics play in the process. Pluralists would argue that our relatively open system of government with multiple points of access for citizens to express their grievances should result in a clear path for problems to get on the agenda. However, Kingdon's model indicates that our relatively receptive system is open to the influence of entrepreneurs and the effects of political forces, such as elections or other events; not all interests get their problems placed on the agenda, but neither is it the case that only some small set of groups or players holds a monopoly on the agenda-making process.

Once legitimate decision makers take up an issue as part of their formal activities, the problem has been placed on the institutional agenda. Evidence for items reaching the institutional agenda is fairly straightforward in some cases. For example, when Congress holds hearings on an issue, when the president or a governor names the issue as one of his or her priorities, or when the Supreme Court decides to take a case on appeal in order to clarify or establish a precedent surrounding an issue, all of these actions indicate that an issue has been placed on the institutional agenda. Even when formal procedural actions are not taken, such as the introduction of a bill in a legislature or the submission of a budget by a president or a governor, less formal actions by powerful decision makers have the influence to move an issue or circumstance beyond the foggy zone of the systemic agenda. For example, when newly elected President Obama gave his first speech to a joint session of Congress at the start

of 2009 and called for an overhaul of the nation's health care insurance policies, it is hard to argue that such an action did not move the problem of having
over 45 million uninsured Americans onto the decision-making agenda. Here
the president was not exercising a formal power (this speech was not even the
State of the Union Address) and no bill was submitted at that time on behalf
of the president (only members of Congress can submit legislation), but the
problem of uninsured Americans was, nonetheless, given a degree of recognition that it previously lacked.

Once a problem is on the agenda, how is it kept in place? There is no guarantee that policy makers will consistently treat an issue as a high priority year
in and year out. Anthony Downs has created a valuable way of thinking about
the nature of agenda items that he calls the issue-attention cycle.[11] Downs
argues that some issues are more likely to remain on the formal agenda, just
as others are doomed to fade away. Even issues that affect small slices of the
population—ones that lack political, economic, or social clout, or that are difficult to address—may first grab lots of attention. But they usually fall off the
agenda because of the cost and inconvenience associated with solving them or
the inability of the affected parties to keep the decision makers' attention. For
example, a series of highly publicized events in the 1960s, including a badly
polluted river actually catching fire, propelled the state of our environment
onto the nation's policy agenda. Although pollution and other environmental
issues have not completely disappeared from that agenda, they got bumped
down the list of priorities once people learned of the difficulties associated
with the proposed solutions to the overconsumption of fossil fuels—such as
giving up their big gas-guzzling cars. After the oil spill in the Gulf, there is a
renewed urgency to protect our environment from the dangers associated with
oil exploration, but it is not clear if the public or decision makers will be willing to make the sacrifices necessary to tame our dependence on fossil fuels and
to strengthen or create new rules that could further safeguard the environment.

Problems have a much better chance of staying on the institutional agenda
if their potential solutions do not greatly disrupt a large part of the population or a subset of the population with extraordinary policy clout. While the oil
spill disaster in the Gulf easily helped grab a spot on the nation's institutional
agenda for a renewed approach to our energy policy, the staying power of the
problems associated with our needs for more fossil fuels may only be as great as
our willingness to sacrifice some consumer comforts and ways of living that we
presently take for granted. For example, the average American household now
owns 2.8 cars,[12] and the average American worker now spends 46 minutes a
day commuting to and from his or her job.[13] A proposal for a national energy
policy that greatly curtailed our dependence on private automobiles as our main
source of transportation, such as the creation of a very high federal gas tax,
would likely be met with anger from consumers, oil companies, auto manufacturers, and elected officials.

Problems are also likely to maintain their position on the nation's
agenda when they are acted upon in the form of ongoing programs at the
state or federal level. The level of poverty in the United States fell during

much of the 1990s through about 2008; in 2009 it spiked upward from 12.7 to 13.2 percent.[14] While government-run antipoverty programs have been commonplace since at least the 1930s, and the problem of poverty has been redefined several times (even the evolution of the names for federal antipoverty programs from AFDC, Aid for Families with Dependent Children, to TANF, Temporary Assistance for Needy Families, indicates a different conceptualization of the problem), poverty is still very real in this country. In the 1960s, President Lyndon Johnson launched a "war on poverty" by creating a number of federal programs—some, like Medicaid, that are run in tandem with the states are designed to undercut poverty. The costs of these programs are very high, especially Medicare, the program that provides health insurance to the nation's elderly. The recently added prescription drug benefit, Medicare Part D, added significantly to the overall cost of the program. While those of us not now benefiting from Medicare and similar programs may gripe about the amount of our taxes that go toward these expenses, a well-entrenched program with a sizeable bureaucracy and a powerful constituency (older Americans) is hard to fight. Even when serious challenges to the existence of antipoverty programs arise, as was the case in 1996 for AFDC, the results have been changes in lines of authority, funding, and benefits, not outright elimination. AFDC was derided as a broken system that allowed "welfare queens" to live richly without doing any work. While abuses of the system were sizeable and evidence existed that AFDC might promote a long-term, even generational dependence on welfare, the call to do away with a governmental role in the antipoverty fight was small. Knocking an idea off the agenda once the problem has been identified and treated by the creation of programs and bureaucratic agencies is no easy matter.

AGENDA SETTING: THE IMPORTANCE OF OUTSIDE PLAYERS

Probably few would argue with the assertion that government can greatly affect the way we live. When the federal, state, or local government changes tax laws, we may be pleased or upset by how our paychecks are affected by the new taxes. In some cases, changes in tax codes can be so dramatic that people can end up losing major parts of their economic worlds. Before the housing bubble burst in 2008, parts of the Adirondack region in New York State saw major upward spikes in property taxes because of the building of new, very pricey homes and the local government reassessment of existing properties at high values because of the "hotness" of the real estate market in the area. Many people living in the area owned their primary residences or vacation homes for generations, but they were hit with very high tax bills that forced some of them to sell their properties. There is no doubt that government can influence how people live and what happens to what is, for most people, their biggest economic investment, their home. But in this example of the real estate boom in the Adirondacks, there are other forces at work. What seemed to be driving much of the boom was an influx of buyers who were seasonal residents purchasing homes that suddenly commanded very high prices. The Adirondacks have a special set of protections under New York State's constitution, making property now developed or open to development in relatively short supply. Add to this a lag in the last time many local communities revalued the properties on their tax rolls and the result was much higher property taxes for all.[15] Yes, the local governments used their power to revalue property to adjust the taxes paid by property owners, but the private real estate market—the buyers and the sellers—played important parts in the spike in taxes. If the buyers did not fancy homes in the mountains with their beautiful vistas and lakes, and the sellers did not need or want to sell their properties, then property taxes would not have risen so precipitously.

This small example probably did not reach news outlets outside of the northeast or even New York, but it offers a much larger lesson about the impact of power on policy. While government does have sizeable and, in some cases, what appears to be near-total control over the direction of policy and policy making, there are far many more influential actors that play their parts, too. Sometimes government instigates policy change, other times it is largely reactive. Figuring out who is able to evoke such reactions to shape desired outcomes is a necessary endeavor because it gives us a sense of who has the power in the politics of policy making.

Not all players outside of government are equally powerful and they seldom maintain the same amount of influence at all times. Keep this in mind as you read about the following selected policy players since they are not presented in an order of "most" to "least" important or powerful. They are, however, the perennial players that often, though not always, gain some level of reaction from governmental decision makers; they are the key components in the agenda-setting part of the policy-making process.

Corporations

Corporations are organizations generally created by private businesses as a means of engaging in trade or commerce. Some corporations are "public," meaning they sell stock in their corporation that the public can buy and sell in a market, such as the trades that take place in the New York Stock Exchange. In this form, the stockholders are part owners of the corporation. Other corporations are "private" and do not offer stocks in the corporation. Both types of corporations seek to earn profits for the owners of the corporation. For corporations, working to influence the policy agenda is a part of doing business, and they devote a sizeable amount of their resources toward lobbying policy makers on the merits of their preferred policies.

The many laws that govern the creation and operation of corporations give these organizations a set of rights and responsibilities in the economic and legal spheres of our lives. For example, corporations can sue and be sued in a court of law. The Supreme Court has also established that corporations have an intriguing characteristic in that they are considered "persons" under the Constitution and are entitled to many protections from actions by the federal and state governments that flesh-and-blood citizens receive.[16] Incorporation is one of many ways that businesses have organized themselves as a means of maximizing profits while seeking to minimize legal and economic risks.

Inexact as it may be, since there are other business arrangements that exist, the business corporation is a fair representative for the power of business and industry in the American economy, our society, and our political system. The business magazine *Fortune* provides a yearly ranking of the top five hundred corporations in the United States based on revenue in the past twelve months. The list contains names that most Americans would be familiar with in their daily lives, including the following top five corporations: Walmart, ExxonMobil, Chevron, General Electric, and Bank of America. A car trip to go shopping with a stop for gas can easily bring a person into intimate contact with these corporations. The rest of the list is populated with equally well-known names that fill our cupboards and make our everyday conveniences of life from dishwashers to jet engines.[17] Another notable feature of the Fortune 500 listing is that many of the corporation names are compounds of two or more company names, such as ExxonMobil and ConocoPhillips. Each of these massive energy corporations had been a smaller, though still sizeable, corporation before they merged together. The trend toward the merger of large corporations into mega corporations accelerated in the 1990s and has produced business entities that affect major aspects of our economy. Simply put, bigger parts of the nation's wealth are now influenced by a smaller pool of corporations.

The impact of corporate power is not an abstract notion that comes into play only for those with big stock portfolios. In addition to perennially being at or near the top of the list of the corporations with the largest yearly earnings, Walmart is also the nation's largest employer.[18] So when a plurality of the nation's workers thinks about their livelihoods, they think about the well-being of the Walmart Corporation. While slowing its pace somewhat by 2007, Walmart continued to expand[19] until the recession kicked in during the fall of 2008. Critics of Walmart contend that its ability to expand and hold economic turf, even during very difficult economic times, forces out other better paying jobs and may hurt or even bankrupt existing businesses in a community. For example, Walmart has been very successful in opening Supercenters containing grocery stores; they use the vast buying power of the parent corporation to sell many items at prices that cannot be met by their competitors. What often happens is that Walmart's gains in a market are at the expense of these competitors who may then go out of business.[20] While this is the essence of how competition works in a capitalist economy, the critics of Walmart note that the employees, some who come to work at Walmart when their previous jobs dry up, often go from unionized positions that offer benefits, salaries, and protections for workers that are not matched by Walmart.[21] None of its roughly 1.3 million workers belong to a union and, according to those who want to unionize its workers, Walmart does whatever it can to keep them out.[22] In another sign of expansion, Walmart has been attempting to offer a host of financial services that banks now offer.[23]

What does any of this tell us about the relationship between political power and the process of agenda setting? As you may recall from the first chapter of the text, the definition of politics is not limited to the things done or not done by government. Politics is about power in the public sphere, and there are other actors that possess power because they can affect what happens in a community, state, or even the nation. A simple test for the presence of power is one that we can derive from a classic formulation by Robert Dahl: "A has power over B to the extent that he can get B to do something that B would not otherwise do."[24] When Walmart's actions change the employment patterns and the number and type of businesses and services in an area, it has a form of power over the people that live in that area. We may view this as a weak form of power, almost like the gravitational pull of the sun on one of the newly discovered bodies at the edge of the solar system. Other factors may be greater than this relatively weak form of power, and existing players and relationships in a community may successfully resist the influx of even frail exertions of power. However, if we look at how communities have dealt with Walmart—and hundreds of other major retail-oriented corporations in the United States—it then becomes clear that power is often on display in the actions of such corporations and the reactions of government to their activities.

Walmart's critics argue that the retailer engages in a game of sleight of hand in which it promises a tax bonanza for the community—think about how attractive a small town's cut of the earnings of a Supercenter might be to a struggling region—and then extracts benefits from the locality or the state in return for coming to town or staying there. One of these critics, Good Jobs First, claims that from 2003 to 2007 Walmart received over $200 million in tax breaks, land grants, and other forms of assistance from state and local governments.[25] Once the store is located in the area, then governments are stuck with the proposition of either losing a good part of their tax base from the earnings of the store if there is a threat to close it down versus complying with requests from the corporation to continue to provide incentives to keep the store open. Even if the rhetoric of those opposed to Walmart and other "big box" stores is overblown and this form of pressure by companies is more subtle and rare than they portray, it still offers a provocative way to view the exercise of even weak power at the community level.

What about the exercise of a more traditional and potent form of power at the federal level? Here we can see corporate action in full flower with Walmart, who is again being singled out because it is the nation's largest retailer, employer, and one of the largest contributors to federal elections. In late 2003, Walmart gave the second largest amount of money to candidates—mostly Republicans—for federal office and stayed in the top tier of givers for the remainder of that election cycle; however, it had not even been among the top one hundred givers back in 2000. In that same time span, Walmart added a staff of full-time lobbyists in Washington, DC.[26] What may account for the increased campaign contributions and beefed up commitment to lobbying? The short answer is that Walmart was seeking to sway policy making by promoting the issues that make it to the agenda—like changes in banking regulations—and by influencing the makeup of those in positions to determine the outcome of the items on that agenda.

Hoping for federal regulators to interpret labor laws in their favor about working conditions and hours, and seeking approval for a plunge into the world of banking, Walmart has had a great deal at stake and could benefit from helpful treatment by decision makers in Washington. This is not to say that when corporations give money to candidates and apply influence via lobbyists that they always get what they want, since this is not the case. However, as many have argued, while they may not win all the time, business and industry have a very good batting average, and even when they do lose, they are often able to gain concessions from policy makers that are surprisingly favorable to their position.[27] In other words, Walmart's attempts to influence the actions of decision makers are good business for the corporation.

The Media

According to the US Constitution's First Amendment, "Congress shall make no law respecting an establishment of religion, or prohibiting the free exercise thereof; or abridging the freedom of speech, or of the press." Clear as day, the framers of the Constitution set out a bold marker for us about the role that the press should play in this democracy. In their day, the press was limited in its ability to transmit ideas to the public because of the slowness and expense of printing and a public that had not attained high rates of literacy. For the framers, this was the press. As slow and limited as it was, they still understood it as a formidable persuasive power, one that might work as a counterweight to the powers vested in the new federal government, and certainly one that would play a role in determining the issues that were part of the policy agenda for the nation.

Today, we live in a communications environment we can modestly describe as "different" from that witnessed or even imagined by the framers. The "press" of 1789 is just part of what we mean when we talk about the media. In fact, a distinction is often made between the news media—what the framers would likely see as the "press"—and the entertainment media. A good argument can be made that the distinction between the two has eroded in the last few decades with the rise of what has been dubbed "infotainment" or "soft news," and this is demonstrably the case. However, whatever the makeup of the news, be it "hard" stories about foreign policy or "soft" news about the latest celebrity scuffle with the law, there is a general acceptance that the Constitution protects the rights of the people to know about both the weighty and trivial by means of an unfettered press. While the American public holds the news media in low esteem, we still support the concept of a free press. However, much has been made by competing news organizations, especially television news divisions and cable channels, about the prospect of

political agendas shaping the news the public consumes. Media watchdogs single out Fox News as an example of a conservative, pro-Republican bias framing news, and Fox News executives have shot back claiming liberal, pro-Democratic bias for rival networks. In essence, both sides are arguing that partisan and ideological forces are tainting the information consumed by the public; in turn, we become part of an agenda-setting process that treats issues as political footballs that are struggled over for political gain, rather than a process that accurately reflects the priorities of the public.

So what? If we went back to the early days of the Republic, we would find that the newspapers of the time often unabashedly showed off their partisanship because political parties financed them. Today, we see some of the remnants of this party connection in the names of newspapers with "Democrat" or "Republican" in their names. What is the harm in having overtly partisan news outlets in contemporary America? There may be little harm, but there exists the possibility that the changes in the communications environment since the days of the framers have made ideological bias in the news media more of a concern. First off, most Americans get their news by watching TV news programs; even with the meteoric rise of the Internet as a news outlet, 71 percent of Americans say that TV is their main source for national news with the Internet coming in at a distant second.[28] While it might be comforting to see the proliferation of news sources via the Internet as the cornucopia of news, the penetration of the Internet into American homes is still not as absolute as it might seem. Additionally, the nature of TV news is, of course, one of image over abstraction, and the underlying force that ultimately drives all news organizations is profit. What viewers will tune in for and what will keep them there is important to editors and reporters who gather and shape the news. Therefore, viewers mostly experience news programs that have images and associated story lines that feature elements commonly found in entertainment programs, such as drama born of conflict or disaster. Even if there isn't a liberal or conservative bias also present within the entertainment values of TV news, discussions of policy are likely to be driven by a "who wins/who loses" mindset. For example, a great deal of the coverage of the Obama administration's attempts to deal with major policy issues in the president's first term—from the US military's role in Afghanistan to the Gulf oil spill and the lingering recession and unemployment—featured analysis of the new policies or changes in existing ones in terms of how they would play out for candidates in the 2010 midterm elections and even for the possible presidential contenders in 2012. If a democracy rests on an informed and engaged public, such a circumstance does not speak well for our current state of affairs.

The other point of concern worth mentioning, that would likely concern the framers, too, is that there is a startling concentration of ownership among news organizations. As was outlined in the discussion of corporations, there has been a spate of mergers since the 1990s that has produced very large corporations, especially in the field of energy production and discovery. The media has also been part of this trend toward mergers. The major broadcast news programs—as opposed to strictly cable or satellite stations—are all now part of much larger "parent" corporations. ABC is owned by Disney and NBC by General Electric. CBS was owned by Viacom until 2006 when it was reorganized as the CBS Corporation, still a sizeable corporate entity, and a separately held company retaining the name Viacom.[29] The two most widely viewed cable news outlets—CNN and Fox News—are owned by Time Warner and News Corporation, respectively. If the parent corporations' interests do not affect the content of news programming under their auspices, then there is no problem. However, it falls into the area of a nondecision to see if either of the parent corporations have attempted to shape news outputs or if news divisions have curbed their journalistic actions because of fear of displeasing the higher-ups in the structure of the company. There is little credible evidence that this has happened, but the notion that it could take place is disturbing.

The rise of Internet-based news gathering and reporting might seem to ameliorate concerns about the concentration of ownership and the effect this trend may have on the content of the news. After all, if the Internet is akin to an open highway with plenty of on and off ramps, then the public should have no shortage of news and information. However, a recent federal study highlighted a disturbing development that the move toward online reporting has had on access to information about politics and policy. The study, commissioned by the Federal Communications Commission, finds that local news organizations—newspapers in particular—have been hit hard by the changes in the public's consumption of news. As we get more of our news from online sources, local papers struggle to compete and cut reporting resources in attempts to remain profitable. Local papers often serve as the source for stories reported higher up in the chain of news dissemination by regional and national news organizations. The findings from the FCC's study include concerns that the vacuum created by the weakening of local news sources may be filled by self-serving interests. According to Steven Waldman, the report's author, "news releases from politicians and policy makers end up having more influence in some cases...contributing to a kind of power shift toward institutions and away from citizens."[30]

Putting these concerns aside, we should note that although the Constitution is absolute about the freedom of the press, in actual practice there is a great deal of control the federal government can exert on news organizations, especially on the business side of their operations; this is particularly notable because of the increasing size of these corporate entities. Congress has recognized the danger of having any one corporation own disproportionate amounts of the news media and has regulated things such as the ownership of local television stations to promote a diversity of ownership and, hopefully, viewpoints. In 2003, Congress was working on legislation that would set a limit on this type of TV station ownership so that no one parent corporation's stations could reach more than 35 percent of homes in the United States. One corporation in particular, News Corporation, would have been injured by this policy because its stations reach 39 percent of households; it would have to sell off 4 percent of its holdings to meet the proposed policy. This loss of the market was highly objectionable to News Corporation's chairman, Rupert Murdoch. Murdoch is an icon in the world of both news and entertainment; he created a global communications empire that features such notable holdings as the Fox Network and HarperCollins publishers. In the fall of 2003, Murdoch—a stalwart campaign donor to conservative candidates—reached out to Republican members of Congress, then in the majority in the House and the Senate, and asked for help. After a good deal of lobbying by News Corporation's lobbyists and the White House, House and Senate leaders who had been pushing for the 35 percent ownership cap changed their minds and upped the cap to 39 percent, the exact level of ownership then held by News Corporation. Critics cried foul and were even more incensed when it came to light that Trent Lott—a key senator in the negations over the legislation who was initially opposed to increasing the cap to 39 percent—had previously signed a book contract with a publisher owned by News Corporation. While not illegal, the business relationship between Senator Lott and Mr. Murdoch's publishing company attracted attention.[31] In the end, the 39 percent ownership cap became law. This is not a case of power over agenda setting, as such, but it is evidence of the potential clout that major policy players can have on the policy outputs of government, and it is not hard see that such power has the potential to influence agenda setting as well.

Interest Groups

Political scientist David Truman argued that all American politics was group politics, meaning that the real power of the public was not that of individuals acting in isolation, but of people coming together to consciously multiply their power by banding together. Interest groups are much studied by scholars of American politics because of their seeming centrality to power in our governmental and policy systems. Broadly stated, groups seek to control the items on the agenda because their existence is based on either the continuance of the issue on the agenda(e.g., groups such as the Children's Defense Fund that advocate for the funding of federal programs to help the poor) or it is based on blocking an item from reaching the agenda(e.g., groups like National Organization for Marriage that seek to keep bills establishing gay marriage from inclusion in the legislative agendas of states).

Citizens are also quite aware of the existence and importance of interest groups. The term "special interest" has become a fixture of our language and has with it the connotation of something unseemly and corrupt in its ability to get more from policy makers than it deserves, most likely because of a group's ability to lavish them with support or other goodies. However, there is an old axiom that people are more likely to pay attention when they are negatively affected by something, that it depends on "whose ox is gored." When people apply the term "special interest," they are mostly indicating that the gains of the group are personally injurious or that they are detrimental to the common good. This idea that groups are powerful because of their ability to produce undeserved or an unfair return for their efforts is one that has its origins in the days that precede the ratification of the Constitution. "Federalist No. 10," James Madison's deservedly famous essay on the power and danger of interests, bluntly defines factions as a group of people "whether amounting to a majority or a minority of the whole, who are united and actuated by some common impulse of passion, or of interest, adverse to the rights of other citizens, or to the permanent and aggregate interests of the community." (Today, we would probably see in modern interest groups like the National Rifle Association and the American Civil Liberties Union what Madison was thinking about in his eighteenth century definition of factions.) Little, if any, good can come from the existence of factions, argued Madison, but we are unable to do away with them; they exist because we have the freedom to allow their existence. The only way to extinguish faction would be to do away with freedom, and that, of course, is not an alternative. Madison's solution to the danger posed by a majority faction is embodied in the structure of the government, and that is to fracture power by way of separated institutions, making it extremely difficult for one faction to easily take control of the direction of the nation. Factions that were smaller in size than a majority of the public would not have enough adherents to gain office in numbers to control an institution like Congress or win the presidency through the somewhat Byzantine structure of the Electoral College.

Shunning the idea of group politics as the work of "special interests" is attractive because it speaks to our political culture's stress on individualism and protections that are supposed to come to all citizens by virtue of the Constitution. However, this may be an overly romanticized point of view since our history is layered with episodes where group action has been necessary to overcome the adversity of entrenched social, political, and economic arrangements. For example, some of earliest salvos against a segregated society that became the Civil Rights movement of the 1950s and 1960s were fired by the National Association for the Advancement of Colored People (NAACP), an interest group founded in 1909. Organized political action highlighted the seriousness of the issues of racism and segregation while helping to draw support and resources for the battles yet to be fought.

The actions of labor unions around the turn of the last century, such as the Industrial Workers of the World (IWW) and the American Federation of Labor (AFL), brought about major changes for working people in the United States, including laws that improved workplace conditions and eliminated child labor. Despite the often violent responses from the owners of mines, factories, and other workplaces, unions persisted in their drive to secure advances for their members. Individual workers had difficult choices to make since they were taking huge risks with their jobs and, in some cases, their own physical well-being if they decided to join a union. However, the risks were offset by the great gains in wages and working conditions that the unions offered. It was only by collective action on the part of union members and their leaders that any gains were won. As with interest groups, labor unions have often been seen as "special interests" that are able to use their power of collective bargaining and tactics such as strikes to wrest more than their fair share from business and industry.

Social Movements

Carl von Clausewitz, an eighteenth century Prussian military strategist, wrote that war "is the continuation of politics by other means." In this much quoted nugget of philosophy, a continuum of politics exists along which there is the somewhat genteel action of "regular" political actors (for example, legislatures, executives, and courts) and further down the line there is the clash of arms (for example, during the Civil War when political opponents actually did battle). Short of actual combat, there is a form of political activity that is outside the parameters of so-called ordinary politics. Protest has always been a major part of politics in this country. The prelude to our independence as a nation included acts of protest featuring the destruction of private property, including the dumping of chests of tea into Boston Harbor. During much of his two terms in office, President Bush was the subject of protests by members of the antiwar movement. Cindy Sheehan, the mother of a young man killed in Iraq, personified this movement and brought intense media coverage to the dissatisfaction many Americans had with the war when she and others camped outside the president's ranch in Texas. Presently, the Tea Party movement has generated very large protest rallies across the nation that may well have a sizeable and lasting impact on both our politics and our policies. The Occupy movement, the liberal/progressive counter to the Tea Party movement, took over parks and other public spaces in 2011–2012 with their protests against income inequality and other issues.

Our history is replete with examples of protest being used by people to maximize their impact on the political process, usually because they are denied full access to the "ordinary" institutions and practices of political life. For example, the civil rights movement in the 1950s and 1960s featured sit-ins, marches, and other forms of "extraordinary" political activity because African Americans were unable to influence decision makers through conventional means. They often lacked the resources or were outright denied the ability to exercise such fundamental rights in our democracy as voting in elections or lobbying. The social or protest movements of the 1960s and 1970s that followed in the wake of the civil rights movement were spurred on by the need to reach the public through protest and to influence decision makers who were unwilling or unable to meet the demands of those calling for women's rights, the end of the Vietnam War, or the improvement of the environment.

Social movement protest can be powerful in helping to place issues on the agenda when it succeeds in reaching a critical mass of the public. When the public starts to understand the grievance of the social movement's participants, they may help further the goals of the movement by providing resources such as contributions of money or services, or they may begin to expect or demand that decision makers in government pursue policies that fit with the goals of the movement. It is hard to measure how successful movements really are in achieving their goals. Would elected officials and others simply have done the "right thing" on their own? Did the protest turn people away from a side of an issue they might have supported because they were offended or worried about the aggressive tone or actions of the protesters? These are difficult questions to answer in measurable terms, but the most important point is that there is a strong belief in the United States that protest and social movement activity work to influence policy making, especially agenda setting.

Because social movements tend to focus on broad and inclusive goals—civil rights for all citizens, improving the environment we all share, stopping a war that deeply impacts our people and our standing abroad—they are quite different from interest groups, which tend to have narrower goals that are often aimed at a smaller slice of the public. However, for all the justifiable importance given to some social movements, in particular to the civil rights movement, not all movements are venerated or even accepted. Much in the way that interest groups are held in contempt by many Americans for their supposed ability to get more than their fair share, social movements are sometimes seen as a perversion of democracy. For example, political scientist Samuel Huntington has argued that social movements undermine good governance because the policies created in response to the wishes of movements cause bloated, inefficient, and expensive government. More generally, movements employing protest are generally divisive because they are boldly forcing the public to take a stand on an issue that will be difficult, traumatic, and costly to change. The tactics and strategies used by movements are designed to confront a public with symbols and actions that are sometimes upsetting and hard to ignore. Because of their very nature, movements may spark the creation of countermovements to oppose the goals of the original movement.

For example, the citizens' councils of the Deep South sprang up in response to the civil rights movement, and the Wise Use movement rose in opposition to the environmental movement.

Citizens

Often lost in the ongoing debates about politics and policy in this country is the role of the citizen. In an odd way, politics and policy making are viewed by many as something that is done by others, and that we are not, ourselves, participants in the political process. Sure, we vote—to varying degrees in different elections—but once the task of voting is done, the stuff of shaping policy is for the pros. Think back to earlier in this text about the idea that there is a "political struggle ends after the election," and you can probably see that if you hold such an outlook, you are more likely to see public policy making as the work of "someone else." Some scholars of democracy support this point of view through a theory known as elitism that, in part, argues democracies are healthy and maybe even better off if just the well-informed segment of the public takes part in political action, such as voting in elections. After all, goes this argument, how does anyone benefit if an uninformed public casts its votes for candidates that support ill-advised or even dangerous policies? Moreover, candidates using the arts of demagoguery to flatter or scare the public into voting for the "wrong thing" may mesmerize voters into participation. The syndicated conservative columnist George Will sharply stated the danger of what he perceives as an overly active public and the do-gooders who seek to increase turnout in elections in the following way: "Such improvers would improve democracy by making voters out of people who are too slothful or uninterested to leave their homes in order to vote."[32]

Apathy and low efficacy do affect the public, but that is not the full story. Surprisingly, the American public is not highly knowledgeable about one of the greatest parts of the Constitution, the First Amendment's guarantee of the right of the people to petition the government for the redress of grievance. Perhaps the language itself does not lend itself to easily rolling off the tongue, but this part of the Bill of Rights is crystalline in its guarantee of our access to governmental decision makers. In a recent national survey, only 3 percent of those sampled knew that the right to petition was one of the rights assured by the First Amendment.[33] Yet Americans do endeavor to directly influence the makeup of the policy-making agenda at all levels of government by their own efforts. The term "grassroots lobbying" was coined to define citizen initiated and executed petitioning of government. If you are "mad as hell" or "glad as hell" about something that the government is doing or failing to do, then your actions to influence the government are in keeping with the term "grassroots lobbying." Citizens visiting, writing letters, phoning, faxing, e-mailing, or instant messaging their elected or appointed public officials are all examples of grassroots lobbying. We are taking part in politics when we do these things, just as much as any member of Congress or any president does when they perform the duties of their offices. This is not to say that we should be naïve enough to think that one citizen's actions have as much impact on policy as the actions of the president of the United States, but we are partaking in politics nonetheless when we lobby at the grassroots level. The public's embrace of social media like Facebook has greatly changed both campaigns for office and the drive to gain recognition for the acceptance of issues as problems and for potential solutions to problems.[34]

There are organized attempts to take the democratic impulse evident in individual and sporadic instances of grassroots political activity and extend and focus them into ongoing campaigns on a range of policy matters. ACORN, the Association of Community Organizations for Reform Now, was an umbrella organization that fit in a unique space between individual political activism and the world of interest groups and social movement organizations. ACORN attempted to provide examples, training, and some resources to help people pursue a wide range of issues from voting rights to fair insurance practices that affect poor to middle-income citizens.[35] (In 2009, ACORN was embroiled in several highly publicized scandals concerning its supposed misuse of federal funds for illegal purposes and partisanship in its voter registration activities. Investigations of the charges exonerated the organization of most egregious charges.[36] The political damage was fatal, however, and Congress even went so far as to pass legislation that removed funding from ACORN. Under great pressure, largely from political conservatives, the organization dissolved in 2010.) US PIRG (Public Interest Research Group) is a similar type of organization that represents a federation of state-level public interest research groups, such as the New York State Public Interest Research Group or NYPIRG. At the state level, PIRGs work to identify issues that affect citizens broadly, especially consumer and health issues, and then they seek to motivate people to partake in the political process in a number of ways, including contacting officials, giving money to PIRGs or other organizations that will lobby on their behalf, signing petitions, or taking part in demonstrations or rallies aimed at the issue.

Organizing individual citizens to sharpen the impact of grassroots political power has become a potent part of the American political process. In fact, professional lobbying firms hired by business and industry—the dominant players in the lobbying world—have copied this form of political activity, and the hallmarks of grassroots political participation are used in an attempt to make their efforts look like spontaneous activity by common citizens. For example, during the 1990s when the tobacco industry was under renewed scrutiny for possible increased regulation of cigarettes, lobbyists set up operations that included mailings to cigarette smokers that encouraged them to send a letter to the federal Food and Drug Administration (FDA) stating their opposition to possible increased regulation of cigarettes as consumer products. The letters the FDA received seemed to come from everyday citizens upset with the prospect of governmental regulation of tobacco use. However, since this campaign was not spontaneous and was crafted by the lobbyists for a client's interest, it is incorrect to label it as grassroots lobbying.

The term Astroturf lobbying was coined to more accurately describe this form of political persuasion on policy making. Astro Turf (the way its manufacturer writes it), one of the first synthetic athletic stadium playing surfaces developed, was needed in the Astrodome, the onetime home of the Houston Astros. The Astrodome is a climate-controlled building whose roof was originally translucent in order to allow the natural grass planted there to get the sunlight needed for growth. The players, however, complained about fly balls getting lost in the latticework of windows that comprised the dome's roof and they were painted over. Of course, the grass soon died and artificial grass was used as a replacement. Astro Turf looked somewhat like grass, especially on TV, but it made for a very different sort of play on the field, as balls tended to roll much faster and sometimes took odd hops when a ball hit to the infield hit a seam in the "rug." In much the same way, Astroturf lobbying looks like spontaneous grassroots political activity, but upon closer inspection it is artificial. Appointed or elected decision makers are left with the dilemma of how to deal with an Astroturf strategy of persuasion. Do they ignore it? This is dangerous if those activated by the lobbying firm are truly in sympathy with that side of the issue. If they respond, large amounts of time and effort will be required. Either way, decision makers take even Astroturf forms of input seriously, because even if it is weakly tied to the public, the potential power of the public to shape policy cannot be discounted.

Other Actors

Lists are tricky things since they imply completeness. One might assume that if it is not on the list then it must not be important. Lists also convey that there is an order or hierarchy among the items they contain. While this chapter may look somewhat like a list—it contains a finite number of actors outside of government and these players are presented in an order—do not fall into the trap of thinking that what you see here is a list. Corporations, media outlets, interest groups, and the public are major players in the world of public policy, but they are not the only ones. For example, Washington, DC, and most state capitols are replete with think tanks—organizations that bring together policy experts from academia and the "real world," often former elected or appointed officials. As the term implies, think tanks allow their personnel to research, write, and talk about their areas of interest. In general, all think tanks are attempting to advance the conversation about a range of policy issues and, perhaps, to form new approaches and solutions to existing or emerging problems. These organizations are often funded by wealthy individuals or larger groupings that may have a partisan or ideological point of view. For example, the American Enterprise Institute and the Heritage Foundation are well known for their conservative ideological bent. The Center for Law and Policy is a recognized purveyor of progressive or liberal views about policy issues. Other think tanks are a bit more difficult to categorize. The Cato Institute professes a libertarian outlook, which sometimes resembles a liberal stance and, at other times, is comfortably conservative. The Brookings Institute is generally more centrist in its staffing and arguments about policy.

Other, less traditional forms of political influence are now here or are poised to make themselves known on policy matters in the very near future. Some examples from the campaign trail in 2008 serve as a possible bell-wether for how bloggers—individuals who are generally unaffiliated with the traditional print and broadcast media outlets and publish their stories as weblogs, i.e., blogs—may influence the policy process in the near term. During the Democrats' hard fought primary contest between Hillary Clinton and Barack Obama, Senator Obama addressed an audience attending a fundraising event for him in San Francisco. The senator had just been beaten by Mrs. Clinton in the Pennsylvania primary and he was trying to explain why such a large chunk of rural and lower socioeconomic citizens did not vote for him. Senator Obama offered that these voters were "bitter" about their lives and, as a result, "cling" to God and guns. These comments drew a great deal of criticism from the Clinton campaign; the Republican presumptive nomi-nee, John McCain; and many others who thought Mr. Obama was deriding the religious convictions and gun ownership of small-town Americans. The "bitter/cling" comments, as they came to be known, were not part of an event open to the press, and in times past they probably would not have made it to the attention of many outside of the room where the fundraiser was held. That same spring, the magazine *Vanity Fair* published a story alleging that former President Bill Clinton was, among other things, having an extramari-tal affair. President Clinton was asked to react to the story by a person in the crowd at one of his wife's campaign events; he denounced the charges and the author of the piece in strong and angry language. What ties the "bitter/cling" comment story together with the story of the angry response from Bill Clinton was that the same person broke both of them. In an unprecedented develop-ment, Mayhill Fowler, a blogger, not a traditional news person, found or helped create new material about key players in the 2008 presidential election and, in so doing, drew the major news organization into coverage of these stories. Will this be the way that new policy issues are discovered or parts of the policy process treated in the future?

CYCLES OF POWER

Also realize that while some of the players discussed in this chapter seem to have more power and resources than others to place and maintain items on the agenda, circumstances can change over time and they can become more or less powerful and resource-rich. In the 1980s and for most of the 1990s, the social movement known as the Christian Right was extremely influential in both electoral and policy arenas, but it seems to have lost some of its punch in recent years. The movement is made up of a collection of Christian faiths and denominations. Its greatest location of strength has been in the southern part of the United States, but the movement is more than a regional phenomenon. The 1973 decision in *Roe v. Wade* was a triggering mechanism for the movement, causing formerly uninvolved clergy and parishioners to turn to politics as a means of undoing the Court's decision about abortion. Other issues stoked the movement throughout the following decades, including women's rights, prayer in public schools, and, most recently, gay marriage. Groups and organizations within the movement, such as the now-defunct Moral Majority and the ongoing version of the Christian Coalition, worked to raise money for favored candidates running in races at all levels of government and to recruit candidates.

By the mid-1990s, the movement was riding a crest of great influence over elections, policy matters, and even appointments to the executive branch and the federal courts. There were many successes to point to as proof of the movement's clout. In terms of electoral politics, the number of elected officials professing membership in movement organizations or association with the movement grew, and numerous state party organizations were dominated by the movement's adherents.[37] Much of this growth parallels and is intertwined with the realignment of the southern part of the United States from an area that was solidly in the hands of the Democratic Party from the period after the Civil War until around the middle of the twentieth century. Race and civil rights helped unravel the Democrats' New Deal Coalition and, by the 1980s, the old "solid South" became the bastion of the Republican Party. But it was not just the South that bore the marks of the movement's successes. In 1988, Pat Robertson, the son of a US senator and a pioneer of evangelical television, came in second behind Vice President George H. W. Bush in Iowa's Republican presidential caucus. His campaign focused on issues of morality, especially opposition to abortion. Robertson's campaign did not prosper much beyond this impressive early showing, but his success was certain proof of the movement's ability to shape the political environment. The eventual Republican nominee George H. W. Bush could not ignore the resources and potential number of votes that were tied to the movement and its issues. In 2000, his son George W. Bush not only understood the power of the movement, he was part of it.

George W. Bush had a spiritual awakening when he turned 40 years old, becoming a born-again Christian.[38] As such, Bush was the obvious candidate for the movement's many followers. He was of their faith and held opinions about abortion and other social issues that were largely in keeping with the movement, yet were presented by Bush in such a way that his positions were not seen as overly strident or fanatical. In his own campaign slogan, often repeated on the campaign trail, then-Governor Bush saw himself as a uniter, not a divider. He was endorsed by the major figures of the movement and strongly supported with money and other movement resources. Once in office, Bush moved to make his commitment to the goals of the movement tangible. He signed legislation to ban a form of abortion that pro-life forces had dubbed "partial-birth abortion." Administratively, the president created a program, which was run from within the White House by the Office of Faith-Based and

Community Initiatives, with the goal of having religious groups provide an array of social services—everything from drug treatment to after-school programs for kids—with funding from the federal government. The president's reasoning was that these organizations were up to the task and to deny them assistance was a form of discrimination based on religion and a waste of committed organizations determined to help with some of our most pressing social problems.[39] Up to this point, utilizing religious organizations for such tasks with federal funds was considered a generally unwise mingling of church and state and something that might run afoul of the Constitution's First Amendment establishment clause. While an unmistakable nod to the movement, the Office of Faith-Based and Community Initiatives (OFBCI) did not seriously advance its key policy goals. Critics and supporters alike noted that the OFBCI failed to put in place tools to measure the effectiveness of their actions. A good deal of surprise met the announcement by Barack Obama in the summer of 2008 that he was keenly interested in not only maintaining, but increasing the importance of the OFBCI if he were elected. Obama, who worked as a community organizer before he became an elected official, had past experience with faith-based organizations and saw great potential for them in the future. He was concerned that stronger barriers were needed to make sure federal dollars were not spent on religious indoctrination or other activities that might clearly cross the church-state divide. Like many supporters of President Bush's faith-based approach, Obama saw its greatest failing in how underfunded the office and its programs had become over the years.[40] In a very curious twist, it is possible that the faith-based approach to social service policy may have its greatest flowering under a progressive-leaning Democratic administration, something that was hardly foreseeable and certainly not called for by the Christian Right.

Some students of social movements believe that movements proceed in a wave-like form, with peaks of action and success along with troughs of waning attention and influence. Samuel Huntington argued that American politics itself follows a cyclical path and that these cycles can affect social movement activity. Ideologically, the nation moves from periods of normality and calm to times when our "creedal passions," something bordering on outrage that fundamental values have been betrayed, are aroused. Once action has been taken to resolve the conflict over these creedal passions, the cycle returns us to our state of equipoise. Huntington's theory does seem to explain why movements rise and fall, but it is not without critics. Charles Euchner notes that it is more accurate to think about politics as evolutionary rather than cyclical. Our goals, problems, procedures, and institutions change, and because of this, there is no reason to assume that the start and demise of movements is caused by the ideological aggravation or satisfaction of the American body politic.[41]

A more convincing explanation is that movements and their attendant organizations are subject to the same political laws as traditional interest groups. While not always a purely linear or precisely predictable evolution, social movements have a discernable life cycle: they are born, struggle to coalesce and organize, and—for a relatively small few—mature into sustainable organizations. This may be especially true for movements that have initial successes that result in political advances, including policy changes. The Christian Right found some early successes in placing their policy goals on the agenda. Some of the goals won by the movement, such as restrictions on access to abortions, were then protected as established policies by a constellation of groups or clienteles. As practitioners of movement politics in the 1960s were fond of saying, a movement is that which *moves* and takes action. If there is no longer a fiercely motivated, and, perhaps radicalized, aggregation of people seeking fundamental change, then is there still a movement? Historical examples indicate that when movements win sizeable victories that change policy and establish governmental structures to administrate related programs, these movements either transition to a mature phase typified by the use of commonplace forms of political activity or the movements wither and are subsumed into other movements, groups, or parties. The labor movement of the early part of the twentieth century is a prime example of some of these possibilities.

Highly radicalized at times, the labor movement won fundamental policy victories in the 1930s when laws were created to allow unions to organize and bargain with employers on behalf of their members. In 1935, the National Labor Relations Board was created in order to more effectively deal with issues directly related to workers and their unions. In their heyday of the 1950s, about 35 percent of the private sector workforce held union membership.[42] Today, unions are ghosts of their former selves, and only 7.5 percent of the private sector workforce is unionized. Part of this atrophying of union strength and membership has to do with the shift of the US economy away from industries that traditionally unionized, such as steel production. Additionally, encouraging workers to unionize in service sector jobs with high turnover rates for employees—think about fast-food outlets and the like—is more difficult than it is for jobs that are viewed as careers, as was the case for many industrial workers in the past. Note too that some employers have been working aggressively to keep unions out of their shops. Walmart managers even went so far as to counsel their workers to vote against Barack Obama and other Democratic candidates in 2008. According to the *Wall Street Journal*, the managers argued that Democrats would make it easier for Walmart workers to unionize and the unions would make Walmart less profitable and, thus, less able to employ workers.[43]

The circumstances that unions find themselves in must be confounding to their leaders. There are policy initiatives in the works that the unions feel are necessary to hold their position but are proving difficult to bring into existence. At the federal level, private sector unions are pushing the Employee Free Choice Act as a way to combat what they see as the antiunion position of major employers. One of the main provisions of the act would allow workers to unionize by marking a card indicating they wish to bring a union to their workplace. If a majority of the workers in a given place did this, the workplace would be unionized. Unlike past practices of union creation that have been overseen by the National Labor Relations Board, "card check" unionization does not make use of elections with secret ballots.

Unions see the card-check system as a way to overcome the difficulties of secret-ballot elections which they claim are more costly for the union and more open to negative pressure by employers on their employees. Lobbyists for major employers argue that the card-check system is too open to pressure from the unions because of the lack of a secret ballot. In a television advertisement sponsored by associations representing employers, the actor who played the crime boss Johnny Sack on the HBO series *The Sopranos* takes on the role of a union tough guy and demands to see the secret ballot of a worker. The implication of the ad was clear: the Employee Free Choice Act will strip workers of basic rights and impose the rule of autocratic and possibly corrupt unions on their workplaces.

As the story of the Employee Free Choice Act indicates, unions have a difficult time connecting to the American public in the ways that they once could. We are in somewhat of a twilight world when it comes to unions and their issues. After all, many Americans probably assume that unions are basic structures of our political and economic systems and, to a degree, this is correct. What is less accurate is to assume that they are invulnerable to change. On one hand, Americans are familiar and even comfortable with the existence of unions and hear enough or guess enough to believe that unions are stable because they are the beneficiaries of government programs, regulations, and laws. On the other hand, however, this familiarity with unions breeds a degree of disinterest in the issues affecting unions. Like many mature social movements that have gained policy victories and had government structurally change itself to respond to the demands of the movement, the labor movement has lost a good deal of its ability to affect policy. It is now part of the policy universe that it fought so intently to change generations ago, and this position at once insulates the gains of the movement while it limits the ability of the movement to expand its goals beyond these victories.

The examples of the Christian Right and the labor movement offer evidence about the variations in the power to influence agenda setting held by outside actors. Many of the factors that influence the policy process itself influence the power of these and other nongovernmental actors. In Chapter 2, power was discussed in terms of the political environment itself using the concepts of elitism and pluralism. The degree of change produced by a policy was the second aspect of power laid out in that chapter. Returning to those ideas here, we can see how these and other factors empower some actors at certain times and weaken them at others. Clearly, social movements, such as the Christian Right and the labor movement, are often cyclical in their ability to influence agenda setting, and movements are not the only nongovernmental actors to feel the impact of forces that are often beyond their direct control. Advances in technology, including the rise of the Internet, have created wholly new players, bloggers, and other elements of the new media for example, and forced existing players to react to the new players while seeking ways to possibly exploit these advances to their own benefit. The loose quality of laws and regulations governing lobbying in the nation's capitol has allowed corporations to continue to wield power and seek comprehensive changes.

CONCLUSION

Agenda setting is about getting attention that may lead to action on a recognized problem. In a way, it is the key to the policy-making process because it acts as a main valve, either allowing or excluding ideas and problems into the flow of the rest of the process. While there are ways to inject items into the process that bypass the typical start with agenda setting, most of what we see as the products of policy making have had their inception by way of agenda setting. Because of its importance to the rest of the progression of policy making, agenda setting is often marked with intense activity by policy advocates, both inside and outside of government. The conflict that ensues is a form of political engagement, with one, two, or more sides seeking to gain acceptance of their problem or issue as ripe for action. Who manages to shape the agenda is often a reflection of resources, such as wealth and political or social status, and how these resources are used.

While the debate over "who wins" is one that pluralists and elite theorists continue to have, the importance of entrepreneurs at this stage is less in doubt. Whether as single individuals, groups, coalitions of organizations, corporations, or mass political movements, advocates for action on particular issues abound within the American political world. Within the government itself, entrepreneurs are at the ready to advocate for the inclusion of an issue on the decision-making agenda.

While it is socially and politically chic to decry the influence of so-called special interests on policy making, much of what we value about democracy is reflected in the policy-making process and, in particular, in the agenda-setting phase of policy making. The interplay among and between interests and their advocates and detractors within government can tell us much about the quality of our democracy. While individual predilections toward the proper role of government and the nature of politics vary greatly, perhaps more today than in the past, we largely share the broad contours of a democracy in which the public and its agents are empowered by the Constitution to bring issues to government for the "redress of grievance," a phrase from the First Amendment. We may not always be reassured by what we see when one grievance and not another is brought to the forefront for redress, since it may seem that power or influence is at play over the public good; certainly this is the case at times, as some of the examples in this chapter illustrate. Yet, even given the cynicism of the contemporary political environment, the idea of getting problems on the agenda for action is one that is unlikely to die since it is accepted as a legitimate and desirable intersection between the people inside and outside of government. Even with the dropping poll numbers for members of government from all political parties and a surge of worry about the debts piled by governments as they attempted to pull out of the "Great Recession," the criticism often leveled at agenda setters was that they were focusing on the wrong issue or problem, not that they should avoid agenda setting in the first place. For example, with public opinion never quite jelling behind the federal economic stimulus policy (formally known as the American Recovery and Reinvestment

Act of 2009),[44] there was a mounting cry that too much money had been spent on programs and actions that plumped up the national deficit without directly focusing on the creation of new jobs. While a great deal was, in fact, contained in the stimulus bill to encourage job creation, the grievance crystallizing among the public was not that government should not act, but that it misidentified the problem or that it failed to produce the proper solution, or both. Certainly, a collection of libertarians and conservative Republicans did believe that less government action and even less government in general was the answer to our economic problems; however, this sentiment did not dominate the thinking of most Americans.

In important respects, agenda setting is a microcosm of our political world where the power of actors varies and there is an often intense struggle over the inclusion of ideas and problems on the agenda. The intensity of this battle is sometimes derived from the stakes held by the players in the outcome in terms of money and other things of monetary value, but it also comes from a conflict over the values held by people in the form of their beliefs. In sum, to paraphrase the noted political scientist David Easton, politics occurs when people are engaged in a contest over the values of society; agenda setting is clearly an arena where this contest takes place, and if we are attentive to the process, we can learn a great deal about the quality of our democracy from what happens there.

SUMMARY

During the problem-identification and agenda-setting stage, outside-of-government actors have the most influence on policy making. Those who have the ability to influence what is seen as a problem and to identify potential solutions to those problems have a great deal of power in our society. There are times when a problem is easily identified and all sides agree that a problem exists. Other times, however, whether or not something is viewed as a problem that requires a remedy by government is less clear-cut. Well-organized groups with large amounts of resources such as money and members may have more sway with policy makers than less organized groups when it comes to problem identification.

Just as the identification of a problem is subject to politics, getting an issue or policy problem on the policy-making agenda is also rife with politics. Power is exerted and exemplified by getting a problem to be considered worthy of a policy solution, as well as keeping a problem from making it to the policy-making agenda.

One of the most influential theories of agenda setting is John Kingdon's model of three streams: the problem stream, the policy stream, and the politics stream. In this model, the three streams are brought together when a policy window, often pushed by a crisis, opens. This model highlights the inexact, and what may at first glance appear to be random, nature of how the policy-making agenda is set, because it provides a way to look at the somewhat unpredictable ways in which problems make their way onto the agenda while highlighting the importance that power and politics play in the process.

A problem has made it onto the institutional agenda once legitimate decision makers take on the issue as part of their formal activities. For example, a policy issue can be understood to have made it to the agenda-setting phase once Congress is holding a public hearing on the matter, a piece of legislation has been introduced, the Supreme Court decides to take the case on appeal, a president or governor claims the issue as a part of his or her campaign platform, etc. There are also less formal ways that issues can be seen to have made it "on the agenda," such as a president using a speaking opportunity to highlight an issue.

Once an issue has made it to the agenda, there is no guarantee that it will stay on the agenda or even progress to the next stage of the policy-making process. Problems are more likely to maintain their place on the institutional agenda if their potential solutions do not have a large disruptive effect on the public or a subset of the public. They are also likely to remain on the institutional agenda if they result in ongoing programs at the state or federal level. Yet, even with these types of assurances, there are many factors, internal and external to government, that contribute to whether or not a problem or issue area continues to receive the attention of decision makers and the public at large.

Outside-of-government players can have a very large effect on the agenda-setting phase of policy making. Corporations, the media, interest groups, social movements, grassroots lobbying efforts, and other actors such as think tanks, all can use their unique positions and resources to influence how and what issues make it onto the institutional agenda and/or what issues and problems do not make it onto the agenda. The amount of agenda-setting success and influence that these various actors have can expand and wane over time, depending on a host of circumstances and pressures that are often beyond their control.

Agenda setting can be viewed as a microcosm of our political environment. Agenda setting is an arena where the power of the actors varies and there is often an intense struggle over which issues and problems are given the most attention. The very nature of our democratic system is vividly on display during this important component of policy making.

DISCUSSION QUESTIONS

1. What role does politics play in the determination of what is a problem worthy of the attention of decision makers and what is categorized as merely a circumstance? What are some of the main factors that elevate circumstances to problems?

2. Many factors are responsible for issues moving from the systemic to the institutional agenda. Actors with resources like money, social status, and well-developed organizations tend to do well in moving their desired issues forward in the policy-making process. What are the other ways that issues arrive on the institutional agenda and do they make up for what seems like an agenda-setting imbalance that favors those with more resources?

3. John Kingdon's model of agenda setting depicts a policy world in which problems, policies (solutions to problems), and politics can exist separately from one another. How is this possible? Does such a model make you feel more or less satisfied with how the agenda is set in the United States? Why is this so?

4. Some issues seem to have a permanent place on the institutional agenda, whereas other issues never break through or, once on the agenda, they fall off. What are the main factors that account for longevity on the agenda? Is the absence of these factors the reason why some issues fall off the agenda, or are there other factors that account for a loss of agenda status? Are there any current issues you see as nearing the end of their time on the institutional agenda?

NOTES

1. Wechsler, Pat. "Coast Guard Forms Panel for Ideas to Mop Up Oil Spill." Bloomberg. June 4, 2010. http://www.bloomberg.com/news/2010-06-04/coast-guard-forms-own-panel-to-probe-ideas-for-cleaning-up-bp-s-oil-spill.html.

2. Dahl, Robert Alan. *Who governs? Democracy and power in an American city.* New Haven: Yale University Press, 1961.

3. Mills, C. Wright. *The power elite.* New York: Oxford University Press, 1956.

4. See the EPA's website for a history of the agency's involvement with PCBs: http://www.epa.gov/history/topics/pcbs/02.htm.

5. Wildavsky, Aaron. *Speaking truth to power: The art and craft of policy analysis.* Boston: Little, Brown and Company, 1979.

6. For a fascinating discussion of how power is exercised by controlling the agenda, see Bachrach, Peter, and Morton S. Baratz. "Two Faces of Power." *American Political Science Review* 56 (1962): 947–952.

7. Caro, Robert A. "Chapter 7." In *Master of the senate: The years of Lyndon Johnson.* New York: Random House, 2002.

8. Cobb, Roger W., and Charles D. Elder. *Participation in American politics: The dynamics of agenda-building.* Boston: Allyn and Bacon, 1972. 86.

9. Schattschneider, F. E. *The semisovereign people: A realist's view of democracy in America.* Hinsdale, IL: Dryden Press, 1975. 35.

10. Kingdon, John W. *Agendas, alternatives, and public policies.* 2nd ed. Upper Saddle River, NJ: Longman, 1997.

11. Downs, Anthony. "Up and Down with Ecology." *Public Interest* Summer (1972): 38–50.

12. "New Study Shows Multiple Cars Are King in American Households." The Auto Channel. www.theautochannel.com/news/2008/02/12/077438.html. (accessed February 6, 2013).

13. "Workers' Average Commute Round-Trip Is 46 Minutes in a Typical Day." Gallup. www.gallup.com/poll/28504/workers-average-commute-roundtrip-minutes-typical-day.aspx. (accessed February 6, 2013).

14. Mutikani, Lucia. "U.S. poverty rate hits 11-year high." Reuters. http://www.reuters.com/article/idUSTRE58943C20090910 (accessed February 6, 2013).

15. "Raising the price on paradise." *The Utica Observer-Dispatch.* http://www.uticaod.com/apps/pbcs.dll/article?AID=/20070527/NEWS/705270354 (accessed June 25, 2007).

16. McCloskey, Robert G., and Sanford Levinson. *The American Supreme Court.* 2nd ed. Chicago: University of Chicago Press, 1994. 88.

17. "Fortune 500: Our annual ranking of America's largest corporations." CNNMoney. money.cnn.com/magazines/fortune/fortune500/2010/index.html (accessed February 6, 2013).

18. Barbaro, Michael. "Wal-Mart's Latest Special: 6% Raises at Some Stores." *New York Times*, August 8, 2006. C4.

19. Barbaro, Michael. "Wal-Mart Cuts Back Expansion." *New York Times*, June 2, 2007. C1.

20. Greenhouse, Steven. "Wal-Mart, Driving Workers and Supermarkets Crazy." *New York Times*, October 19, 2003. http://www.nytimes.com/2003/10/19/weekinreview/19GREE.html?ex=1381896000&en=0d62b20ceed28ce8&ei=5007&partner=USERLAND (accessed February 6, 2013).

21. Ibid.

22. Greenhouse, Steven. "Report Assails Wal-Mart Over Unions." *New York Times*, May 1, 2007.

23. Roane, Kit R. "One more worry for banks: Wal-Mart." CNNMoney. http://money.cnn.com/2010/06/22/news/companies/walmart_banking_services.fortune/ (accessed February 6, 2013).

24. Dahl, Robert A. "The Concept of Power." *Behavioral Science* 2 (1957): 202–210.

25. Good Jobs First. "Wal-Mart Continues to Benefit from Economic Development." Institute for Agriculture and Trade Policy. http://www.iatp.org/news/wal-mart-continues-to-benefit-from-economic-development (accessed February 6, 2013).

26. Hopkins, Jim. "Wal-Mart widens political reach, giving primarily to GOP." *USA Today*. http://www.usatoday.com/money/industries/retail/2004-02-02-walmart_x.htm (accessed February 6, 2013).

27. Hudson, William E. "Chapter 6." In *American democracy in peril: Eight challenges to America's future.* 5th ed. Washington, DC: CQ Press, 2006.

28. "Press Accuracy Rating Hits Two-Decade Low." Pew Research Center. http://people-press.org/report/543/ (accessed February 6, 2013).

29. Alfano, Sean. "CBS, Viacom Formally Split Now Traded Separately on Wall Street, Shares of Two Companies Rise." CBS News. http://www.cbsnews.com/stories/2006/01/03/business/main1176111.shtml (accessed February 6, 2013).

30. Peters, Jeremy W., and Brian Stelter. "A Federal Study Finds That Local Reporting Has Waned." *New York Times*. http://www.nytimes.com/2011/06/09/business/media/09press.html?_r=1&hp (accessed February 6, 2013).

31. Becker, Jo. "An Empire Builder, Still Playing Tough." *New York Times*, June 25, 2007. A1.

32. Will, George. "For the Voter Who Can't Be Bothered." *Washington Post*, January 27, 2000. A27.

33. "State of the First Amendment 2006 Final Annotated Survey (Nov. 11, 2006)." First Amendment Center. www.firstamendmentcenter.org/madison/wp-content/uploads/2011/03/SOFA2006FinalSurvey.pdf (accessed February 6, 2013).

34. Dempsey, Jim, and Dierdre K. Mulligan. "Internet can be a big benefit for democracy." SFGate. http://www.sfgate.com/cgi-bin/article.cgi?f=/c/a/2010/07/03/INAP1E6UCI.DTL (accessed February 6, 2013).

35. "Association of Community Organizations for Reform Now (ACORN)." Center for Constitutional Rights. ccrjustice.org/about-us/movement-support/association-community-organizations-reform-now-(acorn) (accessed February 6, 2013).

36. "Review finds zero ACORN wrongdoing." *USA Today*, December 24, 2009. A8.

37. Wilcox, Clyde, and Carin Larson. *Onward Christian soldiers?: The religious right in American politics*. Boulder, CO: Westview Press, 2006. 90–91.
38. Wilcox, Clyde, and Carin Larson, 50.
39. Black, Amy E., Douglas L. Koopman, and David K. Ryden. *Of little faith: The politics of George W. Bush's faith-based initiatives*. Washington, DC: Georgetown University Press, 2004.
40. Williams, Joseph. "Obama vows $500m in faith-based aid: Analysts say bid signals shift to center." *The Boston Globe*, July 2, 2008. A1.
41. Euchner, Charles C. *Extraordinary politics: How protest and dissent are changing American democracy*. Boulder, CO: Westview Press, 1996. 35.
42. Meyer, David S. *The politics of protest: Social movements in America*. New York: Oxford University Press, 2007. 142.
43. Zimmerman, Ann, and Kris Maher. "Wal-Mart Warns of Democratic Win." *Wall Street Journal (New York)*, August 1, 2008. A1.
44. "Poll: Economy Brings Down Obama's Job Approval Rating." CBS News. http://www.cbsnews.com/8301-503544_162-6199106-503544.html (accessed February 6, 2013).

Policy Formulation and Execution: The Inside Players

Brooks Kraft/Corbis News/Corbis

CHAPTER OBJECTIVES

When you finish reading Chapter 6, you should be able to do the following:

- Identify the politics-administration divide
- Illustrate how the process of policy formulation provides legitimacy for the policies themselves

- Summarize the factors that promote incremental policy making in the US system
- Distinguish between the top-down and bottom-up theories of policy implementation
- Relate the rise of executive power over policy formulation and implementation to the loss of legislative power in these phases of the policy-making process

The struggle to formulate solutions features players from both inside and outside of government, but the location of activity is largely within the apparatus of government. Government controls much of the means of shaping our economic, social, and physical landscape; therefore, our public problems have a natural connection with public officials as problem solvers. The same is true of how policies are carried out; the execution of policy is largely in the hands of government, since our system of laws, including the Constitution, along with our expectations as citizens provides a great deal of power and responsibility to government at all levels. An old saying invoked when something goes wrong helps to sum up this idea: "There ought to be a law!"

In this chapter we turn to two intellectually disparate but practically linked aspects of the policy-making process: policy formulation and execution or implementation. The crafting or formulating of policy is often specific to the policy maker. Legislative bodies, like Congress or a state's legislature, are complex institutions that feature highly structured rules, a hierarchy of power, a specialization of roles for policy makers, and the ever-present pull of constituent politics from the "folks back home" and elsewhere. Legislative bodies are generally more open to public observation than executive branch agencies, and certainly more so than are the courts. The openness that allows us to see the making of policy and, if it is our desire, attempt to influence its shape, also can lead to a dislike of what we see, since all the best and worst traits of human nature are on display. As the nineteenth century Prussian military leader Otto von Bismark may have once said, "Those who like both sausage and law should never see how either is made."[1]

All three branches make policy, just as all three, to varying extents, help carry policy into action. (Legislative bodies have no formal executive power, but can use their legislative resources, especially control over funding, to wield great power during implementation. Similarly, courts use their powers of judicial review and interpretation to influence how policies are carried out.) Moreover, the execution of policy is often done in ways that forge new policies or greatly augment existing ones along the way. Because of this pairing of roles within the same set of players, this chapter presents a view of the policy-making process that first highlights the traditional view of policy formulation as a distinct phase of the process and then moves to the execution of policy with an eye toward understanding how execution can also be a part of the evolution of policy formulation.

POLICY FORMULATION

Gaining recognition for the seriousness of a problem and getting decision makers to start thinking about the extent of the problem are milestones in the policy-making process. The interplay of actors and values can cause intense political friction along the way. But once a problem makes it onto the agenda, the next phase of the policy-making process, formulation, is as politically driven as agenda setting—if not more so. Just how to go about solving a problem is an undertaking that features a range of options. These options must either exist within budgetary, social, and political boundaries or the existing boundaries must be changed. For example, as the nation's economy plodded toward recovery, federal policy makers argued over whether or not a second economic stimulus was needed. There was little debate over the existing economic problems that included high rates of unemployment and a continuation of a weak housing market, but there was a great deal of dispute as to the efficacy and desirability of a second round of federal spending to kick the recovery into gear. Fiscal conservatives, mostly but not exclusively Republicans, foretold of the economic doom that would arise as the nation's budget deficit grew as a result of more government spending. Those in favor of continuing to stimulate the economy via government action, mostly Democrats, viewed the increases to the deficit as worrisome but as a circumstance that would need to be tolerated in order to stoke the economy and bring back jobs. Both Democrats and Republicans viewed any solution as having political effects. A sputtering economy and high unemployment were electoral poison for Democrats going into the 2010 midterm elections when all 435 members of the House of Representatives and one-third of the US Senate would be up for grabs. A change in party control of both chambers looked possible. Republicans hoped that a hard line on spending, even by trying to block legislation to provide an extension of unemployment benefits to jobless workers, would earn them the support of voters who were telling pollsters that they were not happy with the direction of the country. Indeed, the Republicans turned the dissatisfaction with the economy and the federal government's response to the recession and unemployment into the majority in the House of Representatives and a significant gain in their numbers in the Senate.

There is strong evidence that we become highly frustrated with the policy-making process, especially as practiced by Congress, because we assume that once a problem has been identified and placed on the decision-making agenda, a solution should emerge that transcends partisanship and does not show favoritism toward powerful interests. We might call such a model of policy formulation the "civics class" version, since it conforms to what typified the instruction that, until the 1970s or so, high school students received about how government and politics should work in the United States. This "civics class" model is predicated on the belief that something akin to a national goal or good exists and that a solution can be produced by the use of technical and dispassionate reasoning.[2] The reality of formulating policy is that it reflects the political system in many of the same ways as agenda setting.

First, there is no one national goal or good, but a collection of problems that reflect the values and desires of a myriad of people and groups, some with more influence and resources than others. These grievances are often in conflict with one another or are in some way mutually exclusive. For instance, environmentalists and their policy-making champions cringe when an industry with a history of environmental pollution wins a relaxation of regulations, just as industries and their policy-making supporters take umbrage with what are seen as overweening extensions of government power over the private sector when tighter regulations are issued; policy formulation may not always be absolutely zero-sum with one side winning a total victory, but there are usually discernable "winners" and "losers." Second, the process of crafting solutions to problems is also a reflection of our political world. It is especially true of elected officials that they take the idea of representing the interests of their constituents quite seriously and, therefore, these policy formulators battle one another for their preferred solutions to problems. A case in point is the general agreement that our foreign oil energy dependence is a problem, but the solutions are in conflict with each other. Coal states and their representatives are pushing hard for government investment in "clean coal" technology, while others decry any coal energy as too polluting and destructive to the environment and push for renewable energy investment in things like solar and wind power.

Formulating policy means crafting solutions to identified problems. Of course, how you define the problem will frame the acceptable solutions. Was the terrorist attack on 9/11 a crime against US citizens and property or was it an act of war? If your answer, like that of the Bush administration, is "war," then legal actions (such as capturing those who planned and funded the attacks, trying them in court, and possibly sentencing them to death) will not do. If your answer is "crime," the solution will focus on tracking down the "bad guys" and bringing them to justice.

Solutions can come in many forms. Clearly, the **laws** passed by legislatures, like those passed by Congress, are attempts to solve problems. (The legislative process itself, including the introduction of bills, hearings, and floor debates, are all parts of formulating public policy: at each of these stages, the solution can change and evolve.) When presidents issue executive orders directing the federal government to do—or to stop doing—various things, they are also engaging in problem solving.

For example, after George W. Bush was sworn in as president in 2001, one of his first executive orders cut off federal funding to organizations that work overseas to promote family planning, including abortion services (thereby reversing many policies that the US government had been following during the Clinton administration). And, as you might have guessed, one of the first things Barack Obama did when he took office was to reverse Bush's executive order. The **decisions** made by courts, especially the US Supreme Court, are policies, since other branches of government and the nation's citizens are bound by these decisions as though they were laws passed by Congress. When Congress passes legislation that delegates congressional lawmaking authority for specific problem-solving purposes, the actions of the federal government's departments and agencies are also considered binding policies. Such **rule-making authority** allows a department or an agency to pass rules and regulations

THE REGULATION OF WALL STREET AND THE POLITICS OF FORMULATION

The Issue

Should the push and pull of politics end when executive branch agencies are given the task of writing rules to carry out the will of elected policy makers?

The Story

One of the financial problems identified in the wake of what some have called the "Great Recession" of the last few years and taken on by Congress was the use and misuse of financial derivatives. The role of the Securities and Exchange Commission (SEC)—the Depression-era agency of the federal government designed to regulate key parts of the nation's financial sector—in formulating rules to operationalize the broadly constructed charge from Congress is highly illustrative of the political aspects of policy formulation in the bureaucratic arena. In order to understand this particular case, a bit of background information about derivatives is in order.

Derivatives are financial agreements that are somewhat like bets between two or more economic actors, such as corporations or banks. For example, an investor may want to buy what is known as a future (the worth of something at an upcoming time) in a commodity that is dependent on the weather, like oranges. A freeze in Arizona, Florida, or California may radically alter the value of oranges. A derivative could be created between an investor in orange futures and the seller of the future, a kind of guarantee that the value of the future will be safeguarded. (The value of the agreement is *derived* from the value of something else, in this case the value of oranges.)

While this type of agreement has been around for quite a while and probably seems like a reasonable business arrangement to most people, derivatives can also be used to speculate on things of value. Rather than insuring the value of a commodity or other item of worth, it is possible to create derivatives that are largely bets on whether such things will go up or down in their value without actually having to invest in that item or in a future. (Actually owning a part of something or otherwise taking a direct monetary stake in an investment's success is what financial practitioners and those who study economic exchanges refer to as having some "skin in the game." If the business or investment fails, you lose some or all of your contribution.) If you have no "skin in the game," even if the thing of value loses some of its worth, you can still "win" by structuring the derivative agreement to reflect loss rather than gain. Just as you can place a legal bet in Los Vegas that a NFL team will lose by a certain number of points on a Sunday, it has been possible to create derivatives that made money for their creators when parts of the economy lost value. For example, the years preceding the start of the "Great Recession" featured meteoric increases in the price of homes. Real estate was booming! Was the market "over valued," meaning that the prices people were paying for homes was not an accurate reflection of their real worth? Was this boom in real estate based on speculation by investors looking to make a buck on a "bubble" that would someday burst and cause housing values to return to amounts truly reflective of their worth? For those eyeing the real estate market with suspicion and thinking about making some profit by betting on a fall in home prices, the idea of a derivative that would pay if housing prices fell seemed like an attractive one. (Mortgage lenders were heavily into derivatives to protect their loans, too.) When the housing market crashed, many big financial institutions were caught on the wrong side of these bets because they assumed that housing prices would keep going up and entered into derivative agreements that made them liable for a fall in prices. Some of the nation's biggest firms like AIG, the insurance giant, were deeply wounded by derivatives, so much in fact that the federal government had to bail them out so that they would not be financially ruined and further damage the economy by their failure. AIG and other key financial institutions involved in banking, insurance, and mortgages were deemed "too big to fail" and were rescued by the use of money from the nation's taxpayers.[i]

The world of derivatives and other financial mechanisms at the center of the recent economic meltdown was, to many observers, surprisingly under-regulated by the federal government. How could major institutions that have a huge bearing on the nation's economic health be allowed to get themselves into situations where they were so vulnerable to the popping of a speculative bubble? Were these institutions really so big and important to the economy that US taxpayers had to rescue them with mammoth infusions of money, or should there be procedures in place to let them move into bankruptcy in an more orderly way that did not wreak more havoc than necessary on the economy? Recognizing the existence of a problem with an under-regulated financial services industry, Congress passed legislation in the summer of 2010 designed to clean up some of these problems, especially those associated with the misuse of derivatives. The Dodd–Frank Wall Street Reform and Consumer Protection Act, know to most as simply Dodd-Frank, empowered the Securities and Exchange Commission with the task of writing rules to govern the way that derivatives would function in the post-"Great Recession" era. The new rules were to take effect in July of 2011, but this did not happen because the five members of the commission (always split so that no more than three of the appointees are from one political party)[ii] could not agree on the content of the rules they were charged with writing, but they did agree to extend the deadline to produce the rules. Slowness in the writing of rules is not all that unusual, but what is notable is the source of the friction over the rules. As was reported at the time, "The dispute illustrates the political divide that has been brewing in Washington for months as regulators work to roll out hundreds of rules required by the Dodd-Frank financial reform."[iii] The political foment over the formulation of the policies created by Dodd-Frank has come about in some interesting ways. Passed on bipartisan terms after the financial crisis, the formulation of the rules to put the policy into effect was buffeted by the changes in the political atmosphere in Washington, especially after the midterm elections in 2010. Most Democrats pushed hard for the SEC to write stringent rules to check Wall Street and the financial industry, but Republicans—especially new members in the House—were not as supportive of new regulation. In fact, the new Republican House majority worked to trim the budget of the SEC and other financial regulatory agencies as a means of lowering the nation's budget deficit. Adding to the tug-of-war over the direction and the resources available to regulators in charge of formulating the rules for Dodd-Frank was the fact that the term of one of the SEC's members—a Democrat—was to end in the summer of 2011. Any replacement would have to face confirmation by a US Senate with members who might relish a very public fight over a nomination that could serve as proxy for a larger debate over the appropriateness of Dodd-Frank itself, in particular, and over the federal government's regulatory role in general.[iv] As is evident in this example, assuming that formulation is over and done with and that political struggles are not a factor at the rule-making stage is simply not the case.

The Questions

- How did the changes in the political environment brought about by the congressional elections in 2010 alter the way Congress viewed Dodd-Frank?
- Are there problems with unelected members of the bureaucracy writing the specifics of the rules that govern things like the regulation of Wall Street? Should someone more accountable to the public be entrusted with this task?
- Should there be more insulation between overtly political actors, such as members of Congress, and the members of the executive branch that write rules and regulations?
- What input should the public have on the process of rule making?

See for Yourself

If you wonder just how important Dodd-Frank is to the financial community, check out the following website: http://dodd-frank.com/. You might assume that this page was created and maintained by the SEC or maybe by Congress, but it is actually the product of a law firm that seeks to guide its potential clients through the new financial territory created by Dodd-Frank.

[i]Liberto, Jennifer. "Untangling Wall Street's tricky bets." CNNMoney. http://money.cnn.com/2010/04/21/news/economy/derivatives/index.htm (accessed February 11, 2013).

[ii]"Current SEC Commissioners." U.S. Securities and Exchange Commission. http://www.sec.gov/about/commissioner.shtml (accessed February 11, 2013).

[iii]Story, Louise. "Still Writing, Regulators Delay Rules." *New York Times*. http://www.nytimes.com/2011/06/16/business/16derivatives.html?_r=1&hp (accessed February 11, 2013).

[iv]Ibid.

that affect a wide range of our lives, such as imposing standards on the food we eat and the cars we drive. Because thorny problems often require highly skilled and specialized officials to design exceedingly technical solutions—and sometimes because Congress may want to simply pass off a tough, politically charged problem to someone else—the delegation of rule-making authority has become a fact of modern policy-making life.

The Need for Legitimacy

A government's actions during formulation can confer legitimacy on the policies it makes. Legitimacy implies fairness; formal rules and the ability to see the process in action help ensure fairness. When legitimacy is established, people are willing to accept policies, even if they dislike them. Legitimacy is different from **coercion**, which is the threat or actual use of force or punishment to secure compliance with a policy. The most vivid example of such coercion in American history was the action of President Lincoln and Congress in raising armies to crush the South's attempted secession. The seceding states in the South viewed Lincoln's election, by Northern votes alone, as illegitimate. Massive coercion is necessary to obtain compliance with policies that are widely seen as illegitimate, but policies viewed by the public as being fair generally require very little, if any, such action. The fair and open nature of the policy-making process helps ensure that solutions are not favoring one part of society as a payoff or a special favor. If Congress did all its work behind closed doors or if the process by which the Supreme Court renders decisions were to change from case to case, we might justifiably wonder about the legitimacy of the decisions made by these institutions.

The ability of citizens to affect the formulation of policy is also crucial to the legitimacy and stability of any system of government. Openness and rules may be meaningless if the public does not believe that it can influence the solutions that are being crafted to solve problems. If the public beats its fists on the doors of the Congress, lobbying and mobilizing grassroots public relations campaigns, only to have the House and Senate ignore these concerns, the final result will likely be a law that is mocked as illegitimate. This is why most policy makers take great pains to follow the rules of their institutions and, where practical, make room for public involvement. Back in the late seventeenth century, the great political thinker John Locke, who had a major influence on the framers of our Constitution, argued that the people enter into a contract with government by giving their consent to be governed. Locke's argument is still valid: on that consent rests our belief in the legitimacy of the entire process of governing, including the formulation of policy.

Formulation: The Degree of Change Sought

As discussed in previous chapters, the degree of change sought is an important part of policy making and especially germane to formulation. In short, policy change can either promote incremental or non-incremental (sizeable) change to existing policies or situations. How decision makers go about making choices helps to explain the degree of change they ultimately seek. Charles Lindblom depicts a range of decision making using a tree metaphor featuring both a "root" or rational-comprehensive approach in which all possible information and choices are analyzed and a "branch" or incremental approach in which a smaller range of information and options are considered.[3] Lindblom uses these modes of decision making to explain why policy changes are usually small steps away from existing policies, owing to our limited ability to get and process information and to the crosscutting pressures of interests active in a pluralist democracy. The rational-comprehensive approach could lead to grander amounts of change since all information and options would be available to decision makers, not just the narrower range of options depicted by incrementalism. While there are a number of obvious and serious exceptions to the dominance of incrementalism as an explanatory and predictive theory of public policy making, such as the decision by the United States to enter into a global war on terror, incrementalism does an especially good job of conforming to the contours of American politics. The pressures of interest groups, campaigns, and the news media, along with the built-in speed bumps of our system of government, such as the separation of powers and federalism, all point to a process of policy formulation that is likely to rely on debate and deliberation aimed at finding equilibrium more than on sweeping changes.

Clearly, the players, the degree of change sought, and the legitimacy of the process involved in policy formulation are all influenced by or are themselves political factors. As we will quickly see, the implementation of policies is similarly the function of an environment of competition over values and goals in the particular framework of our governmental and political structure.

IMPLEMENTATION

For much of the history of policy scholarship there was an inclination to see the implementation of policy as distant and even disconnected from agenda setting and formulation. Until the early 1970s, there was little scholarly interest in policy implementation. Prior to this interest in policy implementation, the assumption of what is known as the "politics-administration divide" kept many scholars from seeing implementation as a potential area for the study of power relationships. Going back to Woodrow Wilson around the turn of the last century, there was a consensus that the politics of policy making did not extend to the execution of policy. It was thought that the administrators of established policies were largely civil servants who lacked both the political motivation and the discretion to bend policies to their liking. Even if policies were being implemented in ways that differed from the intent of their formulators, the difficulty of investigating the rabbit warren of multiple bureaucracies for evidence of such actions must have seemed daunting. *Implementation*, the groundbreaking work of Pressman and Wildavsky, published in 1973, swept away much of the static beliefs about the political qualities of implementation in their study of a federal jobs program being implemented in California.[4] Following their lead, other scholars began to look at implementation as a part of the policy process containing a vein of information and ideas about the political aspects of policy making. As policy scholar Donald Van Meter noted, "Implementation is the continuation of politics by other means."[5]

Policies are not self-executing, and the degree of variation in how they are implemented is great, resulting in a desire on the part of policy scholars to produce theories that are applicable to more than one or few specific cases of implementation. As Majone and Wildavsky point out, one possible way to understand implementation is to see it in a mechanistic fashion. They dub this the "planning model" in which policy makers produce "clearly stated goals, detailed plans, tight controls and—to take care of the human side of the equation—incentives and indoctrination."[6] The success or failure of a policy is then attributable to how well the planners mapped out the path of implementation or to how closely the implementers hewed to the plan. (Of course, both the plan and the implementers could be at fault.) Majone and Wildavsky see the planning model as faulty because it depicts policies and their implementation as rather static, with implementation having little, if any, influence on the policy itself. Their preferred view is that implementation is evolutionary in the same way that biological evolution is the result of many interactions in the natural world. They argue that, as proffered by the planning model, policy does shape implementation. For example, the recent changes to federal health insurance policy mandated that the states create insurance exchanges that will make it easier for us to purchase private insurance coverage. In this example, the policy formulated by the federal government guides the implementation of the creation of the exchanges by the states. Basic aspects of the creation of the exchanges, such as deadlines for the states putting them into place, were created by the federal policy. For most policies, the objective of the policy itself, who is charged with particular tasks, the amount of authority and discretion they have, and the resources they can use all are fairly basic elements of what policy formulators place in policies on a routine basis. But Majone and Wildavsky also argue that implementation itself shapes policy. "Policies are continuously transformed by implementing actions that simultaneously alter resources and objectives."[7] In terms of the previous example of insurance exchanges, New York, like many states, scrambled to create an exchange that met the basic requirements of the federal law, but the policy allowed a great deal of discretion about how to set up and run the exchanges. One plan offered by the state's governor was to create a public corporation to administer the exchanges and allow input from the insurance industry in their operation.[8] The state may or may not end up doing this, but the federal policy allows sizeable variations in how the states set up and run the exchanges. It is hard to imagine that such variations will not produce differences among the states in how many people buy health insurance, at what price they purchase it, and in the quality of the coverage they secure. These variations are likely to change the perception of the goals and meaning of the overarching policy. In essence, the implementation of the policy will likely change the policy in terms of how it is perceived by its makers and in the ways that it impacts the target population of the policy.

While legislative bodies and courts do occasionally wade into the implementation of policy, it is mostly a bureaucratic endeavor. Policy administrators, often referred to as "bureaucrats," have a number of tools at their disposal which make them important players in the policy process. First, they hold a degree of expertise about the problems, the tools, and the targets of the policy that formulators are unlikely to match. Scientists employed by the Environmental Protection Agency are probably more knowledgeable about the usefulness and side effects of the use of chemical oil dispersants on marine ecosystems than are members of Congress or a president. Thus, an elevated amount of particular knowledge or skill in a specific area is likely to earn bureaucrats some or even considerable deference from others. Most clichés contain at least some degree of truth and, in many instances, "knowledge is power." Second, while roughly ten percent of the upper reaches of the executive branch of the federal government is appointed by the president and must be confirmed by the Senate, this means that about ninety percent of the federal bureaucracy is put in place by way of civil service laws. These laws stipulate that workers must be hired on their merit, often as measured by tests or exams, and not on political considerations. Once hired, the civil servant is protected in his or her job from removal or firing based on purely political motives; they can be terminated or demoted only for cause, such as poor performance or malfeasance. Thus protected from the political tides caused by elections or other political upheaval, federal bureaucrats can settle into careers that are likely to outlast their appointed bosses in the executive branch, a term-limited president, and all but the most tenacious members of Congress. Both of these factors—deference based on knowledge and skill along with a longer time frame—give members of the bureaucracy a view of policy implementation that can differ greatly from elected and appointed officials. This view is often called the department or agency perspective, and it embodies the values, goals, and operational procedures that become part of an agency. Some appointed officials are said to "go native" or to adopt this agency perspective. If there is friction over policy direction between the head of an agency or department and the rank-and-file bureaucrats he or she leads, the agency personnel may grudgingly bear his or her tenure or they may quietly work at their jobs in ways that reflect the agency perspective and not that of the chief administrator of even that of the president.

Policy scholars have investigated the nature of implementation by bureaucracies with an eye toward understanding the successes and failures of implementation. Bureaucracies at any level of government are highly institutionalized, meaning that they are directed toward a basic goal, they have a well established set of rules for carrying out their tasks, they have a hierarchical structure of power and command, and they feature a high degree of expertise and a clear division of labor and job specialization. If you think about a branch of the US military, you can get a good picture of a highly institutionalized organization. Governmental bureaucracies are similarly institutionalized.

Alita Bobrow/Shutterstock

The federal government's Department of Education is clearly arrayed as a hierarchical organization, with the Secretary of Education in charge of a large and highly specialized set of offices and divisions in place to carry out a complex and diverse set of policies. The rules that govern things like the implementation of No Child Left Behind, the federal government's policy concerning public school performance and standards, are vast and explicit.

One of the key attributes of a bureaucracy, the hierarchical arrangement of power, begs a question for policy scholars. Does the successful implementation of policy hinge on proper direction from the top of the organizational structure or do the "frontline" or "street level" bureaucrats at the bottom of the structure; for example, a teacher working to meet the goals associated with No Child Left Behind, play the key role in the implementation of policy?

The top-down approach to policy implementation has much to do with the planning model of implementation in which there is a clear statement of the policy goals, and the execution of the policies in pursuit of the goals is firmly enforced from the leadership of the organization all the way down to the frontline bureaucrats. There is little, if any, innovation or discretion allowed by any member of the organization up and down the ranks.[9] In this view, successful implementation is largely the result of the clarity of policy goals coupled with firm administrative practices. Given the basic premise of this text, that policy is a debate over the meaning and desirability of values, the top-down model's insistence on the existence of clear policy goals highlights its main weakness as a tool to understand or predict implementation. As we have seen, the exact nature of just what we see as problematic and how to go about trying to solve these problems are both laced with struggles over the basic values of our society and political system. The top-down model also

◣ THE POLITICS OF POLICY IMPLEMENTATION

The Issue

Although the implementation of policy may, at first glance, appear to be a simple matter of putting into practice what has already been decided through the political process, even the most agreed-upon policies can become a political battlefront when they are being implemented. How much discretion does the executive branch have in implementing public policies? How can policies that have near unanimous support suddenly become controversial when put into practice? How does politics affect the implementation of policies?

The Story

In late August of 2011, armed federal marshals raided the Gibson Guitar Corporation's factories in Nashville and Memphis, confiscating wood, hard drives, and guitars. This was not the first time such a raid took place. Federal agents also raided the Nashville factory in November 2009 and seized ebony from Madagascar. Gibson officials claim that the raids have hurt their business to the cost of millions of dollars and that the government has not formally charged the company with wrongdoing. Government officials say they were enforcing a federal statute aimed at addressing illegal harvesting of wood products.

The Lacey Act is a century old federal act that was amended in 2008 to combat illegal logging and illegal plant trade around the world. The Lacey Act, originally signed into law by President McKinley in 1900, was the first national wildlife protection statute. It was amended several times, most recently in 2008, and it now protects both wildlife and plants.

The 2008 amendments to the Lacey Act extended the reach of the law to products, including timber derived from illegally harvested plants and brought into the United States either directly or through products manufactured in countries other than the country where the illegal harvesting took place. In addition, the act requires importers of harvested plant products to provide a declaration of the name of the species, the country of harvest, the value, and the quantity of the harvested materials. This means that the end users of wood and other harvested products are responsible for assuring that the wood products they are using are legally harvested.

The Lacey Act amendments were specifically adopted to curtail the devastating effects of illegal logging around the world. Wide-ranging interest groups, including environmentalists, industry, and labor groups supported the adoption of the Lacey Act amendments, and the law passed with strong bipartisan support.

According to federal investigators, the raid on Gibson was clearly warranted because, under the Lacey Act, importers of wood are required to certify the origins of wood products, and Gibson "knowingly imported tainted wood."[i]

Yet, the raids on the Gibson factories have sparked an outcry from those who now see the law as having a detrimental effect on business. Many see the federal government's raid of Gibson as overstepping the intent of the Lacey Act, but federal investigators claim that they were simply executing the letter of the law. They say that the investigation showed that Gibson knowingly imported "tainted wood" and, therefore, committed a violation under the Lacey Act.

Fox News, on the other hand, has even gone as far as to say that the raids were politically motivated, citing the political affiliation of Gibson's CEO. The CEO of Gibson, however, explained in an editorial he wrote for *Huffington Post* that he does not want to see the Lacey Act repealed because of the trouble it has caused for Gibson and other guitar makers, but rather that it should be strengthened to make it clearer to businesses what constitutes a violation of the act.

Other guitar makers are concerned about how they may be affected by the Lacey Act. The National Association of Music Merchants (NAMM), which represents some 9,000 manufacturers and retailers, *wrote a letter* to *President Obama* and every member of Congress complaining about the confusion engendered by the raid on Gibson, calling the Lacey Act "a well-intentioned law, but one with unintended consequences."[ii]

The Questions

- Should the Lacey Act's 2008 amendments be repealed or amended to limit the unintended effects of the statute?
- Were the raids on Gibson politically motivated or necessary under the Lacey Act?
- Did the government overstep its authority in citing the Lacey Act as a reason for raiding the Gibson factories?
- Why is there suddenly disagreement about a policy that had the support of a wide-ranging group of interests?

See for Yourself

Check out the following link for more information about the Lacey Act and the raid on Gibson's factories: http://www.npr.org/blogs/therecord/2011/08/31/140090116/why-gibson-guitar-was-raided-by-the-justice-department

[i]Havighurst, Craig. "Why Gibson Guitar Was Raided By The Justice Department." the record. August 21, 2011. http://www.npr.org/blogs/therecord/2011/08/31/140090116/why-gibson-guitar-was-raided-by-the-justice-department.

[ii]Roberts, John. "After Gibson Raid, Other Guitar Makers at Risk of Breaking Law." Fox News.com. October 5, 2011. http://www.foxnews.com/politics/2011/10/05/after-gibson-raid-other-guitar-makers-at-risk-breaking-law/; "Gibson Guitar Corp. Responds to Federal Raid." Gibson.com. http://www.gibson.com/en-us/Lifestyle/News/gibson-0825-2011/; "Gibson Guitar Raid: A Fox Case Study." Media Matters for America. http://mediamatters.org/blog/201109130020; "The U.S. Lacey Act: Frequently Asked Questions about the World's First Ban on Trade in Illegal Wood." Environmental Investigation Agency. http://issuu.com/eia-global/docs/eia.laceyreport.english.

lacks a good fit with the rather messy reality of our political world filled with influence from other political actors from outside of the process of implementation. Therefore, as tempting as it may be to assume that we can understand implementation as a top-down process, there are many reasons to reject it as an inaccurate depiction of how implementation functions.

Bottom-up approaches offer a very different vantage point for studying implementation, one that begins with the frontline implementer and then traces implementation up the hierarchical structure of an organization.[10] The bottom-up approach focuses attention on a different set of questions: How much discretion do these players have over implementation? What influences from outside actors like interest groups, parties, and the media are effective at the various upward layers of the bureaucracy? If we are looking for the stuff of politics in implementation, the bottom-up approach is clearly a richer one for this purpose.

As much as the bottom-up approach reflects the conflictual nature of implementation in a more realistic manner, it does lack the emphasis on just how much impact the top-tier players of implementation have over the direction of implementation at the lower levels. Clearly, there is room for a combined or hybrid model, and this is the direction being taken by a number of leaders in the area of implementation scholarship, such as Paul Sabatier.[11] Policy scholars have tended to focus on fairly narrow views of implementation, and he advocates a merged view as more accurate. Sabatier's model is one that explains implementation by combining the top-down and bottom-up approaches to implementation, producing a sophisticated, holistic model of this part of the policy process.

We will now turn to significant trends over the last several decades that highlight the importance in the evolution of roles played by the inside players of policy formulation and implementation. A review of these changes will allow us to have a better picture of how political forces and factors shape and are shaped by these policy makers and implementers.

PATTERNS OF POWER: EXECUTIVE POLICY FORMULATION AND IMPLEMENTATION

In January of 2003, the outgoing governor of Illinois, George Ryan, commuted the sentences of every person sentenced to death in his state's prisons. The 167 men and women who were to die would instead serve life sentences. Governor Ryan argued that his review of all these cases pointed out that each contained an element of doubt that was too great to allow execution as the ultimate and irreversible punishment. There was a strong and often highly negative response from many, especially the families of the murder victims involved with the commuted sentences. As one outraged family member stated, "How can one person have all of this authority and power?"[12] Indeed, how is it that a governor can undo what other elected and appointed decision makers have done in keeping with their lawful rights and responsibilities? After all, the laws of Illinois concerning capital punishment were created by the state's legislature in conjunction with the state's executive branch, and the state's court system applied the law in murder cases. While this episode concerning death penalty sentences came as a shock to many, the truth of the matter is that when it comes to commutation of sentences and the ability to pardon—to absolve from punishment for crimes that may or may not have been committed—the power of many state governors and the president of the United States is profound and largely final. The constitutions of the states and the US Constitution are fairly unambiguous when it comes to the powers of commutation and pardon. A careful reading of history underscores this as well. The more compelling aspect of this power is that it is but one example of the magnitude of executive power, and that executive power in other forms has been expanding in the recent past. Given that there are multiple players in both the formulation and implementation of policy, we need to turn to a discussion of who is gaining and who is losing influence as a way to get a more complete picture of the exercise of power in these areas of policy making.

The Rise of the Executive: State Governors

The example of Governor Ryan flexing his executive power in a way that defies other policy makers is not an isolated one. Because of the variations among the fifty states, there is no one template that can be used to chart the rise of the power of state governors. Some come to office in states that have constitutions and other legal structures that make them either weak or strong governors, meaning they have more authority at their disposal to check the actions of others, especially legislatures, or to initiate policies or programs on their own. What is evident is that more states have been willing to provide their governors with the tools of constitutionally and legislatively crafted power over policy, a trend already visible in the late 1970s.[13] A few cases help to map out these changes.

Jeb Bush, brother of President George W. Bush, was governor of Florida from January 1999 through January 2007. Unable to run for a third term because of the state's term-limit law, the office left by Bush was a different position from the one he inherited.[14] By most accounts, Bush fundamentally changed the institution of governorship from one that was often dominated by the state's legislature and undercut by competing interest groups into a much more powerful position of leadership. While many factors account for this, the willingness of the Republican majority in the state legislature to work with the new Republican governor and the readiness of the state's voters to vote for changes that would empower the executive are the two pillars of Jeb Bush's strength in office. Bush was able to gain control over judicial nominations and appointments to the state's university board of trustees, and he then clamped down on pork barrel spending by the legislature. He even took on members of his own party when they failed to toe the line on his most important policy initiatives.[15] It helped that Florida's new term-limits law not only covered the governorship, but the state legislature, too. That ensured that most lawmakers lacked the political experience to outmaneuver an ambitious executive.

The combination of institutional changes, such as control over appointments and nominations and term-limited legislators with fewer political resources than in the past, coupled with his determination to control the agenda of the legislature, made Bush quite powerful as governor. He used this power to cut the size of the state's payroll, lower taxes, and implement a public school testing plan that predated the federal government's foray into this policy area under President George W. Bush.

In 2004, the Brennan Center for Justice, part of New York University's law school, issued a report labeling New York State's legislative process as the "most dysfunctional in the nation."[16] A major reason for this finding is that the state's budget process has been accurately described as "three men in a room," meaning the majority party leaders from the Senate and the Assembly meet with the governor and decide how the state's massive budget will be divided. Each leader—to date it has only been men—bargains for his point of view. The process is not public, and even members of the legislature, especially those in the minority parties, decry these negotiations as unfair and antidemocratic. Given that each of the three players has an actual or de facto veto for any version of the budget that they dislike, it was commonplace during most of the 1980s and 1990s for budgets to come out of Albany weeks and even months late of their April 1 deadline. Part of the problem focused upon by reformers is the particular role of the governor in this process; in New York, the executive provides a budget proposal that is then supposed to be acted upon by the legislature within a few months. In essence, this allows the governor to set the parameters for the fight to come and, because of the short amount of time for the legislature to act, it sets up a game of chicken for all parties in the process to see who will capitulate before the April deadline for adopting the budget.[17] New York governors can also selectively kill budget items proposed by the legislature, a practice known as the "line-item" veto.

Governors have become more powerful in the United States because of a number of factors. First, there have been institutional changes that have given these positions of executive leadership more leverage over the states. The success of Florida's Jeb Bush is a good case in point. Secondly, the devolution of federal power back to the states, such as federal welfare reform in the 1990s, often allowed state governors more discretion over the implementation of policy than had been available in the past. Third, as Ray Scheppach, a dedicated observer of state government, has noted:

> [G]overnors have really just stepped up to the plate. What we've seen over time is this "pushing" on executive authority. I think that's partly due to the fact that we've been able to attract some of the smarter politicians in America. The traditional career path used to be that you'd spend a term as governor and then move up to the US Senate. But now it essentially goes the other way.

Taken together, these three factors do much to explain the expansion of power in the executive branch of many state governments. In reciprocal fashion, legislatures have dimmed somewhat in power as they have been affected by a new breed of state chief executives that have new institutional powers. Certainly, term limits have made legislatures places where the on-the-job training of the legislators themselves creates a fluid environment that favors gubernatorial leadership.

Partisan and ideological changes have been important parts of increased gubernatorial leverage, too. The 2010 elections brought in six new Republicans to states that had previously had Democratic governors, ushering in a GOP majority for the nation's governorships. The policy changes sought by these new governors (and some of their Democratic kin) focused on fiscal reform and budget austerity plans that roiled the political waters of many states. Wisconsin featured a particularly intense showdown between the state's new Republican Governor, Scott Walker, and Democrats in the state's legislature. In fact, the fourteen Democrats in the state's Senate left the state as a way of denying that legislative body a quorum so that it could not act on a budget bill that would remove the right to collectively bargain from the state's public union employees. The Governor and his Republican supporters in the state's legislature said the bill was needed to reign in state spending on employee benefits and salaries, and Democrats and their union supporters countered that the bill was really a means of crippling the unions in the state. Protests over the bill featured thousands of demonstrators, most in opposition to the policy, descending on the state capitol. The impasse over the budget dragged on during the late winter and early spring of 2011 when Republicans in the state Senate modified the bill so that they could vote on it without a larger quorum that would include the fourteen absent Democrats. This action was challenged in court, but ultimately the new policy on collective bargaining was upheld by the Wisconsin Supreme Court.[18]

Governor Walker was not alone in the spring of 2011 in his drive to push divisive policy proposals through recalcitrant state legislatures. Budget bills in Ohio, New Jersey, New York, Maine, Florida, and California featured attempts by governors—some more successful than others—to bring legislatures over to their way of thinking.

The Rise of the Executive: The Presidency

The history of the evolution of the presidency as an inside policy player with great influence over both formulation and implementation is a long one. In sum, for nearly one hundred and forty years the presidency was generally reactive to the US Congress. Of course, there are major exceptions to this statement and it is not hard to produce a list of presidents who clearly bucked the trend, such as Jefferson, Lincoln, and Theodore Roosevelt; all these men either defied the will of Congress, attempted to lead the nation's legislative agenda, or both. These presidents are, however, the short list of exceptions and not representative of the regular state of presidential power vis-à-vis the Congress. Today, most scholars of the presidency would say that the Congress is now subordinate to the presidency or is at least hard pressed to compete with the presidency, especially in the areas of setting the agenda for the nation's policies, but increasingly in the areas of formulation and implementation as well.

If one compares the powers delineated for the Congress in Article One, section eight of the Constitution, it is an impressive list of duties set aside for the nation's legislative body. From the declaration of war to the levying of taxes, the Congress is given an imposing set of tools to control the nature of the nation's policies, both foreign and domestic. In comparison, the presidency is almost impoverished in its lack of enumerated power over policy. Presidents can provide commentary on the state of the union. Presidents can negotiate treaties with other nations, but they have no force until approved by the Senate. Presidents can nominate those who will discharge the will of the Congress in the executive branch, but here too, the Senate must first approve these nominees. Taken all together, presidential power as listed in the Constitution is small and easily checked by the Congress at most every turn. While some early occupants of the office, notably Thomas Jefferson, did challenge and even defy Congress, the predominant view in the first decades of the Republic under the Constitution was that the presidency was limited in power by what the framers carefully planned out in the main articles of our nation's chief governing document. As the nation's political party system came into being—something that was unwanted by the framers because of their distrust of all factions—one party's view of the relationship between the presidency and the Congress is still with us although the party has disappeared. "Whiggish" is a term that denotes a federal government in which the Congress is empowered by the Constitution with the authority and responsibility to lead the nation and the presidency is vastly limited in power; it is a literal interpretation of power as it is enumerated. Some presidents, notably William Howard Taft, were vocal supporters of this governing philosophy. Beyond a philosophical approach to the presidency and an arguably limited office created by the Constitution, the presidency's first nearly one hundred years featured other limitations that kept presidents from extending their power, even if they wished to do so.

The power of political parties over nominations was considerable, if not absolute, until well into the twentieth century. However, over time the parties were remade in ways that turned them into organizations that were more open to the influence of the presidents and presidential nominees and less open to state-level influence. This trend was further helped along by the advent of television and campaigns that employed the "Madison Avenue" approach to reaching the public. Richard Nixon's campaign in 1968 was, in many ways, the first instance of a presidential candidate fully embracing the techniques of advertising in an attempt to win the White House. According to Joe McGinniss, Nixon was sold like a consumer product and repackaged as the "New Nixon," an improved version of the Nixon that lost a bid for the presidency in 1960 and the California governorship in 1962.[19]

The merger of a new nomination formula via direct primaries and the increased use of mass media advertising techniques—especially television—meant that from 1972 onward we were living in a political environment that greatly empowered presidents when it came time to shape the policy-making process. As our only nationally elected official, albeit by way of the indirect method of selection through the Electoral College, presidents were more firmly able to claim a national constituency; they secured nominations without going on bended knee to party leaders and, by using direct appeals to the voters in these primaries, they were increasingly running as candidates with nationwide appeal. When attempting to direct the nation's policy once in Washington, presidents were in a stronger position than Congress when making the case that their view was of the whole field and one that represented the public with greater accuracy. From this position at the center of the nation's political world, presidents gained the leverage to exert themselves more forcefully over formulation and especially over implementation.

At the same time that presidents were garnering more of the spotlight of American politics because of electoral changes, Congress was undergoing a set of changes that in many ways weakened its ability to direct policy making. The undoing of Richard Nixon in the scandal known as Watergate—the president lied to the public and broke the law in the process of a cover up of a host of illegal activities sponsored by the White House, including the break-in at the Democrat's 1972 campaign headquarters in the Watergate business and apartment complex—so damaged the Republicans in the congressional elections of 1974 that it precipitated a major influx of new Democratic members to the House and Senate. These freshmen legislators ran as reformers and did not want to wait around for their turn to "clean up Washington." They pressed for and won an expansion of the number of subcommittees in the Congress. This meant that more members would take positions of leadership as the chairs of these new subcommittees. However, it also created the so-called post-reform Congress in which power was spread out to more members and less easily controlled by party leaders. In short, Congress became more complex and less able to speak with a consistent voice on the direction of the nation's policies. This, of course, worked to favor the presidency, since the office is a unitary one and has far less difficulty maintaining a coherent message and direction on policy matters.

Historically and institutionally, there have been changes to the presidency that have also strengthened the chief executive. As already discussed, for approximately the first one hundred and forty years of the nation's existence under the Constitution, presidents had been playing the game of the politics of policy making with the fairly weak hand of limited powers dealt to them by our founders. Add to this the Whiggishness of many of the occupants of the office, and the transformation of the presidency in the first part of the twentieth century, especially during the 1930s, is nothing short of stunning.

From the inception of the Republic since the Constitution's ratification until the upheaval caused by the Great Depression, the nation largely experienced a policy world in which the federal government carried out its policy mission and the states and localities undertook theirs, with some overlap between the layers of authority. In fact, a more circumspect and stylized version of this relationship that removes the intermingling of shared policy control is known as dual federalism, for its sectoring off of each sphere into its own hermitic container. While the stark relationship portrayed by dual federalism does not seem to have existed in reality, the perception that the federal government should keep to its reservation of power is one that persisted over time. Extensions of federal power and outright grabs for additional and possibly unconstitutional power have been, for most of our history as a nation, noteworthy for their rarity and for how strenuously other political actors tended to push back against these intrusions. For example, President Lincoln's suspension of habeas corpus—one of the most important protections citizens have from abuse of power by the government—in areas in and around Washington, DC, in an attempt to quell spying and further insurrection during the Civil War, was ruled as violating the Constitution. However, this decision by the Supreme Court came after the conclusion of the war when Lincoln was dead. President Truman's seizure of the nation's steel mills during the Korean War to maintain production of military goods during a strike by labor unions also caused tremendous uproar about the expansion powers of the federal government, and there was a similar, if speedier, response by the Supreme Court to halt the president's actions.

The federal government did expand institutionally and in terms of its responsibilities and resources up to the era of the New Deal. The Civil War, the tide of expansion fueled by the industrialization of the nation that followed the war between the North and the South, and the first World War created hardships and challenges that were unknowable to the framers and that required the response of policy players on a scale that could only fall to the resources and prerogatives of the federal government. Still, even with this expansion of federal power and potential, the expectation by many inside and outside government was that the federal role must not expand greatly or, at the least, too rapidly, otherwise, the carefully wrought equilibrium established between the states and the federal government—established by the Constitution and nurtured over the ensuing years—would be wrecked, much to the detriment of the nation and its people. The idea of "states' rights" and a distrust of government in general were not new phenomena in the early 1930s, and the plan of the New Deal to undue such a long-standing relationship was not welcome in all corners.

FDR's first one hundred days is famous for the amount and scope of the legislation introduced and passed by the Congress in response to the president's requests. New policies to regulate the banking industry, put controls on the stock market to limit speculative trading, and restore faith in the value of the dollar were passed quickly. Programs addressing the unemployed and the indigent would soon follow. Farmers, factory workers, school children, artists, musicians, the New Deal's programs made provisions for all of them and more. In this rush to provide for the well-being of the nation's citizens and to reinforce the basic institutions of the economy, the federal government had done more than it had ever done before. For many, it was too much. They were sure that Roosevelt and the Congress had gone too far and, in particular, that the presidency had become too powerful in the process. After all, the Congress delegated a great deal of its authority over policy areas—especially that of commerce—to the executive branch when it passed legislation that created new programs. For example, the National Reconstruction Administration had a great deal of authority over wages and hours Americans worked. As part of the executive branch, this agency and many more like it were working at the behest of the chief executive, the president of the United States. While there is a history of presidents struggling to control agencies with differing policy or procedural goals from the White House, for the most part presidents gain power when the Congress passes legislation that creates a new program or that gives the executive branch the authority to promulgate rules and standards for the execution of broad policy goals. In essence, the Congress delegates to the executive branch some of the power vested in it by the Constitution. For example, much of the impact of the New Deal's programs rested on delegation of the commerce clause, an enumerated power given expressly to the Congress—and no one else—in Article I, section 8 of the Constitution. For the critics of the New Deal, this expansion of presidential power through delegation was a very serious mistake and one that would be nearly impossible to reverse.

Initially, the Supreme Court pushed back against the expansion of federal power embodied in the New Deal, and key programs were declared unconstitutional from 1933 until 1937. However, in 1937, the Court reversed its trend toward limiting federal power when it decided in a set of cases that the regulation of the federal government over important parts of the economy was, indeed, within the bounds of the Constitution. The Court's change of heart has been interpreted in a number of ways: Some say it was an acknowledgement that the political tide had turned after the landslide victory by FDR and the Democrats in Congress in 1936, and the Court was falling into line with the rest of the nation. Others argue that the Court was cowed by FDR's "court-packing plan" in which he unsuccessfully attempted to get the Congress to increase the size of the Court so that he could use the presidential power of appointment to create a pro-New Deal voting block of justices and steer the Court in a new direction. Whichever the case, the Court did validate the expansion of federal power and the delegation of power vested in the Congress to the presidency.

From the late 1930s until the late 1960s, scholars of the presidency would write about the president as a "savior." The presidency was the one position of leadership that could lay claim to a national constituency, court divergent interest groups, and wrangle together a system of political institutions—especially Congress—that were rent with fractures over partisanship and with the basic fault lines the framers built into our system of divided government. This heroic model of the presidency held that what was good for the president was good for the nation and vice versa. In other words, increasing presidential power could only make the nation better, and presidential power was on the increase during this time.

In terms of public policy, oversight is the most basic tool the Congress has for regulating the actions of the executive and it can take many forms including holding hearings, conducting investigations, and using the legislative process—especially action on the budget—to oversee and direct the executive. Knowing this from the inside as one of the most talented and crafty people to ever lead a party in the Senate and as an often-frustrated vice president under John

Kennedy, Lyndon Johnson sought to elude congressional oversight and direction of some Great Society programs by running them from the White House. Johnson's control over the White House was direct and immediate; his control over the bureaucracy of the executive branch was less so. Subsequent presidents have copied Johnson's innovation. The advantages to this form of implementation are that the president can quickly direct changes in the execution of policy and mold the intent of the policy to more closely suit his own policy and political goals. The credit for success is then at the doorstep of the White House and not with the Congress or the bureaucracy. These advantages are also, in many ways, disadvantages. Presidents hear fewer dissenting voices about policies since loyalty is a standard feature of those working in the inner circle of the White House. The unbiased expertise that is supposed to come from a professionalized bureaucracy staffed with merit-based civil servants is lost. If policy goes awry, there is little or no distance between the White House and the failure. Even with these potential pitfalls, presidents have continued to place "marquee" programs in-house because they wish to have close control over them or because they see the political world as hostile toward these policy initiatives and they wish to offer them more protection. For President George W. Bush, the Office of Faith-Based Initiatives was housed within the White House. Its proximity to the president signaled its significance to a constituency—Evangelical Christians—that was very important in supporting many of the president's other policy initiatives over time. This closeness also gave the president greater control over the direction of the policy outputs of the office.

While the overall trend has been for increasing presidential power in terms of public policy making and implementation, there are moments of decline, too. Some declines can be thought of as the necessary trimming of power so that the presidency has a better fit with the Constitution. In the era after President Nixon's fantastic transgressions of law and the constitutional order itself—he declared that the president could not break the law because anything done by the president is lawful—the Congress responded by attempting to reign in presidential power over the budget, war making, and the surveillance of citizens. The Congress, in these cases, was able to respond to the advances of the presidency in ways that were designed to restore the constitutional balance. At other times, the reduction of presidential power, while perhaps more effective, was not as easy to trace. The presidencies of Jimmy Carter, Gerald Ford, and George H. W. Bush were marred by policy failures and eroding public support that crippled their leadership and sent them to defeat in bids for re-election. In these cases, power was not so much chipped away by the actions of another political player, but it was worn away by incompetence or economic and political factors that were often beyond the control of any president. Some scholars, especially those who focused on Ford and Carter, saw the presidency as "imperiled" or "imprisoned" by the impossibility of leadership defined by the expectations presidents had created themselves by stressing the singular importance of their office.

By the time George W. Bush came to the White House in 2001, the power of the presidency had seemed to ebb and flow, with some rejoicing in the apparent resurgence of presidential power under Ronald Reagan. Others were lamenting Bill Clinton's missed opportunities to use his formidable political skills to effectively lead the nation in anything more than minor policy steps toward V-chips to block violent TV programs and school uniforms to curb gang violence. George Bush came to the presidency with a fairly thin résumé as the governor of Texas, a state with a constitution that limits the formal powers of its chief executive. His main domestic policy goal was to reform the nation's public schools by setting national standards that would be ensured by mandatory standardized testing. He called the policy initiative No Child Left Behind, and that is the name of the law passed by the Congress and signed into effect in January of 2002. As for international policy initiatives, the new president seemed to be much less interested in involving himself in diplomacy than had his diplomat father, and he brought many people from his father's administration on board to focus on foreign affairs.

On September 11, 2001, the president's supposed plan for emphasizing the domestic side of his policy agenda was swept to the side by a shocking act of terrorism that killed over 3,000 people in New York, Pennsylvania, and Washington, DC. The nation and our allies around the world reeled at the ferocity and incomprehensible nature of the attacks. The public was bewildered and ready to seek answers for the cause of the attacks and even retribution for the lives lost. President Bush's response was far-reaching. The public was promised definitive action against the "evildoers," and military action against the terrorists operating out of Afghanistan was in the offing. Public opinion polls from this time show robust support for the job the president was doing and for the president himself. Outside of the public's view, the president and his administration moved ahead on actions they believed would weaken the terrorists' ability to operate within the United States, to deal with terrorists for the purposes of gaining intelligence from them for future use, and to incarcerate those who were taking up arms against us. The policy that the president wanted, and that his attorney general, John Ashcroft and, later, Alberto Gonzales, helped to craft and approve, allowed the president of the United States to declare people—US citizens and noncitizens alike—as enemy combatants and interrogate and hold them without any of the procedural safeguards mandated by the Constitution. The president also created a program of domestic surveillance, which included phone taps and the monitoring of e-mail, in which no search warrants were issued by a court. This program, with its direct challenges to the Constitution's Fourth Amendment, went unknown for years until it was disclosed in 2006. The president defended both the bestowing of enemy combatant status and the warrantless wiretap program as necessary tools in the war on terrorism and deflected charges that this was an unchecked expansion of presidential power. The Congress passed legislation in June of 2006 that mostly validated the president's ability to direct the National Security Agency to wiretap without warrants and to monitor e-mail. Many members of Congress may have voted for the legislation in a run up to the midterm elections of that year as a means of warding off charges that they were "soft on terrorism."[20]

The Contraction of Power: The Policy-Making Role of Legislatures in an Era of Executive Ascendancy

Of all the powers listed in the Constitution for the Congress of the United States, there is one that is not expressly stated in our founding document, but is logically necessary for the functioning of the system of separated institutions that must balance their powers with and against one another. The ability to oversee the actions of the executive and judicial branches is more implied than enumerated by the Constitution; it is a function that grew in importance and practicality as Congress became a formalized institution that is based on the functioning of standing committees with identifiable jurisdictions over policy matters and with clear connections to the actions of the executive and the courts. The Constitution does not create an oversight structure or process for Congress, with the possible exclusion of the unwieldy and seldom used power of impeachment. For the most part, the growth of congressional oversight often paralleled expansion of the executive branch from the New Deal onwards. Hearings on bills, investigations into alleged wrongdoing in the public or private sector, and constituent service, such as answering the concerns of the residents of congressional districts or states, are all forms of oversight in that they give members of the House and Senate the means to compile information on what the other two branches of government are doing. For example, if a constituent in a senator's state writes that she is having trouble navigating the changes in the Medicare prescription drug plan, this might be evidence that the agency responsible for implementing this program, the Department of Health and Human Services, is not meeting the needs of its clients. Certainly, a barrage of letters, calls, and e-mails may be evidence that a problem exists. The yearly budgetary process that requires a complicated dance between the Congress and the presidency is a more formalized example of oversight as the Congress seeks to have the president validate his requests for the new fiscal year's spending lines. Part of the process is also backward looking. Congress asks how the current administration has spent money on implementation in the past year.

Oversight comes in many forms and is an essential part of how Congress performs its role as a check on policy making in our scheme of checks and balances. However, there is good reason to argue that this role has been diminished and that the executive branch has been the beneficiary of Congress's loss of power. There are several reasons to conclude that Congress is in eclipse when it comes to its power of oversight. The widest angle view shows Congress as an institution that has undergone tremendous change in the last forty years and beyond. The reforms put in place in the 1970s diffused power in the Congress to an increased number of subcommittees, making the whole body more difficult to lead and less likely to move in the same direction in matters aimed at overseeing the executive. Even before these changes, the Congress was an unwieldy place because it is, for the most part, a majoritarian institution in which the work of the place requires the bulk of the members to agree on the direction of policy and oversight. Think of an ancient galleon manned with rowers who must pull their oars in sync with one another or row about in a circle or splash around aimlessly, dead in the water. Weaving majorities together was somewhat easier to accomplish when parties controlled nominations for the general election and when the parties were able to dole out large amounts of campaign cash for members seeking reelection. Both of these levers of party leadership are but memories of a time gone past. Today, the women and men who are serving in Congress or who wish to do so get nominated by their efforts in direct primaries and raise much of their own funding through the relatively small individual contributions that citizens make within the bounds of the campaign finance laws that govern federal elections. Even the old folkways that socialized members of Congress to see themselves as part of the history and culture of the institution and Washington, DC, itself are changing. For example, in the past it was expected that a new member of Congress would move his or her personal life—including the family—to Washington and that the nation's legislators would socialize with one another, often across party lines. When your kids go to the same schools, when you play softball in the same league, or go to the same house of worship, it tends to draw you together with bonds that are quite strong. Combine the advent of easy air travel to even the farthest reaches of the nation, including Hawaii and Alaska; a Tuesday to Thursday schedule of hearings and floor action that allowed weekly travel back home; and an increasingly antigovernment, anti-Washington feeling among the public, and the result is congressional membership that is less tied to the institution than in the past. This anti-Congress Congress is happy to beat up on itself at election time: "Vote for me! Send me back and I'll make that dysfunctional place work!" With a public that has traditionally been skeptical of Congress—Mark Twain once called it our only native criminal class—a media that is poised to make the most of the scandals that members are often only too obliging to proffer, and the naturally adversarial stance that the executive branch has toward its chief rival for power, the amazingly low view of Congress in public opinion polls is understandable.

However, Congress does operate with rare bursts of cohesiveness. The 1994 midterm elections were truly a sea change as the Republican Party gained narrow majorities in both the House and the Senate for the first time in forty years. The new Speaker of the House was Newt Gingrich and he helped his fellow Republicans campaign on a set of items called the Contract with America. The Contract largely aimed at reforming Congress by moving away from the "bad habits" the Democrats had developed after being in power for such a long time. The House Republicans were unified in the intent of the Contract, by their faith that the public had voted for a major policy change and by their belief in the skill and vision of Speaker Gingrich to keep what he called the "Revolution" moving forward. The Senate had no version of the Contract, and it had no one viewed in such a reverential light as the House Speaker. After some stunning successes in the House and some with the Senate, the "Revolution" bogged down over the Congress's decision to shut down the federal government in a showdown with President Clinton over the budget. The Republicans took the brunt of the blame for the unpopular shutdown, and the

Democrats picked up seats in 1998, something that does not often happen for the party of the president in midterm elections. Speaker Gingrich chose to leave the Congress, and the heady days of the "Revolution" were past. Party unity was reinvigorated early in President Bush's first term when the Republicans regained the Senate in 2002, after briefly losing control of this house of Congress when one of their own, James Jeffords of Vermont, left the party to become an independent and was, for organizational purposes, counted as a Democrat. The scant majorities for the Republicans during this time meant that no dissent could be tolerated, since it was almost impossible to have a party member defect from the party line and still win the day legislatively.

With a groundswell of support for President Bush following the 2001 terrorist attacks, the Republican-led Congress took on a mode of discipline that was quite different from what took place during the Gingrich years, when the Republican majorities were galvanized by opposition to the White House. In this post-9/11 era, the Republican majority was motivated by cooperation and support for the president. In what some Democratic members of Congress and some outside observers viewed as the jettisoning of a vital check on the executive branch, the oversight functions of Congress were seldom exercised. As the enormity of the task of rebuilding Iraq came into focus, along with the harsh reality of battling the growing insurgency, the Congress largely supported the administration's requests for funding and did little to question the planning for the war or its aftermath. In 2005, the devastation of New Orleans by hurricane Katrina turned into a political disaster for President Bush when the slow response to the victims came to rest largely on his shoulders. Again, the Congress stirred little in regard to oversight for the actions or inactions of the executive branch.

A major part of the story for the midterm elections of 2006 was the sense of the public that Congress was not holding the president and the presidency in place (e.g., warrantless wiretaps, the declarations of enemy combatant status) and that it was not holding the president accountable (e.g., the failure to find weapons of mass destruction, the chaos that followed the fall of Baghdad, the lack of response to victims of Katrina). The Democrats won back narrow majorities in both houses in 2006 and quickly began to crank up the moribund oversight functions of Congress. Much in the way Gingrich's Republicans rallied themselves by going after a politically wounded president, so too did the Democrats in their attempt to take on President Bush, whose low poll numbers in the 30 percent range were only made to look good by the even worse poll numbers for Congress. The run up to the invasion of Iraq, the intelligence failures that led to 9/11, the aftermath of Katrina, all of these matters and more were suddenly on the agendas for the committees of Congress.

The more radicalized antiwar wing of the Democratic Party had high hopes for the new Congress, but it did not take long to realize that the same problems that have long plagued Congress—the difficulties in acting collectively, unpopularity of Congress itself, the drive for reelection—were weaknesses that could be exploited by a president who was set on continuing his foreign policy path. President Bush was like a chess player who has only one or a few pieces left on the board, whereas the Congress held many more pieces, but of a lesser value. The president simply continued to make moves that prolonged the game or dinged off the opposition's remaining pieces in a slow and painful manner. A series of reports, some mandated by Congress itself, were often critical of the progress made in Iraq, but the president skillfully held up the nuggets of progress as proof that his policy was working, provided that the Congress did not lose its nerve and foolishly set timetables or cut funding to the troops. The Democrats in Congress did mount efforts to do both of these things, but failed to find the votes to decisively legislate either one of them.

This begs a question: Could the Congress actually have terminated President Bush's policy in Iraq? Yes. If they were to cut off funding for the war and the rebuilding efforts, the president's policy would have to have ended at some point. But publicly, the president saw the war as his effort to secure the nation's future against international terrorism and to remake the Middle East so that there is a pro-Western democracy in the midst of an area of the world that is very unfriendly to the United States and our allies. Prior to the midterm elections of 2006, the president may have also entertained the less idealistic notion that a successful conclusion to the war would help to cement a Republican majority in the nation. No matter what the president's motives, the reality of the situation is that George Bush pinned his legacy as president and, in many ways, the fate of his party's future success to the war; he had little room to back away from that policy because it would reverse years of his insistence that the invasion of Iraq was a war of necessity. The president had the considerable strengths of the modern presidency at his disposal to keep on battling Congress. Moreover, unlike Congress, President Bush was limited to eight years in office, and this time frame shaped the policy environment in ways that highlight the political nature of the issues themselves. With an election looming in 2008 for Congress, but not for George Bush because of the two-term limit, and with no administration official as the heir apparent— the vice president did not want to run for the nomination—the elections for the presidency and control over Congress were very much a part of how President Bush and the Congress had to approach Iraq policy. The Democratic leadership in the House and Senate was both protective of their thin majorities while planning to increase them in the coming elections. To this end, the Democrats adopted a stance on Iraq that featured some failed attempts to set dates to end our military commitment there along with a strategy that sought to shape what the military does in Iraq without setting out timetables for troop withdrawals. This "thrust and parry" of policy fencing by the Democrats with the president and most, but not all of the Republicans in Congress, was a way for the Democrats to try to partly answer the antiwar element of their party while simultaneously inoculating themselves against charges of being weak on terrorism. It was a strategy that produced few tangible gains for the Democrats and one that points out the Achilles heel of Congress when it comes to trying to counter the executive's powers over implementing policy. Both houses of Congress have collective action problems, meaning that their rules require majority support to take positive action. The Senate has additional stipulations, and the will of the majority is not enough to undertake action; an individual senator can scuttle the legislative process. In a sense, a president does not have to lead Congress in the policy process. Rather, a president often simply needs Congress to tie itself up in a series of knots that keep it from involving itself in the president's implementation of policy. The rules of the institution amplify the ideological and partisan divisions in Congress in ways that make it less resistant to the will of a determined president.

Much has been made of the use of signing statements by presidents as a means to reformulate the substance of policy so that it can be carried out in a way amenable to a president's policy goals. Signing statements are used to indicate a president's pleasure or displeasure in signing a bill into law, and they are also used to state whether a president believes the law is constitutional in part or in whole. Historically, presidents have indicated that they would "interpret" how to implement laws they were signing into existence in ways that were not expressed in the legislation itself because they believed that there were constitutional flaws in the legislation. Beginning with President Reagan and greatly accelerating under President George W. Bush, a fundamental reinterpretation of the president's power over implementation and, by extension, over formulation has taken place. President Bush asserted that the president and the president alone was the arbiter of how to execute laws passed by Congress, a concept known as the unitary executive theory.[21] Under this theory, there is little or no role for the courts or the Congress in the implementation of policy. One of the most notable signing statements issued by President Bush obviated a ban on torturing suspects detained on the battlefield in the war on terrorism. The Bush signing statement indicated that the president would use his discretion to apply the law "in a manner consistent with the constitutional authority of the president to supervise the unitary executive branch and as commander in chief and consistent with the constitutional limitations on judicial power." Legal scholars took this to mean that if national security demanded it, the president was reserving the right to ignore the law and use torture to gain information from detainees.[22] While many members of the Congress were outraged by the statement, especially the ban's author Senator John McCain, the constitutional validity of all signing statements remains an open question. President Obama has used the method too, issuing a statement that he would ignore parts of a spending bill that removed funding for "czars" or members of the executive branch with authority over specific policy areas such as the auto industry recovery and health care. President Obama argued that he was not rewriting the legislation, but was exercising his prerogative to manage the executive branch as the nation's chief executive.[23]

CONCLUSION

As this chapter has pointed out, politics has always been a part of making and carrying out public policy. Even more than this, the chapter has argued that politics is a necessary part of policy making and execution because it provides a representative function—however imperfect—necessary for providing legitimacy in a republic. What is relatively new or what seems shockingly recent is that our policy world is far more intertwined with our political world than it was in the past. This is largely a matter of perspective. There is an old tale about the frog that did not know he was being boiled into soup because the water heated slowly until it was too late to escape. In much the same way, policy making and how policies are implemented have become more politicized to the point that some observers react with disgust at the degree of political heat they sense. As you will recall, the developments laid out in this chapter that add up to this politicization were slow to emerge, came to fruition in pieces, or were only recognized for their importance at later dates. We did not undergo a transformation in one day, year, or even decade that suddenly brought us to where we are today. The expansion of executive power and the contraction of legislative influence over policy are tales spanning generations, not news cycles on cable news outlets. Historians sometimes speak of the "great person" theory of history in which one woman or man drives the course of the future. While it is hard to argue that individuals do not make tremendous contributions to what unfolds in history, it is wise to remember that they seldom are as alone as they are depicted. Did FDR single-handedly change the face of politics by ushering in the New Deal? Hardly. Without the support of the parts of the American public that made up the New Deal coalition and the Democrats in Congress that voted for his programs, FDR's bold grip on the direction of the nation's policy would not have existed. Did the substantial expansion of power over domestic surveillance and our civil liberties spring fully formed from the will of George W. Bush? Again, this is hardly the case. The Congress is, depending on your point of view, a partner in these expansions of power by choice or indifference. Little happens in our political system by itself, just as it was intended by the framers.

The formulation and implementation of policy are distinct phases of the policy-making process. Yet, as this chapter has underlined, both phases are linked by the bold changes that have taken place over time to the inner workings of government at the state and federal levels. The players highlighted here—bureaucrats, governors, presidents, and the Congress—all shoulder much of the weight of formulation and implementation. As we have seen here and in other chapters, there is a rather complex set of interrelations among the policy players, the substance of the policies themselves, and the policy-making process. A change in one of the three parts likely means a change in the other two, and this is certainly on display in the evolution of policy formulation and implementation.

SUMMARY

Policy formulation is traditionally viewed as a distinct step in the policy-making process. While players outside of government have more significant roles to play in other parts of the policy-making process, policy formulation is chiefly conducted by the inside-government players, that is, legislative, executive, and judicial representatives and staff. Similarly, when it comes to the execution of public policies, it is the inside-government players that are most responsible.

According to the "civics class" model of policy formulation, once the need for a policy has made it onto the agenda, the solution or policy that arises will be based on dispassionate, nonpartisan reasoning. The reality, however, is that the formulation of policy reflects the political system and politics in much the same way as agenda setting.

Although the nuts and bolts of policy formulation is chiefly the job of inside political actors, in order for a policy to be considered "legitimate," there must be avenues for the public to weigh in during the formulation phase and/or there needs to be a degree of transparency during the policy-formulation process. This is why most policy makers take great pains to follow the rules of their institutions and to allow for public involvement when practical.

Along these lines, the American system of politics and policy making encourages an incremental approach to policy formulation. The influence that outside-of-government players, such as interest groups, campaigns, the media, and the public, can have on the formulation of policy, combined with the built in checks and balances of the American political system, have the effect of encouraging policies that adopt incremental changes rather than sweeping change.

Until relatively recently, policy implementation was viewed by most scholars as a part of policy making that was beyond politics. Although policy implementation is primarily conducted by policy administrators and bureaucrats, there are many ways for politics to affect how policy is executed. Top-down and bottom-up approaches offer different vantage points to understanding how policies are executed, but they are both limited in providing for an understanding of how politics can influence policy implementation.

Changes in the relationship between policy formulation and execution have occurred slowly, albeit dramatically, over the course of American history. Most significantly, the changing roles of the legislative branch and the executive branch at both the state and federal level in the policy-making process have led to the increased politicization of policy making and have blurred the lines between where policy formulation begins and ends and where the execution of policies begin and end.

DISCUSSION QUESTIONS

1. What is the "politics-administration divide" and how has it affected the study of policy making?
2. How does the need for legitimacy affect the process of policy making? Are there any recently created policies that you see as lacking legitimacy? If so, explain why.
3. What is incrementalism, and what is it about our system of government that promotes incrementalism in policy making? What are the potential advantages and disadvantages of incremental policy making?

4. What are the advantages and disadvantages of theories of policy implementation that follow a top-down or bottom-up approach?
5. Has policy making become more politicized in this country over the last few decades? If not, why not? If so, what factors have contributed to this? Are there any specific examples you can cite to illustrate this increased politicization?

NOTES

1. There is a good deal of debate as to the source of this saying. See Shapiro, Fred R. "On Language: Quote . . . Misquote." *New York Times*. http://www.nytimes .com/2008/07/21/magazine/27wwwl-guestsafire-t.html (accessed February 6, 2013).
2. For an extended version of this argument, see Hibbing, John R., and Elizabeth Morse. *Congress as public enemy: Public attitudes toward American political institutions*. Cambridge: Cambridge University Press, 1995.
3. Lindblom, Charles E. "The 'Science' of Muddling Through." *Public Administration Review* 19 (1959): 79–88.
4. Pressman, Jeffrey L., and Aaron B. Wildavsky. *Implementation: How great expectations in Washington are dashed in Oakland: Or, Why it's amazing that federal programs work at all, this being a saga of the Economic Development Administration as told by two sympathetic observers who seek to build morals on a foundation of ruined hopes*. Berkeley, CA: University of California Press, 1973.
5. Van Meter, Donald S. "The Policy Implementation Process." *Administration and Society* 6 (1975): 447.
6. In Theodoulou, Stella Z., and Matthew Alan Cahn. *Public policy: The essential readings*. Englewood Cliffs, NJ: Prentice Hall, 1995. 141.
7. Theodoulou and Cahn. *Public policy*, 143.
8. Crowley, Cathleen F. "Cuomo's plan has bargaining power." *Albany Times Union*. http://www.timesunion.com/business/article/Cuomo-s-plan-has-bargaining-power-1422596.php (accessed February 6, 2013).
9. For a classic example of the top-down approach see Mazmanian, Daniel A., and Paul A. Sabatier. *Implementation and public policy*. Lanham, MD: University Press of America, 1989.
10. For an example of a bottom-up approach, see Elmore, Richard. "Backward Mapping: Implementation Research and Policy Decisions." *Political Science Quarterly* 94, no. 4 (1979): 601–616.
11. Sabatier, Paul A. "Top-Down and Bottom-Up Models of Public Policy Implementation: A Critical Analysis and Suggested Synthesis." *Journal of Public Policy* 6 (1986): 21–48.
12. Wilgoren, Jodi. "Citing Issue of Fairness, Governor Clears Out Death Row in Illinois." *New York Times*, January 12, 2003. A1.
13. Sabato, Larry. *Goodbye to good-time Charlie: The American governorship transformed*. 2nd ed. Washington, DC: CQ Press, 1983.
14. Greenblat, Alan. "Jebocracy: Jeb Bush's eight-year reign in Florida is almost over. Tallahassee may never be the same." *Governing*. http://www.governing.com/articles/12bush.htm (accessed February 6, 2013).
15. Ibid.
16. "New Report: New York's legislative process the most dysfunctional in nation." Brennan Center for Justice at NYU School of Law. www.brennancenter.org/press_detail.asp?key=100&subkey=6939 (accessed August 23, 2007).

17. Hevesi, Alan G. "Hevesi Proposes 21 Measures to Reform Budget Process." Office of the New York State Comptroller. http://www.osc.state.ny.us/press/releases/jan06/012406.htm (accessed February 6, 2013).
18. Davey, Monica. "Wisconsin Court Reinstates Law on Union Rights." *New York Times*. http://www.nytimes.com/2011/06/15/us/politics/15wisconsin.html (accessed February 6, 2013).
19. McGinniss, Joe. *The selling of the President, 1968*. New York: Trident Press, 1969.
20. Nakashima, Ellen, and Joby Warrick. "House Approves Wiretap Measure; White House Bill Boosts Warrantless Surveillance." *Washington Post*, August 5, 2007. A1.
21. "Report of the Task Force on Presidential Signing Statements and the Separation of Powers Doctrine." American Bar Association. www.abanow.org/wordpress/wp-content/files_flutter/1273179616signstatereport.pdf (accessed February 6, 2013).
22. Savage, Charlie. "Bush could bypass new torture ban." *The Boston Globe*. http://www.boston.com/news/nation/articles/2006/01/04/bush_could_bypass_new_torture_ban/ (accessed February 6, 2013).
23. O'Brien, Michael. "Obama signs bill to keep government open, but protects 'czars'." *The Hill*. http://thehill.com/blogs/blog-briefing-room/news/156439-obama-signs-bill-to-keep-government-open-disregards-limit-on-czars (accessed February 6, 2013).

Policy Evaluation

CHAPTER OBJECTIVES

When you finish reading Chapter 7, you should be able to do the following:

- Explain why inside and outside actors both undertake policy evaluation
- Summarize the difficulties found in setting the basic parameters of goals and measurement for policy evaluation

- Distinguish between policy outputs and policy outcomes
- Illustrate how evaluators attempt to control elements of the process and substance of evaluation to influence perceptions of success and failure

Watching economic indicators like the stock market, housing starts, and the nation's unemployment levels for the last few years was likely to induce vertigo in observers. As these indicators pitched up and down, we asked ourselves, "Has the economic crisis stabilized?" Behind this question, of course, was another one: Have the policies undertaken by the US government and the governments of other nations worked to fix or at least stabilize the underlying problems with the world's economy? With jobs, homes, and a multitude of personal versions of the future hanging in the balance, most of us felt the anxiety of waiting to know the answers to these related questions. This chapter is focused on the process of and political factors that surround answering these types of questions, what is known as policy evaluation or an appraisal of how well a solution has worked to solve a problem.

POLICY EVALUATION OR ANALYSIS?

The academic and professional worlds of assessing the effectiveness of policies offer a complex and burgeoning area of the study of public policy. In broad terms, understanding the impacts of policies is done through policy evaluation or by way of policy analysis. While the two terms are often used interchangeably, differences do seem to be emerging between them. Policy analysis is more typically thought of as a form of evaluation that employs the thorough application of social scientific methods and techniques to judge policy success or failure. It rests on the use of quantitative methods of evaluation such as the use of statistical analysis of surveys or other measurable data. Policy evaluation may employ the tools of quantitative analysis but it is more likely to use qualitative methods such as case studies and more anecdotal evidence to draw conclusions.[1] In this formulation, most citizens, journalists, and policy makers engage in some type of policy evaluation on a regular basis, whereas policy analysis is largely the work of academics and professional policy analysts inside and outside of government.

POLICY OUTPUTS AND OUTCOMES

Practitioners of policy evaluation and analysis both concern themselves with the outputs of the policy process and with the outcomes of the process. The outputs of a policy are things like job training programs and tax credits for small business owners. These outputs are generally quite tangible and measureable. We can see the lines in a budget for job training programs, the amount of staff available to train job seekers, and the number of people that use the services offered by the policy. What are harder to gauge are the outcomes or results of the outputs. Does the training program produce clients who are truly more prepared for the challenges faced by today's workforce?

Do these people find jobs that were suitable to them because of the training they received? In other words, does the job training program work? Other questions arise from these: Is the program cost effective? Is the program politically popular? Evaluation of both the outputs and the outcomes of policy are important since the outcomes are largely the result of the outputs. Yet, the struggle over defining the worthiness of policies—the politics of evaluation—tends to focus on the outcomes of policies rather than on outputs. Given this focus, the remainder of the chapter will concern itself with the evaluation of policy outcomes, but keep in mind that they are the result of policy outputs.

Evaluation from the Outside and the Inside

As previously noted, we all evaluate policies. When we hear a story in the news about the results of a program or the actions of government officials, we are likely to at least ask ourselves if that result measures up to our expectations. In a democratic republic, our evaluations of policies do make a difference. If you have ever opened one of the mailings from your member of the US House of Representatives or Senate or from a local official and noticed a survey form concerning issues of the day, you already know that these representatives have an interest in our evaluations of policies. In fact, members of Congress have staff with the specific job of fielding the comments, concerns, and complaints about the operations of the federal government that come from our evaluations. Our evaluations are mostly of the anecdotal kind: we contact our elected officials because some aspect of a program did not work for us, rather than calling or writing because we think the program in general does not work. (Of course, people certainly do let their representative know they do not like a particular policy or program without suffering any personal harm, but self-interest is a very strong motivating factor for contacting one's representative.)

This type of ad hoc evaluation is valuable, but it has severe limitations for policy makers and for those charged with policy implementation. If the goal of policy evaluation is to weed out the poor policies from the better ones in terms of their effectiveness or degree of improvement on the targeted problem, then anecdotal evidence from the public may fail to provide useful evidence. An elected policy maker may get an influx of information from constituents angry about how poorly a program is administered. Continued input like this could lead the lawmaker to conclude that the policy is faulty and in need of revision or termination. But this is a narrow view and one that could be manipulated by what are known as "Astroturf" campaigns. ("Astro Turf" is a brand name for artificial grass. "Astroturf" constituent communication with officials is contact that seems spontaneous but is really generated by a lobbying firm or other organization that specializes in pushing their issue by making it look like grassroots activism.)

While not all organized interests engage "Astroturf" or other duplicitous forms of representing grassroots evaluation and communication, most interest groups do undertake at least some form of policy assessment. Some of this evaluation is innocuous and aimed at simply providing information to group members or other people interested in the group's message. For example, the American Automobile Association (AAA) publishes a monthly magazine in which it routinely evaluates the effectiveness of state and federal policies on things like speed limits and seatbelt use laws on death rates and injuries. There is seldom any advocacy to change or support a policy, just information about the impact of the policy on the drivers. Other organizations are much more aggressive about the use of evaluation for policy advocacy. A good example of such advocacy is the type of evaluations of policies done by privately funded think tanks, sometimes termed policy institutes. Think tanks, such as the liberal-leaning Center for American Progress or the conservative-oriented Heritage Foundation, produce vast amounts of policy evaluations, often quite sophisticated in their use of empirical data analysis, to argue for the creation, continuation, or termination of policies. Labor unions, corporations, and public interest groups also produce policy evaluations that support their own policy goals. All of these forms of outside policy evaluation—from constituent complaints to sophisticated analysis done by highly trained professionals—have their place, but clearly other forms of evaluation are desirable if policy makers are to get the clearest picture of the impact of a solution on a problem.

Inside evaluators abound in the world of policy making. Configured broadly, all parts of government perform some sort of policy evaluation when they carry out their basic functions. The courts hear cases that stem from the creation, implementation, and interpretation of policies. Legislatures hold routine hearings for oversight of the executive branch's implementation of policies as well as have periodic evaluations of reauthorization of funding for ongoing programs run by agencies and departments. At the federal level, Congress created the US Government Accountability Office (GAO) to constantly oversee the implementation of policy by the executive branch. The agencies and departments tasked with policy implementation are required by federal statute to collect and report the results of both the outputs and outcomes of their implementation efforts.

Without a doubt, the inside players of the policy process are required to evaluate the effectiveness of the policies under their purview. While they do this, the outside actors engage in their own evaluation efforts. Each side may have strong motivations to shape the process of evaluation or to interpret the results of evaluation to their own goals. Evaluation is no less a place for us to see struggle over politics than is problem identification, agenda setting, formulation, or implementation. In some ways, evaluation is the most political of the phases of the policy process because so much is at stake. Policies that may contain the very reason for a group's existence through funding or public recognition of their agenda item's worth may be terminated because of negative evaluation. Agencies may lose staff, funding, political clout, or even be done away with altogether if they cannot prove that they are effectively implementing a policy that correctly identified a problem that was mated to an appropriate solution. With this much on the line, the pressures of evaluation are many for all the players involved in the policy process. An often-quoted bit of wisdom from political scientist James Q. Wilson nicely encapsulates the political potential for evaluation:

> First Law: All policy interventions in social problems produce the intended effect—if the research is carried out by those implementing the policy or by their friends.
> Second Law: No policy intervention in social problems produces the intended effect—if the research is carried out by independent third parties, especially those skeptical of the policy.[2]

Much of the potential for variations in evaluations is the result of the substance and process of evaluation itself. In a highly idealized model of evaluation, the following would be present: "The policy goals are always agreed upon, clear, and measureable; the theoretical foundations are sound; the resources committed to the implementation of the program are adequate; the agents of implementation straightforwardly execute the policy makers' intents; the program's target population is willing to participate in the program; the evaluators have the skills, expertise, incentives, and resources to conduct the best possible evaluation."[3] Clearly, this model is one that has little connection to the realities of the political world, but it does provide a set of items that are part of the typical framework for policy evaluators. In particular, evaluators focus on goals and measurements of goal obtainment.

First, policy evaluation is—ultimately—an evaluation of the achievement of goals. Quick reflection on the early chapters in this text will remind you that agreement on the existence and nature of problems is not easily produced because it is largely a contest over the meaning of values and the desires of often self-interested actors. Yet, those engaging in evaluation need some sort of benchmark to measure progress toward solving problems. As you will read in the remainder of this chapter, this most basic part of evaluation can be a highly contentious battle since differences in just what the policy can and should accomplish are the root for judging its efficacy.

Second, establishing goals and benchmarks that indicate progress toward those goals implies that measurements are required to mark the degree of changes observed. While there is no shortage of data on policy outputs, the change brought about by a policy as policy outcomes or impacts is difficult to measure. In the jargon of the social sciences, evaluators need to be sure that their measurements are based on the causal relationship between two variables. Said another way, the measurements must be of factors that really are the result of the policy or program's impact on the problems. This is not as easy as it sounds. Some data is difficult or problematic to collect. It is costly to obtain or just plain difficult to measure with standard research tools like surveys. In the absence of the "right" measurements, evaluators may resort to the use of other means to produce data that are obtainable.

Even if measurements are agreed upon and the data is collectable, the complexity of many policy issues brings into question how well any set of measurements can accurately plumb the effect of policy on a problem. For example, a policy area such drug crime contains a staggering number of factors or variables that could influence the way a policy or program acts on a problem. Drug crime may wane or increase for reasons unrelated to a federal program designed to decrease this type of offense. New sources of cheaper narcotics may be entering the United States, and this supply may cause more drug use and more drug crime. If the measurements of the efficacy of a program do not take into consideration the multitude of factors that could influence the perception of program effectiveness, then any evaluations of success or failure for a policy are suspect.

Related to measurement is an underlying aspect of evaluation, that of costs and benefits. The effectiveness of a program or policy may be great in terms of benefits. The eradication of polio in the United States in the 1950s was a major policy success, basically wiping out a terrifying disease in a short span of time. It was also highly cost effective when the debilitating effects of the disease were compared with the outlay of resources necessary to create and maintain a nationwide program of immunization against the virus.[4] Other policies are not nearly so clear-cut in terms of their benefits outweighing their costs. The recent actions by the federal government to shore up the economy during the "Great Recession" have been derided in some corners as money wasted for bailouts and politically motivated pet projects that did little to help the economy and may have hurt it in the long run by adding to the nation's budget deficit. Other evaluators of these policies see a wildly different picture in which the actions of federal government, however costly in the short run, saved the nation from a 1930s type of economic depression.

Part of the problem with evaluating policies by way of costs and benefits is that the terms themselves—costs and benefits—are open to interpretation and need to be agreed upon before they can be used in an objective way. Who benefits? Must a majority or a sizeable minority benefit from the policy before we consider its impact as positive? What if the promised benefit is only achieved in part? Is there a level of achievement short of total success that is acceptable? If so, what is that level? Who is asked to pay for the benefit? What amount of the resources held by the public must be redistributed in order achieve the benefit? Will all members of the public pay an equal portion or will some pay more because of their greater holding of resources? Agreement can be reached on these questions, but as you no doubt sense from reading them, these are just the types of questions that fuel division because they are derived from basic values. An earlier chapter brought out that the differences in the way that we view the values of freedom and equality form the basis for how political ideology drives the debates we have over public policy making. Yet, evaluators inside and outside of government routinely use the framework of costs versus benefits to evaluate policies. It is worth remembering that costs and benefits are not fixed stars in our political sky, but aspects of evaluation that are subject to the same political forces that shape the other areas of evaluation and the entirety of the policy-making process.

The next section in the chapter uses a set of case studies to apply the basic concepts of policy evaluation just discussed within a more commonly used way of thinking about policy evaluation—that of winning and losing.

WINNING AND LOSING: A VALID FRAMEWORK?

At our core, we humans are goal-directed beings. We seek to affect our own well-being through our immediate actions and longer range plans. Dragging one's self off to a job every day and attempting to squirrel away a nest egg of savings for future needs may not be relaxing or enthralling endeavors, but people motivate themselves for these tasks because their belief is that a cause-and-effect relationship exists between their efforts and some future reward. Since politics and public policy are human creations—a point that is worth reminding ourselves about on occasion—the same cause-and-effect logic that drives our private actions is at work when it comes to our expectations about the actions of policy makers on the lessening or elimination of problems. While few of us are naïve enough to believe that all problems can be completely solved quickly and cheaply, we do hold to a basic faith that action can, under the right conditions, result in improved circumstances.

Successes and failure—winning and losing may also be appropriate in some circumstances—are terms and concepts that fit very neatly with the ideas developed in Chapter 2 about the essentially political nature of policy and policy making. Based on the fundamentals of policy, policy making, policy actors, and the political system that have been discussed so far, it is time to think about how politics informs and shapes how we view the efficacy of policies and those who carry them into being. Doing this provides yet another portal for viewing the intersection of politics and public policy.

The world of sports is filled with memorable moments for fans: the 1986 Mets' victory in game six of the World Series; Michael Phelps shattering records for winning gold medals at the 2008 summer Olympics. Moments like these and our collective celebration of major events like the World Series and the Super Bowl highlight the competitive nature of many Americans. Winning and losing are everyday aspects of life, and without diving into a "chicken and egg" debate over the order of things, other aspects of our experience such as politics in the United States are shaped by this binary view of struggles won or lost. One of the most prevalent uses of this framework for understanding politics is found in the coverage of campaigns for public office. It is no mistake that much of the news media's reporting on campaigns fits under the rubric of "horse race" coverage. If you have ever been to a racetrack or watched a thoroughbred race on TV, you are aware of the terminology and the stock narrative that is used to tell the story of a race. Even before the race begins there is an attempt to "handicap" or predict the outcome of the race based on the past performance of the horses, their level of wellness and fitness that day, the condition of the track at post time, the skill of the jockey riding each horse, and a host of other factors that could affect the outcome of the race; all this preliminary discussion and guessing sets expectations about what will happen. (Of course, this process also influences what gamblers are willing to bet on the horses in the race based on expected outcomes and the possible returns that they will win if they guess correctly. Horses with a supposed better chance of winning will pay a smaller return than those who are "long shots.") Once the race begins, the track announcer "calls" the race, meaning he or she describes the action as the horses move around the track on their way to the finish line. Some horse must lead at some point in the race, and it is possible for one horse to take the lead and not relinquish it over the entirety of the race. Other races may feature a closely bunched group of horses battling it out for position throughout the contest. Still more dramatic might be a long-shot horse that lags behind the others but puts on a burst of speed toward the finish line to win the race. The end result for all these race scenarios is that someone wins and the rest lose.

News stories are, in many ways, like the other stories we have heard all of our lives. They are filled with characters, have a plot to move the story forward, and may use drama or humor to hold our attention. Victory and defeat are some of the oldest plotlines we know of in the history of storytelling. The petroglyphs found in caves and other ancient dwelling places around the world often depict great struggles won or lost. Yet as universal and established as these narrative forms are for most of us, we seldom question how useful they are for understanding politics and policy. True, some have decried the overuse of the horse-race format in campaign stories because it focuses attention on the strategy and conflict of a race and diverts attention from a substantive discussion of where the candidates stand on issues and policy choices. Still, the use of the horse race's winner-and-losers format is unlikely to disappear any time in the immediate future since it works so well for attention getting and sustaining purposes; we like a contest.

However, should we use this format to understand or judge the contests over the creation or augmentation of policy, and should we use it to make sense of the effectiveness of the solutions to problems? One of the trends previously identified in this text has been the use of campaign techniques in the process of governing, what has been called the permanent campaign. Campaigns for office are zero-sum contests with distinct winners and losers. The metaphor of the horse race works well here, but so does the language of the battlefield. After all, the term political campaigning is derived from the term campaign, a word used to describe a segment of a war or other military conflict. If politics is war by other means, then the language of absolutes—victors and vanquished, winners and losers—is appropriate. Or is it?

World War II and the Cold War

Some historians have posited that when nations are beaten on the battlefield, they sometimes win the peace that comes after the cessation of hostilities. For example, the victory of the Allies—largely the United States, Britain and, later on in the war, the Soviet Union—against the Axis powers—Nazi Germany,

Fascist Italy, and Imperial Japan—was a clear military victory for the Allies but had far murkier economic and geopolitical outcomes. The economic problems of the United States and Britain in the postwar era were serious, especially in Britain as the nation attempted to physically rebuild itself after the massive bombing it suffered at the hands of the Nazis. Both the United States and Britain spent enormous amounts of money on the war effort and each nation was seriously in debt as a result. Both countries experienced continued economic and social upheavals as the millions of military service personnel returned home to find economies that were geared toward war production but had not yet made the transition to peacetime industries and services. In the United States in particular, the manufacturing workforce and associated patterns of settlement were markedly changed, at least for a time, by the influx of women and African Americans into the manufacturing sectors. There were postwar scarcities of consumer goods, especially automobiles, and an intense housing shortage.

For many Americans, the 1948 presidential campaign is encapsulated in the iconic image of a smiling President Harry Truman holding up a copy of a Chicago newspaper with the incorrect headline proclaiming "Dewey Beats Truman." Truman's come-from-behind victory is notable for many reasons, but one that is sometimes left out is that Truman had to overcome his association with a very tumultuous economy that, by 1948, had recently featured strikes by workers and large spikes in inflation. Democrat Truman adroitly pinned much of the nation's economic woes on the Republican majorities in the House and Senate. He called them a "do-nothing Congress" for failing to act on his policy initiatives after he ordered them back to Washington for a special legislative session, a charge that seemed to resonate with the American voters.

At about the same time as Truman's victory, the Soviets, our allies who suffered tremendous human losses in their epic battles with the Nazis, were rapidly becoming our chief rivals on the world stage, especially as each side armed itself with nuclear weapons. The threat of the spread of Communism, and, along with it, Soviet influence, began to drive our foreign policy. Europe was devastated by the war, and the peace that ensued was really a transition from the "hot war" of armed conflict between the Allies and the Axis to a "cold war" of tension and suspicion between the United States and our allies and the nations being drawn into the influence of the Soviet Union. The military forces left in place at the end of hostilities by the Allies held the western part of Europe, while the Soviets controlled much of the East. The city of Berlin was dissected into distinct parts, each under the control of either the Soviets or the Allies. As the tensions between the two sides grew, a physical sign of the conflict was put in place. Beginning as barbed wire and then as concrete, the Berlin Wall separated the city in half. Berlin, deep in the part of Germany controlled by the Soviets, was not only sliced in two, it was also cut off from the outside world when the Soviets blocked roads and railways to the city. The United States responded with an immense airlift of supplies to keep West Berlin alive.

The Berlin Airlift was an immediate and dramatic response to what was happening in post-World War II Europe. A perhaps less dramatic but possibly greater impact was a series of actions and programs that, taken together, are known as the Marshall Plan. The plan, named for its chief advocate, General George Marshall, was a highly ambitious plan to rebuild Western Europe as a means of holding in check or containing the spread of Soviet power and influence in all of Europe. The United States spent billions of dollars on the programs of the Marshall Plan. Much of Western Europe was rebuilt, both physically and economically, by these efforts. Germany was carved into two nations—East and West Germany—and West Germany flourished in the postwar era, becoming an economic powerhouse and vibrant democracy. On the other side of the world, Japan experienced a similar economic and political transformation.

Who won World War II? Of course, the Allies triumphed on the battlefield. If we were to measure the physical destruction of a nation as the measure of winning or losing, the destruction of parts of London and other cities are comparable to the destruction of parts of Germany. If the loss of life is the measure of triumph, what does the mind-boggling number of casualties suffered by the Soviet Army tell us? All nations involved in World War II suffered economically. The United States and the Soviet Union became locked into a cold war that drove the foreign policies of both nations and resulted in the involvement of the United States in Vietnam and the Soviets in Afghanistan—two wars that did little in terms of gaining ground in the Cold War while losing a great deal for each nation and its people. While conceptually straightforward, ideas like winning and losing are really not so simple, even in the context of the ultimate struggle of actual warfare.

The Auto Bailout I and II

"America's competitive edge in the world marketplace was sliding, vehicle sales were in an avalanche, hundreds of thousands of workers were thrown out of work; the automobile economy had ground to a halt and corporate losses were running at record levels."[5] There is little doubt that the recession that gripped the United States in the fall of 2008 was hurting many sectors of the economy and, as the preceding quote attests, the automobile industry was especially hard hit. But the quote is not about carmakers' recent bout of trouble; it comes from 1979, when one of the "Big Three," Chrysler, was about to fail. And, as in 2008, an automaker turned to the federal government and asked for help. Congress and the executive branch did provide assistance to Chrysler, and the company survived and became profitable again. Yet, there Chrysler was again in December of 2008, this time along with General Motors and Ford, back before Congress asking for billions more dollars to keep them afloat.

The tribulations of the auto industry in 2008 have some of the same roots as the near collapse of Chrysler in 1979, along with some differences. How the 1980 bailout came about and how well it worked are illustrative of the politics of both and may help explain or predict what Washington may or may not do for carmakers and other major sectors of the economy in the future.

In the late 1970s US carmakers were in a bind that was, in part, their own doing and, in other ways, was outside of their control. Competition from foreign manufacturers, especially Japan, was eroding sales. The federal government responded to the nation's energy crisis of the time in a number of ways, one of which was mandating higher rates of fuel economy and pollution controls for the cars produced in the United States. These actions required carmakers to invest money in new technology and retool some of their production facilities. While these factors were largely outside the control of automakers, other parts of their problems were of their own doing. Chrysler, like other carmakers, was not adapting very quickly to the new reality of expensive gasoline and global competition. They were still building large rear-axle drive cars that got poor mileage when there was clearly a demand for smaller, front-wheel drive cars that were stingy on gas. Compared to some of the imports from Japan and Germany, American cars were not always well designed and constructed. For Chrysler, "customers' complaints about defects became a flood: brakes failed, hoods would suddenly pop open while the car was moving, the car would stall when the driver stepped on the gas pedal."[6] In 1977, the company spent $200 million fixing problems with just two of its models.[7] In sum, Chrysler was boxed in by its own failures and other economic factors such as greater competition from foreign manufacturers, new governmental regulations, a series of energy shocks, and a weakened US economy. When the company began to teeter toward failure, it turned to the one actor—the federal government—that had the wherewithal to save it from collapse.

The parallels between the industry-wide bailout of 2008–2009 and the Chrysler bailout of thirty years ago are striking. Just as in 1979, there was a great deal of angst from many quarters about the most recent bailout. In both instances, a dominant argument against government assistance was that the automakers had to take responsibility for their own missteps and that, perhaps, they should be allowed to go under. This "tough love" approach sometimes envisioned a restructuring of the corporations under a bankruptcy program so that workers would not necessarily be put out of work and car owners and potential owners would still have a manufacturer backing their expensive purchase for work covered under a warranty. Other analysts derided this type of restructuring as too risky; there was less assurance that a car company could emerge from bankruptcy because they are such massive corporations with many outside suppliers and complex labor agreements with their workers. Still others noted that recovery from bankruptcy takes time, and they were concerned that having one or more car companies off-line or operating in a severely weakened state would blow a hole in the nation's economy and lead to further trouble.

The actions of the federal government in 1979–1980 saved Chrysler by guaranteeing that millions of dollars of the company's debt would be repaid by the government if Chrysler could not reorganize itself and become profitable in a fairly short period of time. This was not simply money falling from the sky for Chrysler. Members of Congress were wary of such a gift because it would set a precedent for possible bailouts in the future and it might be a waste of taxpayer money if the company went belly up. The fact that elections for the presidency and the Congress were well underway by this time certainly played a role in the behavior of all sides in this struggle.

The nature of the reorganization and the other strings attached to the guarantees given on behalf of Chrysler were far more constraining than the term "bailout" might suggest. It basically received credit from private lenders with a guarantee that the federal government would back the loans if Chrysler defaulted. In return, its actions would be partially overseen by a federal Loan Guarantee Board. Workers had to suffer pay cuts or no increases to their salaries. State and local governments in the places where Chrysler made cars or components had to kick in $250 million. All of these actions were just prologue to the real task—turning a profit. If there was no profit, then no more loan money would be forthcoming and Chrysler would fail.[8]

The carmaker struggled to right itself and, in a remarkably short span of time, Chrysler was again profitable and paid off the $1.2 billion in federal loan guarantees.[9] New models, a change in management, cuts to the workforce, closing of plants, and a lessening of external economic problems were largely to account for this renewal. By 1985, Chrysler was yet again ranked as one of the fifty largest corporations in the world.[10] From this we might assume that the moral of this policy story is that everyone was a winner! Chrysler won because it survived and was able to rejuvenate its company and its brand, the autoworkers won because they continued to have jobs with Chrysler, the federal government won because it helped solve a major economic problem and demonstrated it could work effectively in this capacity, and the American people were winners because their tax dollars were not squandered. Or, maybe not.

If the Chrysler bailout worked, then why were the carmakers—including Chrysler—back on Capitol Hill in 2008 asking for, yes, another bailout? While thirty years is a long time between infusions of help, some have argued that the 1979–1980 bailout of Chrysler only served to prolong the inevitable changes that would have to profoundly affect the American car industry at some point. If that point arrived in 2008, the actions of the Bush administration may have prolonged the inevitable yet again. Even if we consider the Chrysler bailout as a success at the time, it may have done a great deal of harm for the future, or even our present. As Senator William Proxmire said at the time: "The fact that it worked makes it a much more dangerous precedent . . . If [it] hadn't worked, the next time a situation like that comes up we'd say 'Forget it; that's not the way to go; think of something else.' But now, when there's a national-scale firm in trouble, the word will be 'look at Chrysler'."[11] And in the eyes of some, setting out a safety net may encourage greater risk taking in the future.[12] Seen in this light, winning can be losing if it forestalls an unavoidable change and makes the alterations more difficult or costly in the future. This notion is worth considering as we think about the most recent automaker bailout and the bailout of the financial service and insurance companies that were considered "too big to fail" at the start of the "Great Recession."

In the waning days of 2008, the auto industry put a great deal of pressure on Congress and the Bush administration to get relief as soon as possible. One existing pot of money they eyed was the $700 billion allocated by Congress in the fall of 2008 as a way to unstick the nation's credit markets and keep us from economic ruin. This set of funds was asked for by the Secretary of the Treasury, Henry Paulson, as a way to stabilize the economy by buying up bad debt held by banks and other financial institutions, but not to bailout troubled industries like carmakers. Under the program Paulson was to administer, the Troubled Assets Relief Program (TARP), the federal government would buy up bad loans and other forms of risky debt so that lenders would not go bankrupt. The thinking was that without solvent lenders, all Americans—from major corporations to individuals—would lack access to credit and the economy would freefall into recession or worse. Chrysler, General Motors, and Ford, also known as the "Big Three," went to Washington—first in their corporate jets and then a second time, more humbly, in a fleet of their own hybrid products—to ask for money from TARP or from new appropriations. Before the storm of bad economic conditions hit in the fall of 2008, Congress had already set aside money for the auto industry to help spur its moves toward creating more earth-friendly vehicles. These billions, said some members of the Congress, were already in the pipeline and could be an adequate and quick-acting shot in the arm for the industry. Therefore, little or no additional money was needed at this time. Others said that bailing out the automakers was akin to rewarding bad management and risky corporate behavior. A few senators such as Richard Shelby, a Republican from Alabama, actively worked to block legislation that would have provided more money to automakers. (There was speculation that Shelby's opposition to a bailout was less on ideological grounds than it was on the fact that Alabama is home to Hyundai, Honda, and Mercedes Benz.) Other members of Congress, many of the most outspoken ones from car-making states and districts, pressed for more funding and quick action. John Dingle, a fixture in the House of Representatives for decades and the Democratic representative for the Detroit area, was, not surprisingly, especially vocal about saving US carmakers. The resulting stalemate in the Congress dragged on for a few weeks, with erroneous announcements that a deal was set. After much wrangling about how the program might work and if a "Car Czar" would have to be created to oversee its implementation, President Bush was ready to sign a bailout plan into law, but the Senate could not assemble the votes to pass a version of the House's bill.

Acting on their own, President Bush and Secretary Paulson dipped into TARP and loaned General Motors and Chrysler nearly $14 billion. Members of the president's own Republican Party and some Democrats were outraged at this action, some calling it illegal. Others viewed it as pure politics, arguing that the money amounted to "pork" handed out to a troubled, but still potentially powerful political player with extensive constituencies that got a sweetheart deal. In their opinion, President Bush, walled off from most political payback because he was limited to two terms, was free to hand out the "pork" that members of the House and Senate could not distribute because of possible

Stephen Gibson/Shutterstock

retribution by voters.[13] Indeed, public opinion polls taken around the time of the president's decision in December of 2008 showed a deeply conflicted public when it came to the merits of the auto bailout.

As with the Chrysler bailout of 1979–1980, is this a policy success? At this writing, it appears that both GM and Chrysler are emerging from near financial ruin and are repaying the money given to them by the federal government. (Ford did not initially ask for assistance.) Is this a "win" when compared to what happened in the early 1980s bailout of Chrysler? Chrysler was "saved." Many, but not all, workers kept their jobs, although unions were weakened from the concessions they had to make. States and localities held onto important parts of their tax bases because plants did not close. The federal government looked effective as a problem solver. The public did not lose tax money. And car buyers did not get stuck with cars that would need repairs but had no viable warrantees. Of course, the whole nation benefited because an important part of the economy did not dissolve.

What of the 2008–2009 bailout? There are some similarities in terms of the benefits for companies, workers, states and localities, and car buyers. However, the picture is even less clear in other respects. How effective did the federal government appear during the bailout? A good argument can be made that with a genuinely conflicted public, the Congress reflected their will, and the resulting gridlock on the issue is just the representative and deliberative processes in action. Yet, having President Bush and Secretary Paulson swoop in with bailout money from TARP, something the president initially resisted, has shades of the executive branch saving the Congress from its own collective action difficulties spawned by the political pressures of constituents and other interests.

The auto bailout did keep Chrysler and GM in business, and both companies have repaid much of the nearly $63 billion dollars loaned to them, yet the efficacy of the program is still in dispute. The 2012 presidential campaign featured President Obama defending his actions with the continuation of the auto bailout begun by President Bush and Republican Mitt Romney attacking the policy for its lack of accountability and failure to curtail union benefits.[14] While such debates continue, it is more certain that, success or not, the auto bailout—along with the bailout of specific businesses such as the giant insurance company AIG and the less targeted parts of TARP—set a new standard for governmental involvement in the operations of privately held companies and corporations. As President Bush said at the time, "I've abandoned free market principles to save the free market system."[15]

Losing but Winning? Reforming Social Security

In the waning days of President George W. Bush's time in office, a reporter asked him a predictable question: What was your greatest accomplishment in office? Less foreseeable was the president's answer: The attempt to reform Social Security. This was a rather curious item for the president to pick since his attempt failed and there was no real reform of the nation's Social Security program. The president massed a great deal of the resources of his administration in a effort to take on what has often been called the "third rail" of American politics, an issue area so volatile and dangerous, because of its connections to powerful interests, that messing with the program is akin to jumping down onto the subway tracks and grabbing onto the live electrical element that drives the trains. President Bush did just this; he latched onto the "third rail" and suffered a nasty political defeat as a result. The president pushed for a number of changes to Social Security—the 1930s era program that provides monetary support for retired workers—but the main thrust of his ideas was to create private investment accounts for individuals. (The president used the term "personal" accounts rather than "private" in order to highlight the individual investment freedom citizens would get as a result of his plan. Opponents to the president's proposal used the term "private" accounts rather than "personal" in an effort to paint the policy as a means for individuals to get more than their fair share from the system.) Rather than have all of the money owed to a worker come from the pool of money now being paid by workers as part of their payroll taxes, the president proposed that we could take up to 4 percent of the tax now going toward the traditional pool of funds and invest it in other places, such as the stock market. President Bush reasoned that this would be a better deal for American workers since it is true that over a long view of our economic history, investments in the stock market have easily outperformed the rate of return on the money paid into the Social Security system. The president's opponents quickly opposed this part of his reform plan, arguing that it was far too risky for future retirees and that, in the short run, taking out even part of the money for private accounts that was now flowing into the system would mean a shortfall for existing beneficiaries that would have to be made up somehow.[16] (The record losses for the stock market in the fall of 2008 add some weight to the arguments critics had about the riskiness of personal account investments like the ones proposed by President Bush. Many people with retirement investments in the market had their savings heavily damaged in the market's fall 2008 drop.)

President Bush pushed hard for a reform to Social Security, especially for the centerpiece of personal accounts. The means he used were, to many political observers, the application of campaign techniques to part of the policy-making process. As outlined in an earlier chapter in this text, the president's interaction with the media, allied interest groups, and the public very closely resembled the ways in which a candidate would go about trying to win office. Certainly the president's attempts to "go public," meaning to stoke public sentiment for the reforms so that we would then pressure Congress to move in the president's direction, had all the trappings of a campaign, complete with rallies and town hall meetings along a careful planned route through important states.

However impressive and well planned were President Bush's attempts to shape public opinion and, ultimately, congressional action, they did not work. Members of the president's own Republican Party in Congress began to grouse that the president had not made the case to the public that personal accounts were necessary and harmless and that the real issue should be the solvency of the Social Security system itself.[17] With the Democrats united in opposition to the president's plan, the public unsure and somewhat negative about it, and the Republicans divided about how to rework the proposal so that it might pass, a number of new or expanding issues—such as Hurricane Katrina and the escalating violence in Iraq—helped to push Social Security reform off the national agenda.[18]

Given the clear failure of President Bush's attempt to reform Social Security, how then was he able to claim that it was the greatest accomplishment of his eight years in office? President Bush saw this episode in much the way that one of the early explorers before the age of Columbus might have claimed victory; I did not succeed in the main objective of discovering something new, but I worked toward the goal and survived when others were sure that the attempt itself was deadly. Indeed, this is precisely what President Bush said in January of 2009. The accomplishment was not the achievement of the reform, but demonstrating that reform could be undertaken in the future and, perhaps, at some time to come, reform would take place.

This restricted view of policy success has a good deal of resonance with how scholars of public policy have attempted to weigh the elusive nature of success and failure.

Success and Failure—Moving the Goalposts

There is a very old joke in which a patient seeing a doctor says, "Doctor, it hurts when I move my arm like this." The doctor says, "I can cure that—just move your arm in the other direction!" This bit of silliness underscores the more serious notion that, for a variety of reasons, policy players sometimes reconfigure the meaning of success and failure. But like the doctor in the old joke, the final result is something less than a true fix for a problem.

Many examples of "moving the goalpost" do exist, but it is wise to remember that the complexity of public policy and its highly political nature are likely to mean that even necessary and highly objectively driven reconfiguration of the goals of a policy can strike great political sparks. Certainly, events can and do change the goals of policies. During NASA's attempt to reach the moon in 1970, dramatically portrayed in the film *Apollo 13*, a nearly catastrophic explosion on the spacecraft meant that the mission became no longer to reach the moon but to get the crew back to earth. The memorable phrase uttered by one of the astronauts—"Houston, we have a problem"—has become cultural shorthand for the idea that our plans have just radically changed because of unforeseen circumstances. Implementing policies that continue to move toward unneeded goals or results that will prove disastrous or wasteful are foolish actions. This is not to say that such things do not happen, for clearly they do. Anecdotes abound concerning wasteful government programs such as subsidies for farmers who grow mohair—a natural product that was once essential for the military but has been made obsolete by synthetic fibers. Somewhat comically, we may point to the snuffboxes, the containers for powdered tobacco, which are found by the doors of the US Senate. These boxes are filled on a regular basis,[19] although the decline in the snorting of powdered tobacco probably makes the practice an unnecessary oddity, as are the spittoons found on the floor of the Senate chamber.

We would expect decision makers to adapt to changes in our policy environment so that our resources are not squandered or so that a problem is not made worse. To illustrate, during the transition after the 1992 presidential election, outgoing President George Herbert Walker Bush's economic advisors informed incoming President-elect Bill Clinton that the federal budget deficit was going to be much larger than announced. One of the major elements of Clinton's campaign had been a middle-class tax break to stimulate the sluggish economy. Once the magnitude of the deficit was made known, Clinton scrapped his call for tax breaks and moved toward a number of measures that helped to reduce the deficit. His plan met strong resistance and the budget he submitted containing deficit reduction measures barely passed in the House and only passed in the Senate because of Vice President Al Gore's tie-breaking vote. Some critics of the former president have looked at Clinton's actions not so much as "moving the goalposts," but as a "bait and switch" scheme in which he promised tax breaks but had tax increases in mind all along. While tax breaks are generally quite popular (who does not want to pay less in taxes?), they may be bad policy if they make a problem worse rather than improving conditions. Tax policy is a highly political matter, since a core belief of many in the modern conservative movement and in much of the Republican Party is that lower taxes are a way of lessening many of our social, economic, and political problems. The general thinking along these lines is that more money in the hands of the public means that less government will be needed to provide services, and the smaller the government, the more freedom the people will have to prosper without the burden of taxes and regulation. For many, but not all conservatives, Bill Clinton's decision to abandon tax breaks in 1993 was a very poor policy decision.

In 2009, as President-elect Obama readied himself for office, he began to put forward an outline of his economic policy goals. Without a doubt, the economic condition of 2009 was far worse than that of 1993, yet the shifting policy actions for Obama and Clinton have some similarities. Obama's plan called for tax breaks as part of a stimulus package to try to pull the economy out of a recession. The president-elect's focus on tax breaks for the middle class was not new—it had been a fixture of his two-year campaign for the presidency—but in light of the massive and snowballing federal deficit, members of his own Democratic Party raised objections to his ideas. Obama promised to do something about the large tax breaks given to wealthier Americans during the George W. Bush years, and some of Obama's most outspoken critics viewed his proposal to keep some of these breaks in place for a time as a betrayal of his campaign promises. Some Republicans who had been stalwart champions of lowering taxes during President George W. Bush's eight years in office now became or returned to their roots as "deficit hawks," meaning those who see dangerous consequences in increasing the federal deficit. The sources of this squabbling are many, including friction between the parties, the natural tension between Congress and the presidency, basic differences over economic theory, and ideological beliefs about the proper role of government and the need for taxation. Much the same can be said of Bill Clinton's early rough going with his first foray into federal economic policy making. For both Obama and Clinton, the changes in their goals or means to those goals were met by many—even their supporters—as capitulation or, worse, a betrayal of promised changes. Even when decision makers feel that circumstances require them to alter their policy goals or the ways toward those goals, they risk the backlash of those who see these changes as a sign of weakness or duplicity.

Shifting policy goals may result from changes in social, economic, or political factors, or a combination of all three. While the charge of political influence on goal shifts is very common, it is also difficult to substantiate. As the preceding examples illustrate, partisanship, ideology, or other prejudices shape the perception of goal shift. Are Obama and Clinton pragmatic political leaders who did the best they could for the nation in hard economic times, or are they merely politicians—in every negative sense of that word—who seek political advantage at the expense of ideals and promises? It is an old aphorism, but it does contain a grain of wisdom: where you sit depends on where you stand.

SHIFTING GOALS OF US POLICY IN IRAQ

The Issue

What are the political and policy-related dangers that come with changing the focus of policy goals? Must policy makers always stick with the original goal of a policy for us to view it as a success?

While this text is certainly not about US foreign policy making, an example drawn from our involvement in Iraq provides an especially bold case highlighting the reactions to the possible shifting of goals and how such shifts may be related to various stages of the policy-making process.

The Story

President Bush felt the sting of charges that his administration was changing the goals of our involvement in Iraq to suit developments on the ground. His detractors claimed that the US invasion and subsequent occupation was a failure because the president had to readjust the reason for our being there. Critics of the war have said that first the goal offered by the Bush administration was the elimination of weapons of mass destruction that they claimed Iraqis illegally possessed. When no major stockpiles of useable weapons were found after the invasion, critics noted the administration's shift in the goals of the nation's Iraq policy toward staunching the spread of global terrorism. When it appeared that the US occupation of Iraq may have increased membership in terrorist organizations intent on attacking US troops in Iraq and Americans around the world, the Bush administration—said its detractors—changed the policy goal in Iraq to stability in the Middle East. As Iran and Syria threatened to directly insert themselves in the low-level civil war taking place in Iraq, the Bush administration redrew the policy goals to focus on freedom and democracy for the Iraqi people. Finally, critics contend, with other goals having proved out of reach, the administration took one last stab at redefining the goals by using the military to provide a degree of stability for the Iraqi government so that they could take over the rebuilding of their own nation and we could start to remove our combat troops.

These charges, if correct, illustrate the difficulty of keeping the goals of a policy fixed in one place, time, or one result. If done out of a lack of attention or planning, such gyrations around the center point of the original policy goal underscore fundamental flaws in many if not all of the basic aspects of policy making. Borrowing some of the framework of the policy process model for a moment is a convenient way to illustrate the possible sources of shifts in goals:

• Was the problem correctly identified? Without delving into the briar patch concerning the justifications for the US invasion of Iraq, it is still possible to objectively conclude that the goals of the Bush administration had to shift once no weapons of mass destruction were found.

- Was the solution properly formulated? Many senior members of the US military called for Secretary of Defense Rumsfeld's resignation because they saw Rumsfeld's failure to plan properly for the occupation as the cause of the violent insurgency that followed the invasion. The resignation of Rumsfeld and the appointment of Robert Gates ushered in a policy shift toward the so-called surge, an increase in the number of troops, and a focus on using our forces to take and then hold key segments of Baghdad and elsewhere.
- Was the policy legitimized? The president was able to convince enough members of Congress that he was on the right track in Iraq to keep the funding for the mission flowing, even when there were shifts in the goals of the policy. However, a sizeable number of Americans were not won over by these arguments, and as his administration entered its final year, most Americans did not feel that the war in Iraq was worthwhile. According to an October 2008 Gallup poll, 58 percent of American's believed that it was a mistake to send US troops into Iraq.[i] It is possible that the president's approach to the conflict in Iraq was changed by the opposition to his ideas by both the Congress and the public.
- Was the policy implemented correctly? In the area of armed conflict, this question may be the most difficult to answer. As Union General Sherman noted during the American Civil War, "War is hell." Terrible things happen to innocent people. Some people demonstrate amazing forms of bravery and kindness, while others reveal the all-too human frailties of fear and cruelty. By most accounts, the men and women who have served and continue to serve in Iraq have done so with great professionalism. In all hierarchical organizations, such as the military, any evaluation of the execution of policy should be done at levels beginning above those in the field, since those on the line have little, if any, discretion in how they do their tasks. Given this standard, then, the Bush administration had difficulties with the implementation of its polices, ranging from a lack of oversight and training that led to the abuses of prisoners at Abu Ghraib prison to the inability of US units to get the proper armor-cladding for vehicles needed to carry out patrols. As these failures were uncovered, the negative reactions they produced did alter parts of the administration's Iraq policy and even personnel, as evidenced by the resignation of Donald Rumsfeld.

The Questions

- Are policies somehow flawed if their goals shift over time?
- Do changes in the implementation of a policy in light of unforeseen circumstances affect the legitimacy of that policy?
- Should we assume that those given the task of implementing policies must have the discretion to reshape the goals of the policies to fit the circumstances and resources that exist during implementation?
- Is oversight by Congress less of a concern when it comes to foreign policy? Should presidents have a greater degree of flexibility in the implementation of foreign policy than in domestic policy?

See for Yourself

Watch Bush's War at http://www.pbs.org/wgbh/pages/frontline/bushswar/view/ for a time line of the changes in the focus of US involvement in Iraq.

[iv]"Iraq." Gallup. http://www.gallup.com/poll/1633/Iraq.aspx (accessed February 11, 2013).

Success or Failure—Pulling the Goalposts Out of the Ground

The Chesapeake Bay is a phenomenal body of water on the east coast of the United States. A number of major rivers drain into the bay. It is a gateway to the Atlantic Ocean for commercial shipping and recreational boating. The bay is home to a vast number of species in the water, on the shore, and in the air above. Famous for its seafood and fishing, the bay is also quite polluted, and the once plentiful numbers of oysters and crabs have dwindled. There is no mystery about what has caused these things to happen; scientists are certain that human pollution from sewers, septic tanks, and fertilizer runoff from farming has fouled the water and overfishing has depleted what survives in the bay.[20]

In the 1980s, the federal government's Environmental Protection Agency went to work with state and local governments in the bay area and used millions of dollars of money appropriated by Congress to try to meet goals that would have reduced the amount of key pollutants by 40 percent in 2000. But as the cleanup project went along, it became clear to those involved that it would take more money than first thought to really improve the bay and that a number of powerful interests, mainly agricultural groups, industries, and municipalities, would fight any serious plans to rein in the flow of effluents into the bay. With the goals of the policy drifting out of reach, the EPA's Chesapeake office, the federal body in charge of the cleanup effort, may have first deceived themselves and then sought to fool others.

According to the General Accountability Office and other government investigators, the EPA claimed that it was making substantial progress toward its cleanup goals based on computer models of what could have happened given their efforts, but not on actual measurements of what did happen. When new EPA officials took over the Chesapeake office in 2002, a decision was made to claim that success was in the offing, even when the EPA's own internal data showed that the cleanup was far off track and would require $28 billon to succeed. According to one EPA official, "For us to declare defeat would mean we would have no chance ... of convincing the legislators to give us financing. ... Rather than declare defeat, we should work harder."[21] Apparently the bay is about as dead as it was when the cleanup began twenty-five years ago, but the EPA does not see this as a failure and instead points out that there have been reductions in the amount of pollution in the bay along with other improvements. In essence, they claim that they are succeeding. However, in terms of its overall health, the bay is still on the verge of complete ruin.[22]

Do the EPA's actions show a self-serving tendency to reconfigure the meaning of success for the purpose of holding onto or increasing power? While it may be true that the program was underfunded and under assault by powerful interests, its failure was not preordained; the deception surrounding the difficulty of achieving the goals was a long-term response to the complexity of the project. Even if the solution to the problem was inadequate or poorly conceived, it is hard to justify deception as a response to these shortcomings. This "disregarding of the goalposts" by losing but claiming to win does happen; when it takes place, we are often dismayed that policy makers and administrators would be so crass and self-serving. Yet, the EPA administrator who argued for playing fast and loose with the truth in order to continue to keep the program alive and making even marginal advances does provide a useful point. If political forces are aligned in such a way that the success of a policy is nearly impossible, is it justified for administrators to do what they can with what they have so that at least some good may come from their incomplete actions? The EPA's officials in this example were likely in sympathy with the desire to clean up the bay. While officials are sometimes appointed or otherwise placed in positions because of their opposition to the goals of an agency in order to carry out the contrary views of a president or to play Devil's advocate for a fresh view on the functioning of the agency, it is more common that administrators are drawn to work with goals they see as desirable. Could the EPA's Chesapeake office just have been attempting to surmount impossible political odds while still getting at least a modicum of positive progress from an unworkable policy solution? Expressed another way, can holding the status quo in the face of tremendous social, economic, and political difficulties ever be a policy victory? Clearly Congress and a number of states around Chesapeake Bay do not think so, and these doubts are at the heart of lawsuits by some states and investigations by Congress.

CONCLUSION: THE POLITICS OF OUTCOMES

The political aspects of public policy make judging success and failure a tricky task. All of the examples offered so far in this chapter are attempts to illustrate how the nature of the policies themselves, the actors inside and outside of government, and the policy environment all interact with one another in the course of applying solutions to problems. Just as problems and solutions can be interpreted in light of one's political beliefs, so too can the level of success or failure be affected by our beliefs about what is right and desirable. Table 7.1 is an endeavor to encapsulate the examples presented thus far in the chapter. What you are likely to see when you look at the figure is that, while it does map most of the major forms of policy outcomes in terms of the perception of success and failure as well as their actuality, it also helps to raise a few more points about the political aspects of public policy. The terms "perception" and "actuality" need a bit of attention first.

TABLE 7.1

The Perceptions and Realities of Policy Success and Failure

	Reality=Success	Reality=Failure	Reality=Mixed
Perception=Success	<ul><li>Goals are concretely defined and objectively achieved</li><li>"Win/Win"</li><li>Possible Example:?</li></ul>	<ul><li>Goals are concretely defined but do not solve the problem or cause new problems</li><li>"Winning but losing"</li><li>Possible Example: US economic problems in the post-WWII era</li></ul>	<ul><li>Goals are vaguely defined or shift over time</li><li>"Losing in some ways but winning in others," "Moving the goalposts"</li><li>Possible Example: US policy in Iraq</li></ul>
Perception=Failure	<ul><li>Goals are concretely defined but are not recognized as successes</li><li>"Lose/Win"</li><li>Possible Example: US foreign aid, some anticrime programs</li></ul>	<ul><li>Goals are concretely defined but are not met</li><li>"Lose/Lose"</li><li>Possible Example:?</li></ul>	<ul><li>Goals may be well defined or more broadly articulated</li><li>"Losing, but claiming to win"</li><li>Possible Example: Cleanup of the Chesapeake Bay</li></ul>
Perception=Mixed	<ul><li>Goals are concretely defined but are not met</li><li>Policy maker claims success for attempt</li><li>"Lose/win"</li><li>Possible Example: G. W. Bush's attempt to reform Social Security</li></ul>	<ul><li>Goals are concretely defined, but change OR goals are vaguely defined and shift to fit circumstances</li><li>"Shifting the target," "Losing in some ways but winning in others"</li><li>Possible Examples: Bush administration Iraq policy, Clinton and Obama's first budgets</li></ul>	<ul><li>Goals are vaguely defined OR shift</li><li>"Win/win," "Lose/lose," "Win/lose," etc.</li><li>Possible Examples: Any policy that does not have a finite measure of success</li></ul>

Since absolutes are hard to come by when human perception is involved, let us assume that if a majority of the public and policy makers call a policy a success, it is a success. Also, it can be reasonably argued that when it comes to the success or failure of a policy, reality may be made up of shades of grey rather than the stark black and white of the "truth." However, at least some objective benchmarks are likely to exist to judge the level of success of policy, even if the quality and usefulness of these benchmarks are open to debate. (For example, it is difficult to debate the efficacy of worldwide vaccination programs resulting in the near total eradication of a disease like polio.) If there is a consensus by a majority of objective policy observers and experts that a policy has done what it was created to do, then this gives us a basis to make a claim on the policy's actual success or failure.

One of the most notable features of the figure is that it provides question marks for possible examples of the "win/win" and "lose/lose" varieties. This is the case because these two are largely ideal types. As the examples drawn from the aftermath of World War II underscore, victory may not be absolute or permanent just as it is also true that defeat may harbor the seeds of future betterment. While some examples do exist, such as the efforts to do away with polio and smallpox, "knowing" that a policy has been an absolute success or failure is largely a belief born of conviction rather than a certainty supported by objective facts. There are also several boxes of the "mixed" type that utilize the same possible examples and terms to describe outcomes. This is so because perceptions of success are driven by beliefs in these cases, and the slippery character of the goals and outcomes does not provide a set of objective measures.

What Table 7.1 presents, in general terms, is a view of policy outcomes that underscores the political nature of the policies themselves. It is possible to claim that policies succeed or fail. However, with limited exceptions, there will not be near universal agreement about policy success or failure because the ideological and partisan views of policies in action and the residual attitudes about these policies spawned by the politics of their creation are likely to reinforce preexisting beliefs about the efficacy of the policies. While it has become a truism in American thought that Roosevelt's New Deal saved the nation during the Great Depression, there were and still are sizeable numbers of Americans who see these policies as negative developments that grew government and choked off freedom for individuals. You may be thinking that when confronted with the facts about the performance of a policy, belief will melt away and the truth will take its place, and, in many cases, this does happen. However, our system of policy making ensures that the policies that are made have the imprint of the makers on them. Because of this, the imperfections and inequities of humankind are part of even the most judiciously crafted policy. Returning to the themes established in the earlier chapters of the text, recall that debate, deliberation, and compromise—those essential elements of American democracy—reflect the representative quality of our political system. While we may bemoan the slowness, parochialism, and inefficiency of this system, it is the cost of representation in the policy process.

Since we intuitively and, perhaps, subconsciously see policy as a political substance, are we always predisposed to think negatively about outputs of the process and those who carry policies into action, just as we scoff at policy makers as mere "politicians"? Culturally, our nation tends to downgrade the usefulness or importance of government and policy. Our civil servants are "bureaucrats," a pejorative term in most uses. Appointees are seen as getting "plum jobs" because of their connections or for attributes other than their skills as administrators and leaders. Government itself is unwieldy and wasteful. (A number of idioms come to mind, such as saying "close enough for government work" when someone does a slipshod job.) Policies are "undue burdens" and "red tape." Yet, these default views of policy, government, and those charged with carrying out policy are mostly the creation of our thoughts over more than two centuries as a nation. There are countless jokes and sayings reflecting our dislike or distrust of these matters, yet our most typical experiences with government and its policies are fairly ordinary and benign. We pay our taxes, perhaps grudgingly, but with some general notion that they will go toward that which we could not do own our own, such as plowing the snow from the roads, maintaining parks, or educating our children. Yes, many of us have an anecdote or a few of them about the clerk at such and such a government office that was not that courteous or helpful, but these instances need to be placed in context of all the times, noticed or not, when those carrying out policy did a good job.

All policies cannot be tragically flawed and all those in the government cannot be dreadfully incompetent in all instances. While the opposite is also not likely, it is safe to claim that policies are often fairly well thought out and generally correctly implemented. What, then, is to account for our collective pessimism about the implementation of policy and the quality of the policies themselves? President John Kennedy was fond of saying that success has many parents but failure is an orphan. Policies that fail because of incorrect problem identification, formulation, or bad implementation rightfully attract attention from all the same sources that have been discussed in the preceding chapters of this text that focused on how policy is made. Outside of government, the media, interest groups and their patrons such as corporations and labor unions, social movements, and lesser organized entities routinely blast government policy makers and administrators when things do not go well. There is little wrong with this and much that is good about such actions. Exposing the shortcomings of both the policy and the administration of the policy is a crucial activity in a republic. (It is also something that government itself does on an ongoing basis through activities like legislative oversight.) Many of the turning points of policy change in our history were reached through the efforts of these actors. The civil rights movement of the late 1950s and early 1960s forced the nation to see the inherent inequality in the policy of "separate but equal" that was created by the Supreme Court's decision in the 1896 case of *Plessey v. Ferguson*. The maltreatment of Iraqi prisoners held in US custody was pounded upon by the news media in what seemed like a never-ending slide show of pictures that illustrated the abuses. This pressure caused a number of changes in our detainee policies.

The examples of malfeasance, incompetence, indifference, and countless other shades of poor policy making and execution are numerous and, when exposed, can provide a positive spur toward correcting problems. However, if shortcomings in policy making, implementation, or the policies themselves are inflated or even invented, then a line has been crossed over which the drive for political or other gain has pushed ahead of a utilitarian goal of assuring fairness and equity. Because policy, policy making, and carrying policy into action are all political matters, there is something many players may gain by attacking each of these facets of public policy. Much of our cynicism and dislike about public policy comes from the adversarial exchanges we witness on a daily basis between its creators and its administrators, and those outside of this loop who have a stake in the policies and their impacts. The line is a fine one that separates useful criticism from negativity aimed at gaining advantage. How are we to know the truth of such matters? The golden mean applies here. Complete cynicism would cause us to throw up our hands and say "we can never know." Total faith would lead us to intone "we should never question." In the middle there is room for healthy skepticism; knowing that politics is fully intertwined with public policy should make us aware of the motivations of policy actors and their creations, but does not mean that all policies and their results are necessarily "bad" because of their interconnections with politics. In fact, as has been argued throughout this text, politics is not simply a necessary evil when it comes to public policy; it is the essential stuff of policy in a democracy.

SUMMARY

We all engage in some form of policy evaluation. Much of what we do as citizens when we think about the success or failure of public policies takes the form of ad hoc, impressionist policy evaluation. Policy analysis is a more rigorous form of evaluation, often undertaken by professional analysts inside and outside the government and using quantitative tools of analysis. Evaluation can focus on the outputs of the policy-making process (i.e., the programs created to solve a problem), on the policy outcomes (i.e., the effects that programs have on ameliorating the problem itself), or on both outputs and outcomes.

The evaluation of policy outputs and outcomes is highly political given its potential to affect policies by maintaining, expanding, limiting, or eliminating them altogether. Actors in the policy-making process, both inside and outside of government, have vested interests in the interpretation of evaluation since the continuation of a policy affects the concrete, symbolic, and political rewards and status that actors gain by their position in the policy-making process. Agreeing on goals and benchmarks indicating progress toward goals is as contentious an endeavor as identifying the correct nature of a problem itself. The values, beliefs, and views of the proper scope of governmental action of those involved are likely to shape these most basic building blocks of evolution. Additionally, the means to measure progress toward the solving of problems is often expressed in terms of costs and benefits, two concepts that open up an additional zone of conflict about just what is tolerable and desirable among the many actors in the policy-making process.

The ideas of winning and losing are often used to express our understanding of success or failure of public policies. A basic "horse race" format forms much of our view of policy evaluation and this amplifies its political nature. If a policy fails to deliver the promised result, it may be seen as a political millstone around the necks of its makers. Yet, as straightforward as such a framework may seem on the surface, winning and losing are not easily defined concepts. The range of examples in the chapter that demonstrate the vagaries of a "win/lose" approach illustrate the multiple ways that these terms can be interpreted and manipulated to skew the outcomes and impacts of policies.

While it is tempting to give in to cynicism when faced with the ways that evaluation can be distorted by those who seek to gain political advantage or who are simply motivated by their own political predilections, it is worth remembering that evaluation is not an objective exercise. Evaluation is a reflection on our political selves in all the same ways that the other parts of the policy-making process—from problem identification through implementation—mirror us as political actors.

DISCUSSION QUESTIONS

1. Why do outside actors engage in policy evaluation? What abilities do they have to influence evaluation and what do they hope to gain by doing so?
2. Why is it so difficult to reach a consensus on the measurement of progress toward reaching policy goals? Is there some objective way of creating benchmarks to indicate progress? Do the types of policies that are being evaluated influence what is used to carry out the measurements of evaluation?
3. Policy outputs and policy outcomes are two distinct concepts. Is it more important to evaluate the outputs or the outcomes of the policy-making process? Of the policy examples discussed in the chapter, are there any that you would see as having successful outputs but failed outcomes? Is it possible to have failed policy outputs but successful outcomes?
4. A number of the examples found in the chapter feature policy actors that manipulate the meaning of goals, change the benchmarks for success, or in other ways reinvent the ways evaluation takes place to support their goals or positions. Are such actions ever justifiable? If so, under what conditions or circumstances do you see such actions as having a valid purpose?
5. If evaluation does not always provide an objective picture of the success or failure of outputs and outcomes, is policy evaluation worth doing at all? What potential benefits can evaluation provide to the actors inside and outside of government and to our democracy as a whole?

NOTES

1. For a discussion of the roots of this difference, see Anderson, James E. *Public policymaking*. 3rd ed. Boston: Houghton Mifflin, 1997. 272–273.
2. Wilson, James Q. "On Pettigrew and Armor: An Afterward." *National Affairs* Winter, no. 30 (1973): 133.

3. Nachmias, David. "The Role of Evaluation in Public Policy." *Policy Studies Journal* 8, no. 7 Special Number 3 (1980): 1163.

4. Thompson, Kimberly M., and Radboud J. Duintjer. "Retrospective Cost-Effectiveness Analyses for Polio Vaccination in the United States." *Risk Analysis* 26, no. 6 (2006): 1423–1440.

5. Stuart, Reginald. *Bailout: The story behind America's billion dollar gamble on the "new" Chrysler Corporation.* South Bend, IN: And Books, 1980. 10–11.

6. Hyde, Charles K. *Riding the roller coaster: A history of the Chrysler Corporation.* Detroit: Wayne State University Press, 2003. 224.

7. Ibid.

8. Stuart, 150.

9. Reich, Robert B., and John D. Donahue. *New deals: The Chrysler revival and the American system.* New York: Times Books, 1985. 265.

10. Ibid.

11. As quoted in Reich and Donahue, 270–271.

12. Ibid.

13. Bozzo, Albert. "After Auto Rescue: Bailout Fund Is Under Fire Again." CNBC. http://www.cnbc.com/id/28327001 (accessed February 11, 2013).

14. "Are Obama, GOP hopefuls fibbing on auto bailout claims?" *USA Today.* http://content.usatoday.com/communities/driveon/post/2012/02/fact-check-on-gop-candidate-and-obama-auto-bailout-claims/1#.T5GDftl6nBY (accessed February 11, 2013).

15. Bush, George W. Interview with CNN, December 18, 2008.

16. Edwards, George C. *Governing by campaigning: The politics of the Bush presidency.* 2007 ed. New York: Pearson Longman, 2008. 218–220.

17. Edwards, 268–269.

18. Edwards, 279.

19. "Senate Snuff Boxes." Senate.gov. www.senate.gov/vtour/snufb.htm (accessed February 11, 2013).

20. Fahrenthold, David A. "Broken Promises on the Bay." *Washington Post.* http://articles.washingtonpost.com/2008-12-27/news/36808847_1_william-matuszeski-watermen-cleanup (accessed February 11, 2013).

21. Ibid.

22. Ibid.

The Future of the Politics of Public Policy

CHAPTER OBJECTIVES

When you finish reading Chapter 8, you should be able to do the following:

- Identify the factors that lead to incremental policy making
- Summarize the workings of the prisoners' dilemma

- Illustrate how the basic elements of our political world are relatively stable over time
- Use the concept of political time to show how past instances of policy making are related to present ones

"When life looks like easy street,
there is danger at your door."

−Lyrics from the song "Uncle John's Band" by the Grateful Dead

Uncertainty about the future is a constant part of life. Outside of the pull of gravity and the daily arrival and departure of the sun from the sky, there is much that is open to change in our daily existence. We assume that water is going to flow from the tap in the morning when we prepare coffee or brush our teeth, but there is no absolute guarantee that it will be so. Pipes freeze, water mains break, and bills go unpaid. As the song lyrics found above rather pessimistically attest, even when there is no hazard in sight, the prospect of a problem emerging is always very likely. While there is little to be gained from going around constantly worrying about the possible "danger at your door," the existence of problems is about as near a constant in our lives as gravity or the rising and setting of the sun.

In thinking about the future of the politics of public policy there is no reason to go back to square one and prognosticate about whether or not there will be public problems that require solutions. A simple glance at the front page of your daily newspaper or a look at the first few minutes of a TV newscast will prove this. Nor will politics disappear from policy. This is a good thing. Broadly speaking, politics is the struggle through which our will is expressed. In its various forms, it assures representation and deliberation. Of course, politics does not promise maximum freedom or equality for anyone, and it can be subverted for improper or unwise purposes. Like the existence of problems, the need for politics is about as constant as we are likely to find in our lives. What is more subject to alteration and what will influence how we view problems and policies are the environmental aspects of these constants, including the nature of change, power, and the actors within the policy system.

THE DEGREE OF CHANGE AND THE POLICY-MAKING ENVIRONMENT

The degree of change is a fundamental characteristic of public policy. Incremental and massive changes mark the polar opposites of the continuum of change that can be brought about by the policy process. Sometimes change is highly desirable. The 2008 presidential election featured two candidates, McCain and Obama, who both spoke about bringing change to the country. Public opinion polls showed that the nation was tired of George W. Bush and hungry for someone to tackle the serious problems that lingered or were emerging. To say that 2008 was a "change election" is not a statement that will find many detractors. Certainly the election of Obama, our first African-American president, signaled a significant change in the public's attitudes about race in this country.

At other times, change is far less desirable. For a person who goes to a community food pantry or free soup kitchen for the first time because of a layoff or reduced hours, the change can tear at the person's sense of self-worth and place in the world. For the millions of Americans now finding themselves in such a position for the first time, change is anything but good.

Culturally, America contains conflicting desires when it comes to change. We honor tradition and revere our history, at least in part. Yet, our history is one built on change. It is as though the nation's mantra has always been "bigger, faster, stronger, louder, newer . . . ." We generally seek change as a curative for what ails us when we sense a problem. It is true that there are times when the change called for is to roll back changes in order to return to a time of plenty or peace. In 1920, President Harding campaigned on a pledge to "return to normalcy." In 1980, Ronald Reagan promised a return to the days of a smaller federal government. In 2008, even with its fixation on the future, Barack Obama's campaign tipped its hat to the better economic days of the Clinton years in the 1990s. Indeed, sometimes change is presented as retrograde motion.

The boldest measure of change is not its direction but its degree. A financial crisis, one that may be only eclipsed by the Great Depression of the 1930s, struck the nation in late 2008 and early 2009. The federal, state, and local governments faced a highly uncertain future. What existing programs could continue to receive funding? What new policies would be created to stabilize key parts of the economy? What other policies would be required to stoke the economy so that there would be jobs and continued consumer spending? No matter which level of government is considered or the type of policy considered, the one unifying characteristic of the changes being considered and acted upon was that they were extensive. In the fall of 2008, the Congress passed a $700 billion bailout for the nation's financial sector. At the time, the amount of money was staggering to most people's ears. Newscasters would routinely inject that this was $700 billion with a "B," so that the viewing public would realize that this allotment of money was not a trifling $700 *million*. While both sums are a great deal of money for most Americans, the continual exposure to large dollar amounts—both as spending amounts and as budget shortfalls—may have sanded off the rough edges of the big numbers and, whether accepting of their need or stunned by their magnitude, discussing and thinking about hundreds of billions of dollars or more has become commonplace.

While incremental movement from an existing position is the common degree of change for most policies in the United States, there are times, such as the present, when sweeping changes come about. John Kingdon views these moments as the opening of policy "windows."[1] Like the windows in any house, they are not always open and, like those found in older homes, require a bit of leverage to raise. Kingdon envisions different "streams" of politics, policy, and problems that need to come together in the right amounts and at the right time in order to pop open a policy window. For example, a policy solution often requires a political change in order for the policy to come into being. The recent economic crisis facing the United States produced a boatload of problems, and the entrance of a new presidential administration prompted a majority of the public in opinion polls to feel that these problems would be taken on and maybe solved by new policies and bold actions. Without the weakening economy in the fall of 2008, would this change in party control of the presidency have taken place? What is clearer is that without the myriad economic problems facing the incoming Obama administration, there would have been no need for the new policies swirling around Washington immediately following the new president's inauguration.

In any other time, with a "normal" amount of uncertainty and unease about the future, policy making in the United States might have a suitable fit with the incremental form of policy making that Charles Lindblom used to describe and, in some ways, prescribe for the nation.[2] For Lindblom, our system of public policy making largely "muddles through" a process that produces workable, if not always optimal, solutions to problems. These policies are usually small changes to the existing baseline of what already exists, reflecting the design and evolution of our political system and its numerous and countervailing points of pressure. Vast and sweeping policy change is unlikely in such a world because a form of political centripetal force pushes on the policy-making process in a way similar to how gravity presses us to the earth. Movement is possible, but it will not be great; you can jump into the air a foot or so, but not leap up to the clouds. This containment of the degree of change means continuity in our policies, a general limitation on overly activist government, and a reflection of the general will of the public as expressed through the many channels of representation in a republic. But these are not ordinary times.

While dire predictions abound on the fringes of political discourse—that Obama would somehow end capitalism in the United States, to mention one oft-repeated claim—much of what has come from Washington, the state capitols, and local governments fits with past practices, only this time the changes have come in massive doses. Sluggish economies have been receiving infusions of spending or other versions of a government stimulus at least since the acceptance of the economic theories of John Maynard Keynes in the 1930s. President George W. Bush called for and Congress produced a stimulus package in January 2008 as the economy cooled off. Of course, the underlying problems of that initial cooling period did not go away, and the later crisis required a far more massive stimulus program. While much greater in scope, the actions taken by both the federal and state governments in the wake of the financial crisis were, for the most part, fairly predictable, if still shocking in their extent. This is not to say that innovation did not take place or that none should be expected. What is important to note is that even during times of economic, social, and political turbulence or upheaval, the forms of policy change are often similar from era to era. A concept drawn from the study of presidential leadership is instructive in this regard.

Steven Skowronek posits that individual presidencies can be compared across what he calls "political time," based on the health of the dominant partisan regime in power at the time.[3] Some presidents build regimes or governing coalitions, others preside over established orders, while some struggle in the space between the death of an old regime and the birth of the new. In this way, presidents as distant in years as Andrew Jackson and Franklin Roosevelt can be placed in the same slice of regime building time. Using Skowronek's framework in a slightly different way, it is possible to make the case that policy making fits into a similar set of patterns, at least at the federal level. In times of crisis—political, economic, or social—comprehensive change is far more likely because the established order has broken down. It is as though the gravity of the earth has dissipated for a time and we can now launch ourselves above the treetops. This change may be permanent, but only if the crisis is disruptive enough to require or allow structural changes to what now exists. In 1964 and again in 1965, the Civil Rights Act and then the Voting Rights Act reflected the successful challenges to the social and political order in the United States brought about by the civil rights movement. Perhaps more dramatic still were the collection of economic changes that were part of the New Deal of the 1930s. The creation of the Social Security system for older Americans in jeopardy of living out their years in poverty was unthinkable for most before the Great Depression.

THE APPROPRIATENESS OF POLICY SOLUTIONS

It would be convenient if there were an unambiguous ratio between the intensity of a crisis and the policy response from government. Categorization could then be possible. If we are experiencing an "A level" crisis, then the application of policy "B" is required. Or we could look historically and understand the true nature of a crisis facing the nation by noting the form and scope of the policy response. This can be done, but only to a minor degree, because it assumes that other intervening factors do not exist or are very minor if they are present. Such an approach is similar to that taken by biologists when they place a specimen on the surface of a jelled Petri dish and await the growth of bacteria. Only a controlled environment will grow the sample into its true self. If there is contamination, the outcome of the incubation is unclear. What is policy making but a collection of influences? Because of the politics involved in every facet of the process, there are multitudes of "contaminants" that make it extremely difficult to know if a policy is or was the appropriate response to a problem. The term "appropriate" is suspect in and of itself, too.

TABLE 8.1		
Prisoners' Dilemma		
	Prisoner 2 Confess	Prisoner 2 Profess Innocence
Prisoner 1 Confess	Both get reduced sentence	Prisoner 1 gets reduced sentence, prisoner 2 gets maximum sentence
Prisoner 1 Profess Innocence	Prisoner 1 gets maximum sentence, prisoner 2 gets reduced sentence	Both go free!

Rational choice theorists have attempted to formulate measures of outcomes that objectively evaluate the usefulness of policy choices. In the famous "prisoners' dilemma," two people are picked up by the police and held in separate interrogation rooms. The police have a strong suspicion that both suspects committed the crime, but they lack enough hard evidence to make the case stand up in court. What they need is a confession.

While both suspects are equally guilty, there are different outcomes available to them if they play their roles in certain ways. For "ratting" on one's accomplice, a suspect will implicate him or herself, but get a shorter sentence than if he or she professed their joint innocence. The other prisoner is faced with the same set of choices and possible outcomes. What is the "smart" thing to do? Given the knowledge that one's partner in crime will probably take the route of self-interest, "ratting" is the sure way to avoid the full penalty for the crime, but it is not the best outcome. The "best" or optimal outcome for both would come from each criminal saying nothing or professing their mutual innocence, but this is very risky since if one prisoner makes this claim and the other provides a confession, the full sentence will be given to the "innocent" prisoner. What is likely to happen, say rational choice theorists, is that both prisoners will follow their self-interest and "rat" on one another. Each would then get the suboptimal outcome, that of the reduced sentence, but the optimal outcome of freedom will not come about. The lesson from this exercise in game theory is that human behavior and tendencies lean toward the production of suboptimal outcomes. It is possible to take from this exercise the notion that fuller knowledge about the factors surrounding decisions and how they will produce outcomes will allow us to make better policy choices. However, when are decision makers ever presented with choices that are as straightforward and unambiguous as those found in the prisoners' dilemma? Much of what takes place in the real world of policy making is confusing and highly uncertain in terms of both the factors influencing decisions and what to make of the effect policies have on problems. This is not to say that gaining information about decisions and outcomes is a waste of time, but it should be recognized that even superhuman efforts at the gathering and analysis of data will not necessarily produce optimal outcomes, as is depicted by something like the prisoners' dilemma.

Returning to the term "appropriate" for a moment brings us back to a well-mined vein in this text. Perhaps seeking an outcome that is of a sufficient quantity and quality that it is objectively seen as "best" is an unreachable goal. "Best," like what constitutes a problem and how to go about solving it, is political, too. "Appropriate" implies that a policy solution is adequate to the challenge formed by the problem. It is neither too little nor too much. One of the first tasks facing the incoming Obama administration was crafting a stimulus proposal that would ameliorate the effects of the economic recession either by increasing consumer and business spending, spurring job creation, or both. Many economists, among them some who worked for conservative Republican presidents, advocated a massive stimulus proposal on the order of $850 billion. They said that anything less than this would not have the desired effect on the economy. While this level of spending may be substantively appropriate to the task, is it politically appropriate? Such a spending proposal immediately raised the ire of fiscally conservative Republicans and Democrats in the Congress. The popular media sometimes portrays the two parties as caricatures of their more complex true selves, with the Republicans opposed to most government spending and Democrats free and easy with taxing and spending, but the reality is not as narrow as this depiction suggests. While it is fairly accurate to state that Democrats in Congress have traditionally been more inclined to advocate the use of programs and policies—which do cost money—to solve the nation's problems as they see them, Republicans are not immune to these tendencies either. For much of the first six years of President Bush's two terms in office, the Republicans held the majority in the House and Senate. During this time, the size of the federal government grew and costly programs and policies were put into place, such as the pricey Medicare Prescription Part D program that cost around $40 billion in 2008 to provide senior citizens with needed medicines.[4] Just as labeling all Republicans as fiscally conservative is inaccurate, it is equally imprecise to claim that all Democrats are spendthrifts. Members of the Blue Dog Caucus in the House of Representatives, a group of Democrats, are well-known for their shared dislike of spending that increases the size of the federal budget deficit.

Given well-established viewpoints of many Republicans and Democrats about the undesirability of enlarging the nation's budget deficit, any proposal to spend $850 billion on top of the $700 billion appropriated by Congress in the fall of 2008 was bound to meet with strong resistance. While the need for a stimulus was a widely shared belief in Washington, how big it should be and the target for this influx of spending was in dispute. Any effort to pass such a sizeable spending package was bound to encounter difficulties in Congress, and this one was no exception. Past presidents such as Ronald Reagan and Bill Clinton spent much of the political goodwill they garnered from their elections in efforts to pull the Congress into their respective corners. In Clinton's case, only the tie-breaking vote of his vice president, Al Gore, saved his first budget from defeat. Going all out to win a policy battle is worthwhile if the effort is

justasc/Shutterstock

successful. But what if the endeavor fails? A politically wounded president and a possibly divided Democratic Party in Congress would not be a strong start for the Obama administration. Any policy maker facing a similar financial crisis might see wisdom in seeking a smaller policy goal. In Obama's case, a stimulus package that totaled something much less than $850 billion, perhaps half that amount, would have had an easier time passing Congress. In the end, the bill topped out at $787 billion, including $70 billion in tax cuts. The battle to pass the stimulus was difficult and highly partisan with only three Republicans voting for it in the Senate and with no Republican support in the House of Representatives.[5] This vote made it easy for Republicans to wash their hands of the results of the policy, good or bad. There is some consensus that the stimulus "worked" in that it staved off a more serious economic crisis and that it helped to create millions of jobs. Yet, public opinion on the success of the stimulus is very mixed,[6] and the slow pace of the recovery has given the public lingering doubts about Obama's leadership on the economy. Is it better to seek "half a loaf" because it provides political advantages and the perception of forward movement on a problem even though it is not enough to adequately solve a problem, or is the "adequate" solution one that requires the players to win or lose it all on an all-out bid to go for the bigger prize?

These possibilities about the various paths that could lead to a stimulus package illustrate the place where what is substantively appropriate to the task and what is politically appropriate overlap and may cross-pollinate one another. Recalling the prisoners' dilemma may remind us that even in far less complex situations than what would take place in the struggle to pass a $787 billon stimulus package, the prisoners' lack of complete information and their own self-interest will likely bring them to a fairly undesirable outcome. The level of complexity found in the stimulus struggle easily dwarfs that faced by the two prisoners, and this helps make the prospect for a suboptimal outcome even more likely. The increase in the number of players, the level of uncertainly about both the problem and possible solutions, and variations in how the rules of the process can be applied in pursuit of any solution make the drive toward a stimulus package daunting, indeed. Given all these variables, claims about knowing just what is substantively adequate for solving a problem may be, at best, guesses. The players in the process are likely to know this at some level and such ambiguity provides an additional opening for political calculations in the actions of the players.

The successful creation of policy may not quell feelings that the policy is inadequate, flawed, or politically disadvantageous. The passage of the Patient Protection and Affordable Care Act, often referred to as "Obamacare," was a landmark change in the nation's health insurance policy and one achieved at great political costs to the president and the Democrats in Congress. Backers of the legislation argued that it was needed to control spiraling health care costs, stabilize a sector of our economy that will soon account for nearly one-fifth the money spent in the United States,[7] and assure medical coverage for the millions who lacked insurance. The bill's detractors saw it as a boondoggle; a massively complex piece of regulatory machinery that would stifle the free market and ultimately harm the public. No Republicans voted for the bill and the Democrats were left with complete ownership of the policy. The law was challenged by a number of groups and states. Ultimately, the Supreme Court provided a mixed decision on the law in the summer of 2012, but upheld the constitutionality of its requirement for universal health insurance coverage. With the 2012 elections looming, the political fallout from the law left even Democrats wondering if they did the right thing in crafting a policy that did so much to change the existing system of health care coverage, with some members of Congress openly saying that the policy should have been made "in digestible pieces that the American public could understand and that we could implement."[8] Retiring Democratic House member and health care policy champion, Barney Frank, summed up the situation by stating that "the Democrats paid a terrible price for health care."[9]

Even if we were to know what was "best" or substantively adequate, the influence of politics would not necessarily be muted. (Of course, this does not consider whether or not it should be muted. As has been argued elsewhere in this text, depending on how it is conceptualized, politics is not necessarily a negative factor in public policy; in fact, politics is likely a desirable part of policy making and implementation since it provides opportunities for representation, deliberation, and oversight.) The presence of consensus on a proposal that embodied the "best" solution might actually increase the struggle over its enactment precisely because of this agreement. If all the players agree on the goal, it may free them to bargain harder for particular concessions in the present proposal or for concessions in future dealings on other policies. This is so because it is clear that the other players have a stake in turning the proposal into action. The same principle is at work when buying a car at a dealership. If you walk into a dealership and say to the salespeople, "I really want this car and this is how much I can pay," they are going to try to extract more money from you because they know that you truly want the vehicle. If a potential buyer enters the showroom and says, "I was considering getting a different car, but I am not really sold on any of your models" and the buyer does not state what his or her budget limit is for a car purchase, the salespeople will have to be willing to cut their profit margin to reel in such a shopper.

In such a situation there is also likely to be a sense on the part of all actors that since the general goal is agreed upon, then there should be bargaining and maybe a chance of using the policy-making process to allow everyone involved the chance to get a bit more for themselves and their constituents. This is fairly typical in the legislative process, for instance, when Congress is reauthorizing existing programs and members place amendments or riders in a bill so that they can either symbolically or concretely gain an advantage from the legislation that was not there in the first place and which may not be all that germane to the main intent of the bill. For example, in the struggle over the reauthorization of the federal highway legislation in 2004, Senator Judd Gregg, a fiscally conservative Republican from New Hampshire, introduced the "Public Safety Employer-Employee Cooperation Act of 2003," an amendment that would, if passed, give police and firefighters the right to form unions.[10] What did this have to do with the amount of funds each state would receive from the reauthorization of the highway fund? Nothing, but that was not the point. Senator Gregg wanted to use the amendment to get a better funding deal for his state, and the amendment was a way to hold the bill hostage until he did. In the years just after 9/11 it was nearly impossible for anyone to cast a vote in an election year that might be construed as harming firefighters and police officers, but few Republicans would be interested in voting for an amendment that bolstered the power of unions, a traditional foe of the party. Gregg boxed in his party and its leadership in the Senate. In the end, his gambit did not pay off; his state had one of the lowest payouts for highway funding in the new act.[11]

In sum, in terms of the substantive appropriateness of solutions, the future of policy making in the United States is highly likely to feature a mixture of incremental and more comprehensive degrees of change. Lindblom's ideas about muddling through are usually applicable in describing and, to a less certain degree, predicting what will happen in the future. Most existing programs that provide services for a large section of the public or that are deemed essential to the nation's well-being are likely to continue, albeit with fairly minor programmatic and budgetary changes. This is less a prediction than a restatement of what always has been. Even in a crisis, like the one in which we recently found ourselves, the ossification of decades of programs and policies often dating back to the New Deal era has produced stability or stasis in US policy because the interests and institutions that hold a stake in the continuation of these policies and programs have grown in around them in a protective shell. This inertia is hard to shake and only at times of crisis or lower level conflict does it wane. In 1996, Bill Clinton did sign into law a welfare reform bill that did away with Aid for Families with Dependent Children (AFDC) and created Temporary Assistance for Needy Families (TANF) in its place. The change was large and quite noteworthy in a number of respects, not the least of which is that the new program gave a great deal of control over welfare policy to the states, control that was previously held by the federal government. Also important is that the change was precipitated by a major electoral victory in the US Congress for the Republicans in the 1994 midterm elections. Add to this the fact that Democrat Clinton probably wanted to remove the issue of what to do about the nation's troubled welfare system as an issue from the 1996 presidential election. Furthermore, such policy change as large in scope and impact as this one might have been easier to pull off because it affected mostly the poor in this country, a part of the population that is generally unable to shape or deflect shifts in policy because of its lack of organization and political clout.

Massive, comprehensive change is possible in the future. The passage of the Patient Protection and Affordable Care Act in 2010 is a clear example of such a change in the recent past. As noted earlier in this chapter, it is possible to think about political time as well as time in the familiar mode of a continuous progression of days, weeks, months, and years. These eras of political time revolve around the creation, maintenance, and ultimate decay of governing coalitions. Franklin Roosevelt and Andrew Jackson exist in the same epoch of political time because they are regime builders. They put together new party organizations or revamped those in existence while drawing in support from many additional sources for their visions of governing and policy. While crisis provided the targets for action in Roosevelt's case and less so in Jackson's, it was the successful construction of a governing coalition that allowed for successful policy making aimed at solving those problems. The key to understanding if comprehensive policy change is possible for the future is not that massive problems now exist that would seem to require concomitant policy solutions. That is only half the equation. The ability to overcome the intentionally fractured system of governing we have in the United States comes not from the ferocity of the challenges or the "rightness" of the possible solutions. Rather, it comes from politics, because only through the political forms and processes at our disposal in this country can fundamental changes to our social, economic, and—yes—political orders take place and be sustained. Short of the successful building of a governing regime that can last longer than the life span of the immediate dangers surrounding us, US policy making is likely to remain in an incremental mode, even in the face of crisis.

A LESS POLITICAL POLICY WORLD?

> What the cynics fail to understand is that the ground has shifted beneath them—that the state of political arguments that have consumed us for so long no longer apply. The question we ask today is not whether our government is too big or too small, but whether it helps families find jobs at a decent wage, care they can afford, a retirement that is dignified. Where the answer is yes, we intend to move forward. Where the answer is no, programs will end.
>
> —President Obama's inauguration speech, January 20, 2009

One striking feature of public opinion around this time of change in the nation's capitol was a hope that our politics would change. Perhaps that, if not eliminated, politics would be a lesser factor in policy making and governing during the difficulties presented by the financial crisis that greeted the incoming presidency of Barack Obama. The newly sworn-in president seemed to say as much in his inaugural speech when he spoke of old political arguments no longer applying because of the change in circumstances attributable to the crisis. Like most of the men who have attained the presidency, Obama has a fairly keen understanding of politics and we can assume that he knows that change is not synonymous with elimination. His call to change as a main campaign theme might be interpreted by some observers as a desire to do away with politics, but a closer reading of Obama's early actions as president indicate that he was seeking to reorder the political aspects of the nation's policy making and governing, not eradicate them entirely.

During the period of time before his first inauguration, much was made of President Obama's reading Doris Kearns Goodwin's, *A Team of Rivals*, her history of President Lincoln's tenure in office in which he surrounded himself with many of his political competitors, including some who sought the presidency that he ultimately won in 1860. Would Obama do as Lincoln did and place rivals, even from the opposition party, in his cabinet? His chief rival for the Democratic Party's nomination was Senator Hillary Clinton, and Obama did select her as his secretary of state. He also included a few Republicans in his cabinet, the most notable being Robert Gates as secretary of defense, a holdover from George W. Bush's administration (later replaced by a Democratic Party stalwart, Leon Panetta). These are noteworthy actions for any president because they intimate a willingness to govern in ways that break with traditional partisan viewpoints. However, while it is interesting to try to draw parallels between one president and another in this way, the political, social, and economic environment must be considered in such comparisons. Lincoln served in office during a crisis that dwarfs what any other president, with the possible exception of Franklin Roosevelt, has experienced. The survival of the nation was truly at stake. Like all presidents, Lincoln had to work with the political materials around him in his time, and we cannot know what his second term in office would have brought to the nation in terms of either policy or style. We do know that his Republican Party became increasing factious after his death and, while it held power for much of what scholars demark as the third and fourth party eras (roughly 1860–1932), this was anything but a time of decreasingly partisan policy making and governing. Lincoln's presence through his second term and even beyond might have changed this outcome only to the degree that he could have built a governing coalition that could survive the end of the war and the pains of reconstruction. He may have been able to firmly imprint the party with an inclusive and less partisan governing style. Lincoln's election in 1860 is one of two "classic" or "complete" realigning elections, 1932 is the other, which are agreed upon by most scholars. As FDR was able to build a long-lasting coalition out of not just his election but Democratic policies in the years following 1932, so too Lincoln could have possibly created a long-lasting force in American politics and policy.

The story line is almost too tempting not to write. Two unlikely and generally unknown politicians from Illinois seek the presidency. Both are tall and considered to be eloquent speakers. They come to office in a time of national crisis. They are considered by some to be beyond partisan politics. (There were some party scholars who described the 2008 election as the beginning of the post-partisan era when partisanship would be a lesser factor in our politics; they saw Obama as our first post-partisan president.) While the similarities are often intriguing, they are also generally superficial. A key distinction between Lincoln and Obama's election is that 1860 was a true realignment of the party system and 2008 was not. In 1860, an existing party, the Whig Party, was displaced by the newly formed Republican Party. The main characteristics of realignment, including a clear and polar opposite stance on the major issue or issues of the day from the other party or parties and a wholesale shift in party identification from one party to another by the public, are not comparable between 1860 and 2008. In terms of the vote itself, while Obama's margin of victory is impressive given the closeness of a number of the most recent presidential contests, it is nowhere near the order of magnitude of FDR in 1936, LBJ in 1964, Nixon in 1972, or Reagan in 1984. John McCain clearly lost the 2008 election, but he still garnered a solid share of the popular vote. Was Obama's victory a partial realignment or what some have dubbed a secular realignment in that it encompasses some of the aspects of the full-blown item but not all of them? This may be so, but partial realignments, if real phenomena, produce circumscribed policy changes and are of shorter duration than their complete versions. The colossal gains made by the Republican Party in the midterm congressional elections of 2010 and the bruising fights over health care reform, the nation's debt ceiling, and the "fiscal cliff" point to very short and very partial political changes wrought by the election of 2008.

Short of a full realignment then, could the parts of our present political system be welded into a governing coalition that is comparable with that of Franklin Roosevelt? Andrew Jackson was able to do so even without the environment bestowed by a classic realignment. The answer is yes, but the experiences of the Obama administration highlight the extreme difficulty that awaits anyone that embarks on such an endeavor. Our temporal moment in history is very unlike that of the 1930s or 1830s when government was small, did less, and had fewer responsibilities placed on its shoulders. Our system of government and the policy-making process taking place within it and affected by our political system are much like the systems of the human body. Over time, parts of our circulatory system—akin to human veins and arteries—have become clogged and even lost some of their elasticity. Undoing these internal, systemic problems may be as weighty a task as dealing with the other problems that exist outside these systems but that still must pass through them for resolution.

CONCLUSION: WITHER POLITICS?

Will policy making and policy itself be less tied to politics in the future? Drawing on what was established early on in this text, let us hope not. If by "politics" we mean the struggle over direction and substance of policy, then policy without politics in a democracy is undesirable and nearly unthinkable. Politics is seldom ever absolutely zero-sum in the American version, especially the politics of public policy making and implementation. At its best, politics provides representation of a diverse set of viewpoints and interests through debate and deliberation, two activities that can improve the quality and legitimacy of policies themselves. Politics can also provide necessary oversight for existing programs and policies while injecting new ideas into old areas of debate.

Rather than turning up our collective noses at the thought of a future that must include politics as part of our policy world, it is potentially encouraging to know that our policies will remain, at their core, the result of a highly political process. A politics-less policy-making and governing process in the United States would be the work of machines, not people living in a democracy. For all of humankind's faults, our governments, politics, and our policies are a direct reflection of who we are.

SUMMARY

While the future of policy making and politics is, of course, yet to be written, there are basic trends in both that are highly likely to carry on. For good or ill, our pattern of incremental policy making is almost certain to continue, given our pluralistic arrangement of power and our fragmented system of government. The political world spun into motion by James Madison, featuring a multitude of competing factions in a large republic and the ability of ambitions to counteract ambitions, is still with us. While world-shattering governing and policy-making regimes born of crisis and political upheaval do mark our history as a nation, they are exceeding rare. Even recent events related to the "Great Recession" produced far less policy experimentation and changes away from solutions used in past economic crises than might have been expected. The patterns of our policy-making system are strongly ingrained by our political institutions, practices, expectations, and beliefs.

Much like our past, our future of policy making is likely to feature a sustained struggle over the appropriateness of solutions to chronic and newly emerging problems. It is tempting to make assumptions about a shared common or national "good." However, a quick reflection on the main theme of this text—that policy making is a political endeavor— should remind you that widely shared agreement on the means and ends of public policy is rare; it is differences of partisanship, ideology, and the meaning of basic values that drive much of what we want and the ways that we go about trying to reach those goals. Moreover, even if a "common good" were to exist, we would be hard-pressed to produce policies that did more than approach the "best" results. The complexity of problems, crosscutting political pressures, and limits on resources place us in a policy-making world akin to the captives of the prisoners' dilemma.

At the outset of this text it was argued that politics is not a dirty word, especially if it means advocating for best interests of others. Our current political world is raucous and fast paced, with overblown rhetoric and often topped with a dollop of anger. While the ferocity of some aspects of our politics is hard to ignore, it is of our making. This means that the ways we practice politics—including how we make policy—is as likely to change for the better as it is for the worse. One thing that is more certain is that politics is essential for policy making in our republic because politics is the only practical means of securing our democratic ideals of representation, debate, and deliberation.

DISCUSSION QUESTIONS

1. How do incremental policy changes reflect our political structure and system of politics? What are the advantages and disadvantages of incremental policy making? Are the policy responses to our most recent economic crisis and the changes to the nation's health care insurance laws evidence of incremental or non-incremental policy making?
2. Are we living in a moment of political time that mirrors other periods in our history when we were shaken by crisis, or is it impossible to compare our current political circumstances to those of the past? Depending on your answer, are there recent policy changes that reflect your position about political time?
3. Is it possible to ever "solve" most public policy problems in ways that produce the "best" results? Why or why not? What examples, from now or in the past, can you provide to support your position?
4. Would you want our policy-making process to be less political? Explain what you mean by political as it relates to representation, debate, and deliberation.

NOTES

1. Kingdon, John W. "Chapter 8." In *Agendas, alternatives, and public policies.* Boston: Little, Brown, 1984.
2. Lindblom, Charles. "The Science of Muddling Through." *Public Administration Review* 14, no. Spring (1959): 79–88.
3. Skowronek, Stephen. "Presidential Leadership in Political Time." In Nelson, Michael. *The presidency and the political system.* 8th ed. Washington, DC: CQ Press, 2006.
4. Cauchon, Dennis. "Medicare drug program snips $6B from year's tab." *USA Today,* October 31, 2008. A1.
5. Gay Stolberg, Sheryl. "Obama signs huge stimulus bill." *New York Times,* www. nytimes.com/2009/02/17/world/americas/17iht-18webstim.20260581.html (accessed February 11, 2013).
6. Lynch, David J. "Economists agree: Stimulus created nearly 3 million jobs." *USA Today.* http://www.usatoday.com/money/economy/2010-08-30-stimulus30_CV_N.htm (accessed February 11, 2013).

7. Young, Jeffrey. "Health Spending Will Account for 20% of U.S. Economy by 2020, Study Shows." Bloomberg. http://www.bloomberg.com/news/2011-07-28/health-care-projected-to-be-one-fifth-of-u-s-economy-by-2020.html (accessed February 11, 2013).

8. Pecquet, Julian, and Sam Baker. "Democrats expressing buyers' remorse on Obama's healthcare law." *The Hill*. http://thehill.com/blogs/healthwatch/politics-elections/222719-democrats-buyers-remorse-on-obama-health-care-law (accessed February 11, 2013).

9. Zengerle, Jason. "In Conversation: Barney Frank." *New York Magazine*. http://nymag.com/news/features/barney-frank-2012-4/ (accessed February 11, 2013).

10. Panagopoulos, Costas, and Joshua Schank. *All roads lead to Congress: the $300 billion fight over highway funding*. Washington, DC: CQ Press, 2008. 97.

11. Panagopoulos and Schank, 167.

INDEX

Note: Page references with letter 'n' followed by locators denote note numbers.

A

AAA. *See* American Automobile
    Association
AARP. *See* American Association
    of Retired Persons
ABC, 82, 111
Abortion, 134
    Courts decision, 120
    partial-birth, 120
Abrams, Samuel J., 79n12
ACF. *See* Advocacy coalition
    framework
ACORN. *See* Association of Community
    Organizations for Reform
Actors, political, 57
Advertising techniques, 149
Advocacy, 62–64, 99, 168
Advocacy coalition framework, 61–64
AFDC. *See* Aid for Families with
    Dependent Children
Affordable Care Act, 16, 69
Afghanistan, 21, 111, 154, 174
    military's role in, 111
AFL. *See* American Federation of Labor
Agenda
    decision-making, 103–104, 124
    formal, 104
    institutional, 103
    legislative, 148
    national, 180
    systemic, 103
Agenda-making, 103
Agenda setters, 124
Agenda setting, 101–105
    citizens, 116–118
    corporations, 106–109
    interest groups, 112–114
    outside players, 105–119
    media, 109–112
    social movements, 114–116
    success, 126
Agricultural and residential pesticides, 84

Aid for Families with Dependent
    Children, 45, 105, 202
AIG, 88
Alfano, Sean, 111n29
American Association of Retired
    Persons, 27
American Automobile Association, 168
American Civil Liberties
    Union, 113
American Civil War, 184
American democracy
    elements of, 8
    understanding of, 3
American demographics, 76
American Enterprise Institute, 118
American Federation of Labor, 114
American Idol, 40
American politics, third rail of, 179
American Recovery and Reinvestment
    Act, 123–124
Amnesty, 4, 81
Anderson, James E., 62n28
Andrews, Edmund L., 22n17
Antidemocratic, 147
Anti-Federalists, 71
Antipoverty programs, 105
Approaches
    microeconomic, 63
    process-oriented, 56
    theoretical, 102
Aristotle, 36
Armed conflict, 184
Articles of Confederation, 70, 82
Assimilated immigrant groups, 42
Association of Community
    Organizations for Reform, 117
Astro Turf, 118, 167
Authoritative societal creation, 10
Auto bailout, 174–179
    Chrysler, 174–175
    Ford, 174
    General Motors, 174

Automobile economy, 174
Autonomous actors, 60
Axis powers, 172

B

Bachrach, Peter, 7, 43, 44, 101
Baker, Sam, 201n8
Bank of America, 107
Bankruptcy, 31, 136, 175
Bankruptcy bill, 31
Baratz, Morton S., 101
Barbaro, Michael, 107n18, 107n19
Baumgartner, Frank R., 61
Becker, Jo, 112n31
Berlin, Isaiah, 32n34
Bernstein, Barton, 52n10
Big box stores, 108
Big Three, 174, 177
Bill of rights, 71, 116
Bin Laden, Osama, 83
Black, Amy E., 121n39
Blue-collar tradition, 42
Blue states, 74, 79
Border Protection, Antiterrorism,
        and Illegal Immigration
        Control Act, 80
Boston Harbor, 114
Bozzo, Albert, 178n13
Branigin, William, 70n2
Brennan Center for Justice, 147
British Petroleum, 70
Brookings Institute, 119
Brooks, Jennifer, 31n33
Budget austerity, 148
Budget deficit, 133, 137, 170
Bureaucracy, 105, 141, 153
    federal, 22
    key attributes, 142
    street level, 142
    upward layers of the, 145
Burkhalter, Sarah K., 73n4
Bush, George, 4–5, 16, 21, 25–27,
        31, 52, 80–81, 89, 114, 120–121,
        153–154, 157–159, 177–181,
        183, 199
Bush, George H. W., 20, 21, 120, 181
Bush, Jeb, 146, 147
Bush administration, 22, 45, 52, 83, 88,
        134, 176–177, 183–184

Business community, 27, 80
Business spending, 199

C

CAFE. *See* Corporate average fuel
        economy
Cahn, Matthew Alan, 140n6
Campaigns and Elections, 15
Campaign techniques, 25, 172
Campaign theme, 204
Capitalism, 85, 196
    free market, 86
    nature of, 86
Capitalist economy, 107
Capitalistic, 10
Capital punishment, 41, 146
Capitol Hill, 26, 50, 77, 79, 176
Card check unionization, 122–123
Carmaking states, 177
Caro, Robert A., 101n7
Carson, Rachel, 54, 84
Carter, Jimmy, 153
Cauchon, Dennis, 199n4
Categorizing policies, 54
Cato Institute, 118
CBS Corporation, 82, 111
Cell phones, 8, 81–82
Center for Law and Policy, 118
CFPB. *See* Consumer Financial
        Protection Bureau
Checks and balances, 72–73,
        155, 161
Chevron, 107
Children's Defense Fund, 113
Christian Coalition, 120
Christian faiths, 119
Christian Right, 119, 121–123
Chrysler bailout, 174–179. *See also*
        Auto bailout
Cigarette taxes, 55
Civics class model, 133, 161
Civil Rights Act, 16, 197
Civil rights activists, 102
Civil rights movement, 72, 114–116,
        189, 197
Civil rights policy, 102
Civil servant, label, 24
Civil service system, 24
Civil War, 71–72, 114, 120, 151, 184

Clean coal technology, 134
Clinton, Bill, 21, 27, 44–45, 47, 75, 78,
    119, 154, 181–182, 199, 202
Clinton, Hillary, 119
Clinton's health care policy
    proposal, 30
CNN, 82, 111
Cobb, Roger W., 102n8
Cohen, Michael D., 58n19
COLA. *See* Cost-of-living adjustment
Cold War, 21–22, 172–174
Collective action problems, 158
Communication, 2, 11, 81–85, 87, 91,
    109–110, 112
Confederal system, 70
Confessore, Nicholas, 79n10
Congressional authorization, 16
Congressional behavior, 60
Congressional districts, 155
Congressional elections, 78, 150
Congressional legislation, 44
*Congress: Keystone of the Washington
    Establishment,* 60
Connecticut, 42
ConocoPhillips, 107
Conservatism, 34
Conservative ideology, 34
Conservative movement, 34, 71, 181
Constitutional authority, 159
Constitutional convention, 70
Constitutional limitations, 159
Constitutional scholarship, 70
Constitutional validity, 159
Constitution Amendments
    First, 109, 116, 121
    Fourth, 16
Constitution's ratification, 71, 150
Consumer Financial Protection Bureau,
    22–23
Consumer Price Index, 48
Consumer Protection Act, 23, 136
Consumer spending, 199
Contract employees
Contract workforce
    off-budget, 24
    rise of, 24–25
Cooper, Helene, 23n18
Corporate average fuel economy, 99
Corporate power, 107

Corporations, 106–109
Cost-benefit analysis, 59–60
Cost-of-living adjustment, 48, 50
Court packing plan, 152
Credit card interest rates, 31
Credit crisis, 89
Crisis managers, 96
Cross-cutting pressures, 50, 139
Crowley, Cathleen F., 140n8
Cuban Missile Crisis, 52
Cultural change, 20
Culture war, 18, 74–76, 79, 91
Cynicism, 28, 124, 190–191

D

Dahl, Robert Alan, 42, 43,
    97, 108
Davey, Monica, 148n18
Decision makers
    access to, 98
    action by, 103
    attention of, 126
    elected, 118
    formal, 102
    governmental, 7, 99, 106, 116
    legitimate, 103, 126
    political, 101
    powerful, 103
    public policies, 9
Decision-making
    agenda, 133
    models, 48
Degree of change, 40, 44–53, 59, 64,
    123, 138–139, 169, 194–197
    incrementalism, 48–53
    minor adjustments, 45
    non-incremental, 45–48
DeLay, Tom, 79
Democracy
    elements of, 188
    intricacy of, 11, 15
    nature of, 3
    perversion of, 115
    pluralist, 139
    political activities, 11
    pro-Western, 158
    representative form of, 8
    version of, 33
Democratic ideals, 207

Democrats
    1932 election, 46
    1992 election, 78
    1998 election, 157
    2006 midterm election
    2008 election, 76
    2010 midterm election, 133
    2012 election, 76
    budget deficit, 199
    health care, 201
    House control 2006, 73
    Iraq stance, 158
    liberal cultural warrior, 74
    New Deal Coalition, 120
Demographic changes, 80–81
Dempsey, Jim, 117n34
Derivative agreements, 136
Dewey Beats Truman, 173
Dissatisfaction, degree of, 56
Dodd-Frank Wall Street Reform,
    22, 136
Domestic surveillance program, 16
Donahue, John D., 176n9
Downs, Anthony, 104
Drug crime, 170
Dual federalism, 71, 150
Duintjer, Radboud J., 170n4
Dye, Thomas R., 42

E

Easton, David, 19, 20, 48, 55,
    56, 64, 125
Economic arrangements, 114
Economic crisis, 86–87, 89, 166,
    196, 200
Economic depression, 170
Economic goals, 19
Economic indicators, 87, 166
Economic meltdown, 136
Economic recession, 59, 199
Economic relationship, 11
*An Economic Theory of
    Democracy,* 59
Economy, 85–90
Edelman, Murray J., 54n12
Edwards, George, 26n23, 27, 180n16,
    180n17, 180n18
Eilperin, Juliet, 18n6, 77n9
Elder, Charles D., 102n8

Election
    campaigns, 25
    congressional, 150, 205
    culture war, 79
    federal, 156
    midterm, 76, 78, 111, 133, 137, 154,
        156–158, 203
    presidential, 8, 75, 81
    secret-ballot, 123
Electoral College, 72, 113, 149
Electoral politics, 28, 36, 79, 120
Elite-based theories, 51–52
Elite dominance, 42, 51
Elitism, 116, 123
Employee Free Choice Act, 122–123
Employees
    contract, 22, 24
    federal, 21–24
    high turnover rates for, 122
    private sector, 22
    public union, 148
Energy policy, national, 104
Enlightenment thinkers, 46
Environmental disasters, 96
Environmental Protection Agency (EPA),
    98, 141, 185–186
Equality, 33–34
    advancement of, 31
    core beliefs in, 31
    economic, 33
    guarantees of, 10
    of outcomes, 33
    political, 33
    process view of, 33–34
Equal outcomes, 33–34
Euchner, Charles C., 121
Executive Reorganization Act, 25
ExxonMobil, 107

F

Fahrenthold, David A., 185n20
Faith-based organizations, 121
Family planning, 134
Fascism, 10
Favoritism, 133
FCC. *See* Federal Communications
    Commission
FDA. *See* Food and Drug Administration
Federal-Aid Highway Act, 19

Federal Communications Commission, 111–112
Federal Constitution, 70, 72, 82
Federal deficit, 182
Federal economic stimulus policy, 124
Federal gas tax, 104
Federal health insurance policy, 140
Federalism, 46, 69–72, 139
  aspects of, 70
  dual, 150
  dual theory, 71
  nature of, 72
Federalist No. 10, 33, 45, 82, 85, 113
Federal policy makers, 48
Federal power, expansion of, 151
Federal regulators, 109
Federal Reserve, 89
Federal system of welfare, 16
Federal tax credit, 100
Federal troops, 47
Federal workforce, 22, 24
Financial crisis, 87–88, 136, 195, 197, 200, 204
Financial regulatory agencies, 137
Financial system, 89
Fiorina, Morris P., 60, 79, 80
Fiscal cliff, 28, 205
Food and Drug Administration, 117
Ford, Gerald, 153
Fortune, 107
Founding Fathers, 6, 8
Fox News, 110–111, 144
Frank, Barney, 201
Freedom, 32–33
  definition, 32
  negative view of, 34
  versions of, 32
Free market, 34, 86, 90, 92, 179, 201
Fuel economy, 100, 175
Fuller, Richard, 55
Fundamental values, 121

G

GAO. *See* Government Accountability Office
Garbage can model, 58–59
Gay marriage, 113, 120
Gay Stolberg, Sheryl, 200n5
Gear, L. L., 8n3

General Accountability Office, 185
General Electric, 107
Geopolitical units, 70
Germany, 173–174
  splitting of, 174
Gibson Guitar Corporation, 143–144
Gingrich, Newt, 21, 33, 77, 156
Gingrich's Republicans, 157
Global warming, 51
Goals
  achievement of, 169
  basic, 59
  domestic policy, 154
  economic, 19, 182
  establishing, 169
  inclusive, 115
  national, 133
  political, 153
  presidents, 26
  procedural, 152
  unreachable, 199
  utilitarian, 190
Goldwater, Barry, 76
Gonzales, Alberto, 25, 154
Goodling, Monica, 25
Goodwins, Doris Kearns, 204
Gore, Al, 21, 181, 199
Government
  actions of, 54–55
  activist, 35, 196
  bureaucracy, 141
  city's, 43
  divided, 26, 76–77, 152
  expanded, 23, 28, 34
  expensive, 115
  functions of, 53–54
    distribution, 53
    redistribution, 54
    regulation, 54
  layers of, 36, 82
  local, 98, 105–106, 185, 195–196
  modern libertarian/limited, 34
  municipal, 70
  national, 71
  new federal, 109
  new form of, 71
  outputs of, 19
  policy-oriented, 18
  populate, 6

Government (*continued*)
  power of, 69
  program-oriented, 18
  responsiveness of the, 74
  role of, 17, 32, 34
  role played by, 20
  shadow, 23
  size, 21–24
  smaller federal, 195
  sweep and creation, 48
  transformed, 36
  unified, 78
Government Accountability Office, 168
Grants, Pell, 32
Grassroots evaluation, 167
Grassroots lobbying, 126
Great Britain, 72
Great Depression, 45–46, 86, 150, 188,
  195, 197
Great Recession, 41, 87, 92, 124,
  135–136, 170, 176, 206
Great Society programs, 71, 153
Green, Donald P., 60n23
Greenblat, Alan, 146n14
Greenhouse, Steven, 107n20, 108n22
Greenhouse gasses, 51
Gregorian, Vartan, 33n36
Guest worker, 4–5, 80–81
Gulf of Mexico, 70

H

Hamilton, Alexander, 6
Handgun control, 51
Handguns, ban on the sale of, 51
Health care coverage, 30, 86, 201
Health care reform, 6, 16, 70
  insurance, 69, 72, 78, 205
  legislation, 69
Health care system, overhaul of, 48
Health insurance, 30, 59, 69, 105,
  140, 201
Heritage Foundation, 118, 168
Heffner, Richard D., 33n36
Henninger, Daniel, 14n1
Hidden workforce, 22
Hierarchical arrangement, 142
Hispanic voters, 81
Holistic system, 19
Hoover administration, 46
Hopkins, Jim, 108n26

Hostilities, 26, 173
Hot-button policy areas, 4
House Majority Whip, 79
House of Representatives, 18, 72, 133,
  167, 177, 199–200
Housing bubble, 87–88, 105
Housing values, 136
Hudson River, 98
Hudson, William E., 109n27
Human values, 29–35
Hunter, James Davison, 74
Huntington, Samuel, 121
Hurricane Katrina, 28, 157, 180
Hybrid cars, 58, 99–100
Hyde, Charles K., 175n6
Hydroelectric power, 99
Hydrogen-powered fuel cell vehicles, 99

I

Ideology, 29–35
Illegal logging, 143
Illegal plant trade, 143
Immigrants
  illegal, 81
  from Italy, 43
  rights of, 80
  from Russia, 43
Immigration, 4–5, 53, 70, 72,
  80–81, 91
  illegal, 4
  legal, 4
  reform, 5, 81
Immunization program, 170
Income inequality, 114
Incrementalism, 48–53, 61, 139
  types of, 48
Industrial Workers of the World, 114
Institutional characteristics, 91
Institutional components, 23
Insurance, 30, 59, 69, 78, 88, 104–105,
  117, 136, 140, 176, 179, 201
Intelligence failure, 54, 157
Interest
  aggregate, 113
  clients, 118
  entrenched, 51
  multiple, 47
  organized, 30, 50, 167
  powerful, 133, 179, 185–186
  scholarly, 139

self-serving, 112
shared, 82
special, 4, 113–114, 124
Interest groups, 2, 6, 10, 18–19, 26–27,
        61, 73, 78, 98–99, 112–115,
        117–118, 121, 126, 139, 143,
        145–146, 152, 161, 168, 180, 189
    activism of, 27
    allied, 180
    coalition of, 27
    competing, 146
    conservatively oriented, 78
    demand of, 19
    divergent, 152
    environmental, 73, 98
    importance of, 113
    modern, 113
    pressure from, 6, 139
    role of, 26
    sophistication of, 18
    traditional, 121
International politics, America's
        rival in, 21
Internet, 2, 81–83, 110–111, 123
    -based communication, 81
    news gathering, 111
    rise of, 110, 123
Iran, revolution in, 99
Iraq, 158
    Bush policy, 158
    danger to US, 45
    free, 31
    invasion of, 44, 157–158, 183
    rebuilding, 157
    WMD issue, 28
Iraqi prisoners, maltreatment of, 189
Iraq war, 27
Irving, Will, 81n14
Italy, immigrants from, 43
It's Even Worse Than it Looks, 79
IWW. *See* Industrial Workers
        of the World

J

Jackson, Andrew, 197
Japanese automakers, 100
Jefferson, Thomas, 6, 28, 46, 149
Jenkins-Smith, Hank C., 61
Jindal, Bobby, 70
Job creation, 125, 199

Jobless workers, 133
Job training, 166
Johnson, Lyndon, 76, 105, 153
Jones, Bryan D., 61
Jones, Jeffrey M., 74n6
Judicial nominations, 146

K

Kennedy, John, 52, 152–153, 189
Kerry, John, 26, 28
Kingdon, John W., 58, 59, 103, 125, 196
Knowledge of power, 44
Kony 2012, 84
Koopman, Douglas L., 121n39
Kopicki, Allison, 81n14
Korean War, 151
K-Street, 78–79

L

Labor movement, 122–123
Labor unions, 189
Lacey Act, 143–144
Larson, Carin, 120n37
Lasswell, Harold Dwight, 3, 4, 9
Lasswell's formula, 4
Leadership
    campaign mode of, 27
    Democratic, 77, 158
    executive, 147
    gubernatorial, 148
    presidential, 197
Lee, Christopher, 22n16
Legitimacy, 138
Lehman Brothers, 88
Levinson, Sanford, 107n16
Lewis, David E., 25n22
Liberalism
    modern, 34
    traditional, 86
Liberty, meaning of, 32. *See also*
        Freedom
Lichtblau, Eric, 16n3
Light, Paul C., 22, 23
Lindblom, Charles E., 48, 50, 139,
        196, 202
Line-item veto, 147
Loan money, 89, 176
Lobbying, 11, 16, 19, 30, 78–79, 97,
        106, 109, 112, 115–118, 123,
        126, 138, 167

Locke, John, 8, 138
Lowi, Theodore J., 17, 53, 55
Luntz, Frank, 26
Lynch, David J., 200n6

M

Macro change, 47
Madison, James, 45, 51, 59, 71–72, 82,
    84–85, 113, 206
Madison Avenue approach, 149
Maher, Kris, 122n43
Mann, Thomas E., 27n30, 79n11
March, James G., 58, 60
Marshall Plan, 174
Mass society, 81
Matthews, Donald R., 77
McCain, John, 205
McCartt, A. T., 8n3
McCloskey, Robert G., 107n16
McGinniss, Joe, 149
Media, 109–112
Media attention, 26
Media watchdogs, 110
Medicare Part D, 105
Meier, Kenneth J., 63
Meyer, David S., 122n42
Microtargeting of voters, 15
Middle-income citizens, 117
Military-industrial complex, 21
Mills, C. Wright, 42
Moe, Terry M., 25n22, 60n22
Monetary policy, 89
Mortgage
    crisis, 89
    lenders, 136
    meltdown, 87–88
Moynihan, Daniel P., 18, 19, 20, 23, 36
Moynihan, Pat, 36
Mufson, Steven, 70n2
Mulligan, Dierdre K., 117n34
Mutikani, Lucia, 105n14
Myers, Richard, 55

N

NAACP. *See* National Association for
    the Advancement of Colored
    People
Nachmias, David, 169n3
Nakamura, Robert, 56

Nakashima, Ellen, 154n20
NAMM. *See* National Association of
    Music Merchants
NASA, 181
Nashville factory, 143
National Association for the Advancement
    of Colored People, 114
National Association of Music
    Merchants, 144
National Labor Relations
    Board, 122
National Organization for
    Marriage, 113
National Reconstruction
    Administration, 151
National Rifle Association, 113
National Security Agency, 154
Natural disasters, 54, 97
Natural tension, 182
NBC, 14, 82, 111
Negative liberty, 32
New Haven, 42–43
News Corporation, 111–112
New York State Public Interest
    Research Group, 117
New York Stock Exchange, 106
New York Times, 16
Nixon, Richard, 18, 73, 76, 149–150,
    153, 205
No Child Left Behind, 142, 154
Nomination fight, 21
Nondecisions, 7, 9, 43–44, 52
Non-incremental change, 45–48,
    51, 61
Non-incremental policy, 59, 64
Nozick, Robert, 33n37
Nuclear power, 99
NYPIRG. *See* New York State Public
    Interest Research Group

O

Obama, Barack, 6, 28, 81, 119,
    121–122, 134, 159, 195, 204
O'Brien, Michael, 159n23
Occupy movement, 69, 114
OFBCI. *See* Office of Faith-Based
    and Community Initiatives
Off-budget, 22–24, 36
Office of Faith-Based and Community
    Initiatives, 121

Oil exploration, 104
Oil scarcity, 99–100
Oil shock, 99
Oil spill, 70, 97, 104, 111
Olsen, Johan P., 58
On-budget, 22–24
Openness of pluralism, 51
Ordinary politics, 114
Organization of Arab Petroleum
        Exporting Countries, 99
Ornstein, Norman J., 27n30, 79n11
Oval Office, 96
Overpriced homes, 87
Ownership cap, 112
Ownership society, 31–32

P

Panagopoulos, Costas, 202n10, 202n11
Parenti, Michael, 42
Partisan antagonisms, 73
Partisan conflict, 77
Partisan roadblock, reality of a, 47
Partisanship, 18, 24–25, 36, 46, 79,
        110, 117, 133, 152, 182,
        205–206
    level of, 18
Party affiliation, 3, 47
Party-line voting, 18, 76
Patient Protection and Affordable Care
        Act, 69, 201, 203
Patterson, David, 73
Paul, Ron, 20, 34
Payroll taxes, 179
Pear, Robert, 50n9
Pecquet, Julian, 201n8
Permanent campaign, 25–29, 36, 172
    prevalence of, 36
    techniques of the, 27
Personal freedom, 31–32
Peters, Jeremy W., 112n30
Phases model, 56–57
PIRG. See Public Interest Research
        Group
Planning model, 140
Pluralism, 43–44, 51, 61, 123
    conceptualization of, 43
    critique of, 43
    openness of, 51
Pluralist theories of power, 64
Polarization, 76, 79

Policies, efficacy of, 171
Policy advocacy, 20, 36, 99, 168
Policy change, without
        realignments, 47
Policy entrepreneurs, 58
Policy evaluation, 11, 190–191
    from inside, 167–171
    from outside, 167–171
    policy outputs, 166–171
Policy formulation, 133–139
    degree of change, 138–139
    legitimacy, 138
    Wall Street regulation, 135–137
Policy goals
    implicit, 18
    shifting, 182
Policy implementation, 139–144
    bottom-up approach, 145
    planning model, 142
    politics of, 143–144
    top-down approach, 142, 145
Policy maker
    advancement goals of the, 5
    federal, 133
    as government, 20–29
Policy making
    agenda-setting phase, 124, 126
    arenas of conflict, 18
    check on, 155
    component of, 126
    contemporary state, 35
    degree of change, 138–139
    direct involvement, 27
    elite theories of, 51
    environment, 74, 80, 83–84, 86,
        89–91
    fundamental aspect, 10–11
    incremental, 206
    influences on, 11
    legislative, 16
    machinery of, 46
    meaning of, 19
    model, 48, 59, 63
    outcomes, 64
    outputs of the, 4
    phases of, 17
    political aspects of, 140
    political form of, 36
    politicized, 11, 17–18, 24, 35
    politics of, 139

Policy making (*continued*)
  progression of, 57
  realm of, 6
  structure of, 68–90
    communication, 81–85
    demographic changes, 80–81
    economy, 85–90
    federalism, 69–72
    political culture, 74–80
    separation of powers, 72–74
  understanding of, 64
  views of, 58–63
    advocacy coalition framework,
      61–63
    garbage cans, 58–59
    Punctuated-Equilibrium, 61
    rational choice theory, 59–61
Policy monopoly, 61
Policy players, orientations of, 35
Policy promotion, 25–29
Policy solutions, 86
  appropriateness of, 197–203
  concomitant, 203
Political activism, 117
Political actors, 4, 10–11, 48, 50, 57,
    114, 145, 151, 161, 191
  conservative, 50
  job of, 161
  regular, 114
Political competitors, 204
Political crisis, 45
Political culture, 74–80
Political damage, 117
Political earthquake, 46
Political engagement, 124
Political fallout, 201
Political friction, 17, 133
Political goodwill, 199
Political hurdles, 6
Political ideology, 10, 34–35, 170
Political influence, degree of, 51
Political liberty, 86
Political motivation, 139
Political payback, 177
Political persuasion, 118
Political revolution, 90
Politics
  compartmentalized, 2, 9
  constituent, 132
  contemporary, 36

  continuation of, 114
  definitions of, 3, 9
  electoral, 28, 36, 79, 120
  influence of, 11, 201
  international, 21
  level of, 52
  meaning of, 9–10, 15, 122
  nature of, 10, 124
  nexus with policy making, 27
  ordinary, 114
  partisan, 205
  policy as, 3, 10–12, 14–15,
    40, 50
  real, 17
  role of religion in, 82
Politics/administration dichotomy, 6
Politics-administration divide, 139
Politics and Policy, 15–17
Pollution, 99–100
Pope, Jeremy, 79n12
Positive freedom, 34–35
Positive liberty, 32
Post-partisan era, 6, 205
Post-reform Congress, 150
Power Elite, 42, 52
Power, energy
  hydroelectric, 99
  nuclear, 99
  solar, 134
Power patterns, 145–159
  contraction of power, 155–159
  legislatures role, 155–159
  Presidency, 148–154
  State Governors, 146–148
Power, political, 40–44
  abuse of, 83, 151
  atypical form of, 44
  concentration degree of, 42–44
  corporate, 107
  cycles of, 119–123
  degree of, 42
  division of, 68, 91
  economic, 42, 174
  elements of, 51
  expansion of, 147, 160
  formal, 40–42, 52, 104, 154
  formidable persuasive, 109
  governmental, 16
  hierarchical structure of, 141
  informal, 40–42

judicial, 54, 159
nature of, 3, 10, 12, 42, 44
pluralistic arrangement of, 206
real, 5, 112
residual, 71
Power shift, 112
social, 42
traditional form of power,
    form of, 108
trimming of, 153
unconstitutional, 151
unilateral, 52
Pragmatism of political culture, 35
Prescription drug program, 7
Prescription drugs, 27, 105
Presidency, 148–154
2012 Presidential campaign trail, 33
Presidential contest, 205
Presidential nominees, 149
Presidential power, 148–149,
    152–153
Press freedom, 112
Pressman, Jeffrey L., 139
Private economic activity, 87
Private ownership, 85
Private sector unions, 122
Proactive policy, 20, 36
Problem identification, 14, 85, 97–101,
    125, 168, 189, 191
Problem recognition, 103
Problem solvers, 96
Problem solving, 74, 134
Pro-Democratic bias, 110
Program effectiveness, 170
Progressivism, 34
Protest movements, 115
Public announcements, 41
Public Interest Research Group, 117
Public opinion polls, 154, 195
Public policy
    definition, 7–9, 29
    meaning, 20
    public part of, 8–9
    views of, 57–63
    wonkish side of, 17
Public relations campaigns, 138
Punctuated-equilibrium, 61, 63

Q

Quantitative approaches, 60

R

Racial
    antagonism, 81
    segregation, 71, 102
Ragsdale, Lyn, 25n21
Rational choice approaches, 60
Rational choice theory, 59–61, 64
Rational-comprehensive approach,
    48, 139
Rationality project, 60
Reagan, Ronald, 21, 71, 154,
    195, 199
Reagan era, 20
Real-estate agents, 88
Real estate market, 105, 136
Realignment, 46–47, 120, 205
Reality programs, 40
Real politics, 17
Recession
    stimulus packages, 182
    tax breaks, 182
Red staters, 74
Red states, 79
Reduction of greenhouse
    gasses, 51
Reform
    bankruptcy, 31
    federal welfare, 147
    financial, 136
    fiscal, 148
    health care, 69, 72, 78, 205
    health care insurance,
        6, 16
    immigration, 5, 81
    welfare, 44
Regulation
    banking, 109
    federal, 54
    immigration, 80
    lax, 96
    new governmental, 175
    relaxation of, 134
    tighter, 134
    tobacco use, 117
Regulatory policies, 73
Regulatory power, 69, 86
Reich, Robert B., 176n9
Religious indoctrination, 121
Religious organizations, 121
Republican House Whip, 77

Republican Party, 4, 25–27, 34, 45–46, 76, 80–81, 120, 156, 177, 180–181, 204–205
  1994 midterm election, 156
  2010 midterm election, 76, 205
  ability to win presidential election, 81
  business community support, 80
  discipline, 26
  dominant, 46
  guest worker policy, 4
  macro shifts, 46
  presidential nomination, 34
  TARP, 177
  tax concessions, 181–182
Republican pollster, 26
Republican principle, 45
Republican Revolution, 26
Republicans voting, 200
Rights
  basic, 123
  civil, 115, 120, 189, 197
  fundamental, 115
  individual, 86
  lawful, 145
Riker, William H., 59
Risen, James, 16n3
Risk-adverse actors, 50
Risk diversification, 88
Roane, Kit R., 108n23
Robertson, Pat, 120
Rokeach, Milton, 10
Romney, Mitt, 14, 21, 81, 179
Roosevelt, Franklin, 197, 203–205
Roosevelt, Theodore, 148
Rule-driven institutions, 9
Rule-making authority, 134
Rumsfeld, Donald, 184
Russell, Richard, 102
Russia, immigrants from, 43
Ryan, George, 145
Ryden, David K., 121n39

S

Sabatier, Paul A., 61, 62, 145
Sabatier's model, 145
Sabato, Larry, 146n13
Safety net, 27, 31, 176
Satellite phone, 81
Satellite stations, 111

Saudi Arabia, 83
Savage, Charlie, 159n22
Scandals, 117, 156
Schank, Joshua, 202n10
Schattschneider, E. E., 102
Scheppach, Ray, 147
Schulman, Paul A., 47
SEC. *See* Securities and Exchange Commission
Securities and Exchange Commission, 135–136
Separation of powers, 72–74
Shadow government, 23
Shapiro, Ian, 60n23
Shear, Michael D., 70n2
Sheehan, Cindy, 114
Shelby, Richard, 177
Silent Spring, 84
Simon, Herbert A., 60
Sinclair, Barbara, 76
Skocpol, Theda, 30n32
Skowronek, Stephen, 197, 201n3
Sluggish economy, 181, 196
Social contract theory, 8. *See also* Locke, John
Socialism, 10
Social Movement, 3, 11, 114–116, 121, 123, 126, 189
Social networking, 2, 82
Social scientist, 10
Social security, 26–27, 31–33, 48, 50, 179–180, 197
  campaign techniques, 180
  payments, 48
  reform, 26, 180
  solvency of, 180
  taxes, 31–32
Social service policy, 121
Social values, 91
Societal change, 36, 86
Solar power, 134
Solar system, 108
Soviet Union, 172
Space program, 47–48
Special interests on policy making, 124
Speculation, 100, 136, 177
Speculative trading, 151
Spiritual awakening, 120

State Governors, 146–148
Steinhauer, Jennifer, 23n18
Stelter, Brian, 112n30
Stimulus package, 182, 196,
    200–201
Stock market, 87, 90, 151, 166,
    179–180
Stone, Deborah A., 30, 33, 36, 57, 60
Strip workers, 123
Stuart, Reginald, 174n5, 176n8
Student loan programs, 32
Study of Administration, 6
Survivor, 40
Swiftboating, 28
Systems Analysis of Political Life, 19

T

TANF. *See* Temporary Assistance
    for Needy Families
TARP. *See* Troubled Asset Relief
    Program
Tax
  breaks, 21, 108, 181–182
  codes, 105
  credit, 166
  money, 178
  penalties, 69
  policy, 47
Team of Rivals, 204
Tea Party, 20, 69–70, 114
Teaser rate, 88
Temporary Assistance for Needy
    Families, 45, 105, 202
Terrorism, 16, 98, 102, 154
  global, 183
  international, 158
Terrorist attacks of 9/11, 21, 26,
    45, 55, 59, 83, 89, 102, 134,
    157, 202
Textbook approach, 56–57, 63
Theodoulou, Stella Z., 140n6
Theory of Political Coalitions, 59
Thompson, Kimberly M., 170n4
Thucydides, 10
Tobacco use, regulation of, 117
Tocqueville, Alexis de, 33
Troubled Asset Relief Program, 19,
    177–179
Truman, David, 112

U

Unconstitutional preemption, 69
Undue burdens, 189
Unemployment benefits, 133
Unions, 151
Unitary executive theory, 159
United Nation, 16
USA PATRIOT Act, 59
US presidential elections, 8

V

Vaccination programs, 188
Value orientations, 35
Vanity Fair, 119
Van Meter, Donald S., 140
V-chips, 154
Viacom, 111
Vietnam War, 28, 115
Von Clausewitz, Carl, 114
Voting rights, 117
Voting Rights Act, 197

W

Wall Street Journal, 122
Wall Street regulation, 135–137
Walmart, 107–109, 122
  assistance from government, 108
  land grants, 108
  tax policy and, 108
Warner, Time, 111
War on poverty, 105
War on terrorism, 159
Warrick, Joby, 16n4
Washington, George, 6, 76
Watergate scandal, 150
Weapons of mass destruction, 28
Wechsler, Pat, 96n1
Welfare benefits, 45
Welfare policy, 203
Welfare reform bill, 202
Whiggishness, 150
Whig Party, 205
Who Governs, 97
Wilcox, Clyde, 120n37
Wildavsky, Aaron B., 98, 139, 140
Wilgoren, Jodi, 145n12
Will, George, 116
William, H. Riker, 59

Williams, Joseph, 121n40
Wilson, James Q., 55, 64, 169
Wilson, Woodrow, 6, 139
Wind power, 134
Wiretap program, 16, 154
Wise Use movement, 116
Women's rights, 120
Workers' union, 41
World Trade Center, 83, 102
World War II, 172–174
   Fascist Italy, 173
   geopolitical outcomes, 173
   hostilities, cessation of, 172
   Imperial Japan, 173
   Marshall Plan, 174
   Nazi Germany, 172

   nuclear weapons, 173
   Soviet army, causalities, 174
Wright, Mills, C., 42, 43, 51, 52

Y

Yom Kippur War, 99
Young, Jeffrey, 201n7
YouTube, 35, 84

Z

Zengerle, Jason, 201n9
Zero emission cars, 99
Zero-sum, 3, 15, 134,
    172, 206
Zimmerman, Ann, 122n43